INCREDIBLE JOURNEY THROUGH LIFE *with* CHRIST

INCREDIBLE TESTIMONIALS OF MY LIFE

HENRY L. ODOM
with God

MESSENGER OF GOD
THOMASVILLE, NC

Published by Messenger of God
2114 Lancey Dr.
Thomasville, N.C. 27360

Publisher's Cataloguing-in-Publication Data
Odom, Henry L.

Incredible journey through life with Christ : [incredible testimonials of my life].
[Thomasville, N.C. : Messenger of God, 2005]

p. ; cm.
ISBN: 0-9765463-0-2

1. Spiritual life—Christianity. 2. Christian life. 3. Christian biography. I. Title.

BV4501.3 .O36 2005
248/.4—dc22 2005-921464

Printed in the United States of America
09 08 07 06 05 • 5 4 3 2 1

To God

Out of my heart, I proclaim this book to be dedicated unto God Almighty for providing me with his knowledge to write his holy word.

Contents

Foreword

This incredible book of stories from God is being published to inform the entire world, churches, and family of the amazing and incredible power of the Holy Spirit from the Almighty Heavenly Father, and from our Lord Jesus Christ. To bring you peace, love, and joy down in your heart, soul, and mind. These stories came to me beyond my knowledge and understanding. I had no knowledge of my own to write anything with this kind of magnitude involving the power of the true living God. When God spoke to me and said write a book. I said, "Lord, I can't write" God said I will provide you with the Spirit and my knowledge to write what I tell you. I am here to tell you everything written in this book is from the hand of the true living Jesus Christ. Writing God's words in this book has been one of the most incredible and rewarding things I have ever accomplished in my life. And knowing God was right there with me leading and guidance me in everything involving these stories. When God told me to write this book and said it would go out to the entire world, I didn't really understand the magnitude of this project, not until two years later when He informed me how many copies would be sold.

While in service, God showed me the conduction of the world involving the rich and the poor, and then He led me to North Carolina and said go into all the churches, give testimony, and feed my people, and there I saw the conduction of God's house. I saw that some churches are losing ground and losing the war to Satan. He is in full control because he knows the future plan of God is coming back for His church. We the church must be more involved in supporting the poor, lost, and hurting family. Satan doesn't have to work hard because he has us just right where he wants us. God's love for His church has not changed, but we have change doing things our way. He knows we have failed Him. This book is written because God is calling on churches to ask Jesus Christ to clean their hearts and prepare themselves for the future coming of the Lord. God spoke and said; "I am coming back for My church." He is also calling on families marriages to turn themselves over to the Lord to change their hearts, and let Him be the head of the family and church. There are many churches that are supporting the needs of the people, but they are so far apart, and this is why Satan can easily take advantage of us. God's plan is for all churches to come together for the perfecting of the saints, for the work of the ministry, for edifying the body of Christ, and for breaking down barriers of man-made denominations, races, and colors. Come together and study the true word of God and the Holy Bible and let Jesus Christ teach us how we must unity our hearts together as one body of our Heavenly Father.

This book is written from the King James version of the Bible, and it is writing from the word of God Almighty that He spoke. All through this book God handwriting appears, because I didn't write all of this book , God spoke to me and said this is His handwriting. He spoke to the person who corrected some of my writing and said the same thing. This book is alive because of this true, loving, amazing, awesome, and incredible Almighty God, who is alive in heaven and earth.

God's Spoken Word

ON 29 **October, 2000,** I was at work talking to a student about God. His Holy Spirit came upon my soul so strong tears were coming from my eyes, before I could ask God, what this meant these words came out of my mouth "Incredible Journey through life with Christ." The Holy Spirit was upon my body so powerful I had to leave my post and go into the bathroom until the spirit calmed me down. I came back out and the Holy Spirit suddenly came upon me again and said "write a book of His Word and my life story. I thought write a book!" "Lord, I don't know how to write." Then He brought this to my mind, I gave my prophecy and disciple the inspiration of My Holy Spirit and knowledge to write my Holy Bible, "I will place the same Spirit in your heart, mind and soul to write this book." This book will be published the way my Bible is published and it will go out to the entire world. The Holy Spirit came upon me again like fire shooting up in my bone. During this time, I felt the Holy Spirit tell me what my calling was in life to publish my life story so that the Powerful Holy Spirit and the grace of God will touch My people. I Pray these stories will open up your hearts to let the power of the Holy Spirit come upon you with peace, joy, and confident that you will stand on the Holy hand of the Almighty God. These stories are to bless your hearts with understanding and knowledge of the mighty power of the most high God.

When I stop to think of all the things the Almighty God has brought me through, I started to praise the mighty hand of Jesus with my whole heart, which has unbelievable love for my soul. Oh God, if I could praise your holy name with my whole heart, mind, soul, and strength I could not praise you enough for all you have done for me.

In the Holy Bible it is written in **Luke 4:18**, "The Spirit of the Lord God is upon me; because the Lord hath anointed me to preach good tidings unto the meek; he hath sent me to bind up the broken-hearted, to proclaim liberty to the captives, and the opening of the prison to them that are bound."

Only God Can Change Your Bad Habits

EVER SINCE I was thirty years old, I always felt God's calling for my life, which I found out at age fifty-seven. When I was growing up, my mother, father, and grandmother taught me valuable lessons about what is right and what is wrong. My father and grandmother put the fear of God down in my heart and soul. As I grew up in age I was drafted in the army, I started drinking alcohol and smoking cigarettes, trying to be like my friends, but I got ill several times, so I had to quit. I continued to drink beer until one day in 1979, as I was outside cutting grass, I came in and opened a cold beer and took one drink. I thought I was going to die because I could not breathe. The beer would go down. It scared me so bad I gave it up. The Lord had his hands upon me and delivered me from these bad habits.

My heavenly Father, I thank and praise your Holy Name because you are worthy to be praised for saving me from my bad sinful habit. I would buy a pack of cigarettes and smoke three or four and that would leave a bad taste in my mouth, so I gave it up, and God took the taste out of my mouth. Whenever I would start doing something wrong the Spirit would come over my heart to let me know this was not right. During these times, Satan was tempting me. Oh Lord, I am so glad I know Jesus Christ as my savior, because in **Isaiah 41:10,13** says, "Fear thou not; for I am with thee: be not dismayed; for I am thy God: I will strengthen thee; yea, I will help thee; yea, I will uphold thee with the right hand of my righteousness. For I the Lord thy God will hold thy right hand, saying unto thee, Fear not I will help thee." **Psalm 54** says, "Save me O God, by thy name, and judge me by thy strength"

Oh God, I praise and bless your holy name for your precious blood and the lamb of Christ. I thank you for redeeming me with the salvation of grace and mercy, and for your inheritance in the hope of your resurrection power. By your Son Jesus Christ, you have given me power, faith, and the truth of your word to be a minister of the Gospel to spread your Good News.

I Was Controlled by God's Guardian Angel

AT TWELVE years old, Christ saves me as my personal savior. I grew up in a little town called Emporia, Virginia. After high school, I moved to Washington, DC and met a girl who later became my wife. Eventually, she moved to Philadelphia, Pennsylvania. During the winter of 1965, I decided to visit her one weekend. I arrived at her house about 8:00 p.m. on that Saturday night, I stayed up mostly all night. That Sunday, she and I spent the day visiting friends. I departed back to Washington about 7:30 p.m. I was on I-95 South about 800 p.m. around 8:15 p.m., I began to feel sleepy so I slapped my face to wake up. At 8:30 p.m. I was driving asleep.

My girlfriend called my name and I woke up heading straight for the rail and down in the water. The next thing I knew, I found myself headed straight on I-95 South. God had sent my guardian angel to save me. He used my girlfriend's voice to call me. God put me back on the highway without me getting hurt or into any danger. God promised He would stay right by my side and He would not leave me nor forsake me because I am His son. This is one of God's greatest blessings He has for my life. When His blessings come, I must thank the Almighty God at all times. He has a plan for my life that is amazing. God knows the direction of my life.

The Almighty God saved me by the blood of the lamb. There are times when God sends us through danger to strengthen our faith in Him. I can say I found confidence and courage in Jesus Christ to stand along with Him. My Lord saves me because He loves me, and He said love my people like I love you, and my heart is burning with overflowing love for all of God's people. Oh Lord, if I could take the world's sins upon my soul, the way you took my sins on the cross, I would do it that all peoples would be saved by your grace and salvation. Oh God, continues to help me to love your people more each day of my life. I will praise your holy name every day because I love you with my whole heart, I will never leave you

Luke 2:8-9,13 says, "And there were in the same country shepherds abiding in the field, keeping watch over their flock by night. And lo the angel of the Lord came upon them, and the glory of the Lord shone round about them; and they were sore afraid. And suddenly there was with the angel a multitude of the heavenly host praising God, and saying. Glory to God in the highest, and earth peace, good will toward men."

God, Hope, and Mercy Will Save You

BEFORE ENTERING the service I took the test five times and failed. On August of 1967, I was drafted into the United States Army. In September, I was sent to Fort Bragg North Carolina, for my basic training. While I was there they gave me another test. During our first overnight training, it was in the winter and very cold. During the day we conducted field training exercises that continue on into the night tell 11:00 p.m. We arrived into the bivouac area and set up our sleep tent, I was very cold and my finger was hurting, and it kept me awake all night. I said "Lord, I can't stay out here another day, so help me Lord." The next morning it was so cold, and I was shaking when the sergeant called my name and said you have KP duty. "I said, Thank you, Lord Jesus," because I would get warm. Then I felt guilty because I just had KP duty two week ago and it was not my time. I got on the truck and I didn't say anything; I went and performed KP duty. All that day I was worried the sergeant would come and say he made a mistake. When my unit came back from the field I was glad and began to praise the Almighty God for saving me from the cold. Lord, I don't understand these things; all I can say this is why you are the true living God. **Psalms 50:15** "says, "And call upon me in the day of trouble: I will deliver thee, and thou shalt glorify me." **Psalms 46:1** says, "God is our refuge and present help in trouble."

The next phase to be sent off to advanced training there were 250 soldiers. The Vietnam War was going on and the Army needed ground troops. The platoon sergeant and platoon leaders called off all the names except three. 247 soldiers were scheduled for Jungle Warfare Advance Training at Fort Pock, Louisiana. I was standing there hoping and praying they would not send me to Fort Pock. I was one of the three left. We were sent to Fort Rucker, Alabama, for aviation training in helicopter operation mechanic. God brought it to my attention that He saves me by retake the test, by giving me the knowledge to past the test to become a helicopter mechanic. I could not hold back the tears of joy and knew that God was with me all the time covering me with His Holy hand.

In **Psalm 34:6-7** say, "This poor man cried, and the Lord heard him, and saved him out of all his troubles. The angel of the Lord encamped round about them that fear him, and deliver them." The mighty hand of God was guiding my life. God is already with those whom he saves, because God lives in the temple inside our hearts. Whenever we are be patient with Him, He is always there with his angels to guide us and lead us, for He knows what's best for our lives. Whenever God give us a mission we should do our best, because we never know what Christ may have for us the next time. For this I will praise Him with my whole heart, thank Him according to thy loving-kindness: according unto the multitude of the tender mercies, what He has shown unto me. It was the power in the blood of the lamb that set me free, and the power of his Holy Spirit was directing my life. God wants me to tell you, put your trust in the hand of the saving grace of God, and He will be your comfort all the days of your life, give Him your trouble, have faith and trust in him. **Psalms 27,** says, "Be of good courage, and he shall strengthen your heart, all ye that hope in the Lord."

Hope is desire with the expectation of obtaining what is desired, or believing that it is obtainable with trust and reliance. In the New Testament, Christian hope should always be connected with the return of Jesus Christ at the end of the age and the resurrection of the dead. This hope is anchor down my soul and I will be steadfast within my faithfulness in Christ Jesus until He come.

My Guardian Angels Save My Soul

APRIL OF, 1968, my first month in Vietnam, I arrived in Long-Ben. One afternoon as I looked up, I saw all those airplanes coming from north. I asked the sergeant what was going on and he said that they were bringing bodies out of Lia-kay. That is where the morgue is located. "Then he toll me, this is where you are going." The next day I arrived at Lia-kay, with the 163rd Assault Helicopter Company.

The next morning, six solders were scheduled for In-Country Orientation Training; the platoon leaders took us to a place where a large bunker was underground. We stayed there overnight and the next morning we were to police call (pick-up trash) and burn human waste. There were two hundred soldiers standing around and I was the one singled out to burn human waste. I got in the group to police call. The sergeant picked me out of all those soldiers at once, as if he knew me. When he turned his back I slipped back into the group again. I had my back turned to him in the midst of the other solders, so he grabbed me, pulled me out and led me to the door, and said go and burn the waste. I was wondering how could he pick me out of two hundred soldiers so quickly? I went and picked up a five-gallon can of gasoline. As I was walking toward the rear of the building, a Vietcong rocket flew over my head and hit a tree where the soldiers were on police call. It exploded in the midst of them killing and wounding over half of them. That sergeant must have been a guardian angel sent by God, because if I had not done what I was told I would have been killed along with the other soldiers. I got up and ran into a bunker. There, solders had been seriously wounded by the rocket and they were in real pain. The Soldiers were still coming into the bunker, one soldier came and stood in front of me, screaming and holding his arm. there was a big hole in his back where my hand could pass through, but there was no blood. I said to him, you have a hole through your back; he looked at it and collapsed and died right in front of me. I got sick and was screaming Get me out of here; I can't take it any more, "Oh Lord why did so many have to die?"

I was calling on my mother to help me, and then they took me to the hospital. I told the doctor I wanted to go home because I could not stand the sight of all the people dying. They gave me some pills, and after about two weeks, I was all right. Oh Lord God, you have saved me from the hand of Satan. Oh God you knew what was going to happen before it happened, and you sent your angel down to save my soul. I said. Lord Jesus, how can I praise and thank your Holy Name? You are an amazing and incredible God; your grace and mercy endure forever, Oh holy hand of the Almighty God, I thank you for saving me one more time. Lord, you love me more than I love you. Lord God, clean me of all my sins and make me more Christ like every day. **Psalm 41:2** says, "The Lord will preserve him, and keep him alive; and he shall be blessed upon the earth and thou wilt not deliver him unto the will of his enemies" It was amazing how God saved me from the hand of Satan, so I was waiting whatever he had for my life I shall be ready. **Psalm 51:14** says, Deliver me from blood guiltiness, O God, thou God of my salvation: and my tongue shall sing aloud of thy righteousness." Both riches and honor come of thee and thou reigneth over all; and in thine hands are power and might; and in thine hand is to make great, and to give strength unto all.

Lord I pray for those family of the soldiers who lost their life during that tragedy war, that you will comfort their heart with love, peace and joy.

My Guardian Angel Protected Me from Rockets and Bombings

My third month in Vietnam, one evening around 9:00 p.m., the Vietcong started launching a rocket attack on our position. At the same time the U. S. Air Forces were retaliating bombing the Vietnam position, which was more than a mile away from our unit location. Hot debris and shrapnel were flying all over the place. The soldiers ran out of the building into the bunker. It was dark and I got a little confused about entering into the bunker. I could hear the shrapnel flying all over the place. When I finally got safely into the bunker, they asked me in disbelief, "Why didn't you get hit?" I said "I don't know," "I can't believe it. I thought I would be hit or killed and this could have been the end of my life."

All I could say was God had mercy on my soul and covered me with his holy hands. Then I said to myself, "Oh, He even sees me in the dark? At night I'm immersed in the light." Lord God you saw my need in trouble and you covered me with your holy hands. It was the power of Your mercy that brought me out of the pass way of Satan. It is God who delivers us from our trouble, so we must always show Christ we love Him by doing the will of God by spreading the Good News of God's word and how He is always there to rescue us during our need in prayer. The wicked enemies may come from the east, west, south, or north, the enemies may camp around my soul, and flames of fire may come after me, but when God Almighty has your name written down in the Book of Life in there no power on earth that will defeat you. Oh Master, I praise your holy name for the loving protection you have provided for my soul. Lord, you are teaching me how to stand when trouble is all around me. Lord, I know my enemies will rise up against me, and I pray my strength and courage will increase day by day, that I may walk in your footstep. Oh Lord, in my time of stress and need, will you hear my prayer, morning, day, and night? I will direct my prayer unto you, Oh Lord, I thank you for not delivering my soul without cause to mine enemy.

II Samuel 22:2-4 says, "The Lord is my rock, and my fortress, and my deliverer; The God of my rock; in him will I trust; he is my shield, and the horn of my salvation, my high tower, and my refuge, my savior; thou savest me from violence. I will call on the Lord, who is worthy to be praise: so shall I be saved from mine enemies." When the wave of death compassed my soul, the Lord covered me with His Holy Hands, so I will sing praises to the name of the Lord highest, I will praise thee, Oh Lord, with my whole heart and show forth all thy marvelous works.

The Mercy of God Saved Me from a Test Flight

DURING MY six months in Vietnam, one of our helicopters was in for service maintenance. After completing the maintenance and technician inspection, the helicopter was ready for takeoff. I was scheduled to go on the test flight. When the pilot started the helicopter I said, "Wait. I'm going to get my gear." When I came back they had taken off and left me. I said, "Why couldn't they wait for me? Lest than three minutes." The helicopter was gone for over thirty minutes; it was overdue back to the base. An hour went by with no radio communication from the helicopter pilot. My superiors decided to send out another helicopter to look for it. Then the news came back that the helicopter had crashed or had been shot down by the Vietcong, and all were killed. That could have been the end of my life, but God had mercy on my soul and made them leave me.

It was not God's plan for me to be on that flight because if He were not on my side, Satan would have taken my life long ago. God is all knowing, and always knows what is ahead of us. Because He is the God, who guides our life through this whole world day by day, I thank him. God directs our every move; he warns us time after time, so be ready at all times because we never know when death will come our way. Make sure you are seal in salvation of God. Always be ready to give an account of yourself, and be patient, be faithful, and trust in the Almighty Lord Jesus

Christ. When God saves His people from the snare of Satan, it is according to His master plan of every one blueprint He has for the purpose for your life. "My heart is glad, and my glory rejoiceth: my flesh also shall rest in hope." Through this our purpose in life is to be used by God. Our life will continue adversity along with trial and temptation, but God will mold and shape us the way He wants us to be before He will send us out to do His will. These are some things God has sent me through, and he has given me strong faith with encouragement, confidence and love with understanding of the true word of Jesus Christ.

I will praise Christ Jesus every day of my life because He has comforted my soul. When I am sad or frightened, this reminds me that all I need to do is open myself to the Lord and His love will wrap around me like a warm comforting blanket. Oh what a mighty God I serve. God still has more work for me to do. In **Psalms 91:1-4** says, "He that dwelleth in the secret place of the most high shall abide under the shadow of the Almighty. I will say of the Lord, He is my refuge and my fortress: my God; in him will I trust. Surely he shall deliver thee from the snare of the fowler, and from the noisome pestilence. He shall cover thee with his feathers, and under his wings shalt thou trust: his truth shall be thy shield and buckler." **II Samuel 22:26** says, "with the merciful thou wilt show thyself merciful, and with the upright man thou wilt show thyself upright."

Lord I pray for the family of those soldiers, who lost their life during that tragedy war, keep them in perfect peace and good health.

I Was Covered by the Blood of the Lamb

DURING MY ninth month in Vietnam, amazing things were still happening. It was the start of the Tet Offence. Fighting was going on down in the delta. The time was about 9:00 p.m. at night when my commander's helicopter had maintenance problems.

My superiors asked me to go down and repair the helicopter. We took another helicopter on the way down, I saw red tracers coming up to the helicopter. There are five rounds between each tracer. The helicopter was not hit it was unbelievable. We arrived down in the delta and I was up on the helicopter performing maintenance. The sergeant reached up and snatched me three feet down onto a steel slab, right on my back. I had my flight helmet on and I could not hear what was going around me. I said why did you pull me down and then I saw flashes of fire. He said the Vietcong are shooting rockets on our position. Rockets were falling all around us. I heard someone scream. I was lying on the steel slab calling my mother and asking God to save me. I went to get up to run, but the sergeant grabbed me by my leg and pulled me down. As soon as he did, a rocket came right over my head and exploded. If I had stood up, I would have been killed. Oh Lord God, I thank You for that sergeant. There was a fence about fifty yards away surrounding the U. S. compound. The fence was about six feet high and with bar wire on top making it about eight feet.

When the Vietcong stopped shooting, the U.S. started shooting back at the enemy, and I immediately got up and started running toward the fence. The next thing I knew I was inside the compound inside the operation office. It was blackout and it was hard to see anything; it was incredible how I found myself standing inside the right office I never seen before. The other soldiers came in and wondered how I got in without the gate being open. They didn't see me go over the fence and I couldn't explain. I know without a doubt that God is an incredible God; he holds the key to my future. It was not by my power, but the mighty power of God that lifted me over the fence and place me inside the operation office, which was amazing. Only God knows what he has in store for my life. I will praise and thank Him all the days of my life because He has blessed and saved my soul. The Lord new I was in great distress, He knew the enemies were closing in on my soul. I was at a point where only my God could deliver my soul from the hand of my enemies, so I was afraid and called upon the Lord. Oh Lord I am down here and my enemies are closing in on me. Oh Lord please hears my prayer, hear my voice, hear my cry.

I could feel the earth shaking each time I heard a rocket explode. Oh Lord doesn't leave me, but cover me with your holy hand. I will call upon the Lord, who is worthy to be praised: so shall I be saved from mine enemies. The sorrows of death compassed me, and the flood of ungodly men made me afraid. For I have kept the way of the Lord, and have not wickedly departed from my God. Lord Jesus I will stay under the blood and Satan can't do me any harm. I will pray under the blood and the world can't do me any harm. I will stay right by your side and you will cover me with your Holy hand. Oh Lord how I love you, you are my rock my salvation you are my way to the promise land. **Psalm 6:9** says, "The Lord hath heard my supplication and will receive my prayer."

Psalms 91:7-12 says, "A thousand shall fall at thy side, and ten thousand at thy right hand; but it shall not come nigh thee. Only with thine eyes shalt thou behold and see the reward of the wicked. Because thou hast made the Lord, which is my refuge, even the most High, thy habitation; there shall no evil befall thee, neither shall any plague come nigh thy dwelling. For he shall give his angels charge over thee, to keep thee in all thy ways, they shall bear thee up in their hands, lest thou dash thy foot against a stone."

My First Marriage Didn't Last

DURING MY eleventh month in Vietnam, June 1965 I was married to my lovely wife, the one I visited in Philadelphia. This was a joyful year we had together, so we had talked about buying a house, but in June of 1967 I received my draft noticed for the army. In August of

1967 I was called to serviced and was sent to Vietnam in April of 1968, to fight in the war. During my time there, I was a helicopter mechanic, and also I was in charge of NCO club.

I would send most of my money home; my wife was to use some and put the rest in the bank to purchase a home when I returned. While I was there, the soldiers were scheduled to perform outer perimeter guard duty at night three times a year. On my last night out, in February 1969 at about 10:00 p.m. it was just getting dark At about 10:30 pm a shot went off so we jumped up and picked up our weapons, thinking someone had spotted the enemy, so we were looking and waiting for the enemy to show up. At 10:40 pm the phone rang. The sergeant answered, and said three bumpers down the line a soldier had received a Dear John letter (I want a divorce) and had shot and killed himself. A strange feeling came over my soul, and then I said that soldier was crazy, because I would never do anything like that.

As I write this story, the Holy Spirit is upon me. The next month in March, 1969, I received a Dear John letter, and the first thing that came to my mind, was that soldier who killed himself. In April, 1969, I departed Vietnam and returned home. I had six months remaining in service at Fort Lewis, Washington. When I got home, my wife told me she did not love me anymore. I said "What did I do to cause you to not love me anymore?" She said, "I love someone else." I will never know how a woman can reject a man who never did anything to cause the problem. The letter I received from her had no indication. To my knowledge, everything was going great, all the time she would send pictures of herself, and mentioned in mail a house she had looked at. I was puzzled trying to find out what went wrong. I talked to one of my friends, and I could not believe what I was hearing. It was almost unbearable. I had sent about four thousand dollars to my wife to put down on the house that we planned to buy, but she used the money completely out of our plan. Later on, I found out that she was spending money just as fast as I could send it home. I saw one of our good friends who got married a year before us, and she told me she had broken up with my wife because of the comment she had made when she was at her house. I asked what the comment, she told me that my wife said that she wished I would be killed so she could receive my insurance money. When I heard this, it felt as if someone had driven a stake through my heart. It was unbelievable. I would often wonder why God put me through this, plus the war. I said to God, Why did you save me and let all the other soldiers die and get hurt? I am still waiting on the Lord to tell me my purpose.

In May, of 1969, when it was time for me to report back for duty, I saw her and said I needed some money. The next day we went to the bank and she gave me seven hundred dollars, so I asked how much she had left, and she said she only had a thousand dollars. I never told her what I heard, or what she did with the money. I said give me the other three hundred dollars; she got upset and said what I am going to live off. of I got upset and said, "You have a job and you stay with your sister." After arguing, she gave me the threes hundred dollar, so I left for duty. I could not hate her; I could not judge her I left it to God who has the right to judge. God knew my heart that I still loved her which after what she said and what she did. I have God to keep me safe and sound and I thank Him for bringing me back alive.

As I began to tell some friends about my marriage, they said "Why, you let her get away with that;" you should have killed her or committed bodily harm to her. I said to them, "What would I gain if I did this to her? I am a heavenly child of God; why do this and lose my soul?" When I finished my tour of service and returned to Washington, DC, I saw her again and said to her, I still love you, so let's try to get back together. She said; I like you very much, but I love my friends more than you. "So we were separated and later divorce." Be strong and have courage, fear not, don't be afraid, for the Lord thy God, He will go with thee, he will not fail thee, nor forsake thee. **Deuteronomy 31:6** say, "Be strong of a good courage, fear not be afraid of them: for Lord thy God; he will not fail thee, nor forsake the." **Psalms 92:11-15** says, "Mine eye also shall see my desire on mine enemies, and mine ears shall hear my desire of the wicked that rise up against me. The righteous shall flourish like the palm tree: he shall grow like a cedar in Lebanon. Those that be planted in the house of the Lord shall flourish in the courts of our God. They shall still bring forth fruit in old age; they shall be fat and flourishing; to show that the Lord is upright: he is my rock, and there is no unrighteousness in him.

My Guardian Angel Was Watching Over My soul

During my tenth month in Vietnam, I had to work late one night and that morning I was the only soldier left in the building. Around 9:00 a. m, I heard a loud crash and I jumped out of my bed and ran outside and saw two helicopters had crashed three feet from my building. God was right there beside me. We lived in a rubber tree plantation; trees were located all around the building. When the helicopters collided in the air, they started falling directly toward my building. Before reaching the building the two helicopters collided into the trees, falling three feet short of my building. Only the amazing hand of God could have saved me, those trees were there for my protection. This was another horrible situation I had to witness. Eight soldiers were killed and their bodies were separated apart hanging up in the trees. When the helicopter collided together, they went into a spin and ended up in the trees. I had seen so much killing, this did not bother me, so my hearted became harden. My God is an everlasting God full of grace and mercy; He has put me through so many situations that have brought me so close to death.

Oh God I thank you, for you are an incredible God whom I will praise. Lord God, I praise your holy name once again because you looked down upon my soul. I thank the powerful hand of the Lord for my salvation. He stretched out His mighty hand and saw my affliction, He had compassion on my soul. I thank the awesome power of the Almighty God for saving my soul one more time. He could just as easily snuffed out my life, but for His glorious grace, mercy and His perfect love He has for my soul. **Psalm 40:11** says, "Withhold not thou thy tender mercies from me, O Lord: let thy loving kindness and thy truth continually preserve me." Oh God I will trust in the true living God, I have strong faith in my heart, I will stand on the promise of God, because you are a greatest God who have poured out your love upon my heart, mind, and soul. **Jeremiah 15:21** says, "I will deliver thee out of the hand of the wicked, and I will redeem thee out of the hand of the terrible." I have learn how to put my trust in the holy hand of you Lord, because there is no one on this earth who could save me from the terrier of this war, Jesus Christ.

God Can Transform Our Hearts and Minds into love

DURING MY eleventh month in Vietnam, my section would have a cookout for us once a month. On Saturday nights a Captain who was a medical doctor about six foot one around 220 pound and who would always come around to eat and drink without helping us pay for food and beverage. For that reason, I hated him. I truly did not like this officer at all because he was a cheapskate. That Saturday night we were cooking and the food was ready to eat. I looked up and here came that captain, "I said Give us some money or you have to leave you cheapskate." He came up to me and knocked me out. When I came to myself, something strange was happening that I could not explain. We started talking and eating to gather and had a good time with no hate in my heart toward him. My chin was sore, so the doctor treated me. I had been transformed by the power of God. **Romans 12:2** says, "And be not conformed to this world: but be ye transformed by the renewing of your mind, that ye may prove what is that good, and acceptable, and perfect will of God."

The captain and I became the best of friends. It was amazing and I didn't know what had happen to me. Lest then one half hour I went from hating to loving him, it was more than incredible. It was the holy hand of God who put the love in my heart for other. Father, these things that were happening to me were beyond my wildest imagination because my friends could not believe or understand what they had seen. They were shocked to see me talking to him the way I was. I had love in my heart for him and this was one of the strangest things that ever happened to me.

I was taught growing up you should not hate your brother or sister; you should love them no matter what they do. Why did I change so quickly? All I know is God is an amazing God.
II Corinthians 13:11 says, "Finally, brethren, farewell. Be perfect; be of good comfort, being of one mind, live in peace; and the God of love and peace shall be with you."

God Knew the Outcome of My Flight

AT THE end of my twelfth month in Vietnam, my time was up and I was scheduled to depart in that morning. There were two helicopters that were schedule for Long Bend, where I was scheduled to go, for my departure back to the U.S. That morning somehow my paper work was not completed and I had some equipment to be turned. The helicopter departed as scheduled without me. I thought to myself, "I don't want to stay here one more day; I wish all my requirements were completed so I could have departed." Around 10:30 a.m., it was reported that those two helicopters had crashed or shot down. My commander scheduled a flight for the next morning. Only God knew what was going to happen to that first flight, sometimes He delays us because He knows what is ahead of us. God wants us to stay beside Him and walk wherever He goes. He said, "If you abide in me I will abide in you and I will cover you with my Holy hand, I will be your shelter your rod your staff." God is my Father, so where He leads I will follow. The marvelous hand of the everlasting present of the love-kindness of Christ Jesus saved my soul. I praise and give thank to him for delivering me from that flight. He shielded me because He knew the outcome. The blood of the true living lamb of Christ Jesus had redeemed me. I was set free from the hand of Satan. **Galatians 1:4** says, "Who gave himself for our sins; that he might deliver us from this present evil world, according to the will of God and our Father." Lord God you have brought me this far and I will stay right by your side. There were times when I didn't know how I was going to make it; you were right there all the time to see me through. Lord God, I thank you with my whole heart. I praise and bless your name for saving me one more time. Sometime I wonder why you saved me. What is it about me that you are saving some one like me?

I am no better than my friends who didn't make it through. Lord, I don't understand, but I know that you are in charge. **Psalm 101:6** says, "Mine eyes shall be upon the faithful of the land, that they may dwell with me: he that walk in a perfect way, he shall serve me." **Exodus 12:13** says, "And the blood shall be to you for a token upon the houses where ye are: and when I see the blood, I will pass over you, and the plague shall not be upon you to destroy you, when I smite the land of Egypt." Lord God, I pray you will have mercy and grace upon all soldiers who are still alive from that terrible war, where so many lives was lost. Those who are remaining Lord I pray you will lay Your Holy hand upon their soul and comfort them, heal them and keep Your loving arms around them. O Lord give them peace of mind, and Lord I pray those who don't know You will seek Your Holy face and ask for forgiveness of sin and receive a eternal life in heaven.

In the Valley of Death My Guardian Angel Was There

AFTER LEAVING Vietnam, I was stationed at Fort Lewis, Washington. It was July, of 1969, and I had three months remaining in the Army. One morning the pilot, crew, chief and I were scheduled to take a flight to Yakima, Washington. On the way to Yakima, we wanted to fly up and around Majestic Mount Rainier so we flew up as high as we could. It got so cold; we flew off to the side down through a valley. The valley was about a half mile deep and two to three hundred yards wide. We were flying along, and the draft was so strong it began to pull the helicopter down and we could not fly up.

We were so frightened we started praying. Trying to keep the helicopter up caused us to use more fuel. As time passed by, the fuel gauge was showing close to empty and no end in sight. I looked out to see the grounded, it was so far down I could barely see ground. There "Oh God, we are going to fall, I was afraid, for the flight schedule was about thirty minutes long, After about forty five minutes, we were still in flight under a heavy downdraft, and no one could hear us on the radio. I was praying for God to save us. I though this would be the end of my life and that I would never see my family again. All of a sudden, we came out of the valley and there was a fuel pump sitting out in a field from nowhere. It was amazing. We fueled up and continued on our way to Yakima. "Oh thank you God for saving us on this day. Lord God, you are the most incredible God in the whole wide world and in heaven. Lord God, I love my guardian angel that you sent down to bring us out from the valley of the shadow of death. I thank you Lord for hearing my prayer and rescuing us from the hand of Satan. Lord God, you must have something special for our lives. Who else in heaven could have guided our lives the way you did. I thank you with all my heart for your extraordinary grace and mercy, that you have shower down upon my soul.

Oh Lord how can I thank you? I will praise your holy name every day and night. Lord, there is no way I can ever thank you for what you have done in my life, for the love you have covered me with and the knowledge and understanding you have given me. I will never stop being a witness by telling everyone how I met Jesus. October, 1969, was the end of my first incredible experience while in service. Oh God, what an amazing and incredible Journey through life with you Lord Jesus Christ.

Psalms 23:1-6 says, "The Lord is my shepherd; I shall not want He maketh me to lie down in green pastures: he leadeth me beside the still waters.

He restoreth my soul: he leadeth me in the paths of righteousness for his name's sake. Yea, though I walk through the valley of the shadow of death, I will fear no evil; for thou art with me; thy rod and thy staff they comfort me. Thou preparest a table before me in the presence of mine enemies: thou anointest my head with oil; my cup runneth over, surely goodness and mercy. Shall follow me all the days of my life; and I will dwell in the house of the Lord forever."

God Gave Me Light to Overcome Darkness

DURING MY time in Vietnam, I didn't try any marijuana. For some reason it never appealed to me. There was a rumor going around the company area that I was part of the Criminal Investigation Division (CID). When soldiers would stand around in a group and saw me coming, they would disappear in fear. They thought I was spying on them to see if they were involved in smoking marijuana. It continued until I completed my tour in Vietnam. I thought this would cause them to stop smoking. I returned to Washington, D.C. and remained there until 1970. I never did try any during my time there. There was a lot of smoking marijuana going on. I departed Washington in the summer of 1970 and moved to Chicago. I attended college and worked fulltime. Marijuana smoking was all over the city; it was not that common to see someone standing on the corner smoking. I was working and going to college, I did not have much time to go out.

The summer of, 1971, I had already met two brother, who became good friends. We had been discussing going out clubbing, so one Saturday night they asked me to come by their house. They had something they wanted me to see and try. I went and when I arrived, I asked them what they wanted me to try. They said we had to go up in the attic. They went and brought some marijuana. This was my first time seeing marijuana. So they fixed it up and offered me some. I said no, so they started smoking. They said, "Come on it's not strong. It wont hurt you," so "I said, Why not." After smoking it I did not feel anything, although they told me they felt good. They offered me another one and I said no. We arrived at a club. I was drinking while standing up talking to a girl I had just met. All of a sudden, my legs started to get weaker and I became dizzy. I reached over to put the glass down and my eyes went black. I don't know what happened to the glass.

I called my friends to help me because I could not see for about thirty seconds. My eyes went from seeing black to seeing red. It was a sea of blazing fire burning; I started screaming for somebody to help me. Someone lead me outside. All I could see was a sea of fire burning. I heard voices screaming but I did not know if the people were in the club screaming or the people screaming in the fire, I was so frighten I was calling on God to help me, I didn't know what to do.

Revelation 20:10 says, "And the devil that deceived them was cast into the lake of fire and brimstone, where the beast and the false prophet's are, and shall be tormented day and night for ever and ever." I pleaded with the Lord to give my eyesight back and in return I would never smoke marijuana again. For the next five minutes, I continued to see fire blazing. I believe God was showing me a glance of hell. I am here to tell all who smoke marijuana or disobey God, I pray to the Almighty God that you will refrain from your evil ways pray and turn to the one and only true living God and ask for forgiveness of your sins. Because if you saw what I saw that night, you will live for God forever and never turn back. Then my eyes started getting better so I was well enough to drive home. Oh Lord, if I was not a child of God, no telling where my soul would have been. All I can say is there is no place on this earth where I would rather be than in the kingdom of God with your glorious peace down in my soul.

I thank you for your awesome power. **Isaiah 9:18a** says, "For wickedness burneth as the fire: it shall devour the briers and thorns, and shall kindle in the thickest of the forest." I stayed in Chicago until December of 1972 and I never did smoke any more marijuana again. I departed Chicago and moved back to Maryland. When I visited friends in Washington, D.C., it seemed like everybody was smoking marijuana. None for me! Being around friends smoking it made me sick. I lost friends when they started smoking, for I would leave. To this day, I have never tried smoking again. Thanks to the Almighty God for His saving Grace and mercy for not letting me get involved with marijuana. I thank God for having mercy on my soul and showing me what hell was like. I thank you for delivering me from the pit of hell. God is the only one who can clean us from our sins, not ourselves, nor the doctor, nor the government. It is the one who put us on this earth; He is the only one who has the power to overcome all of our sinful trouble.

Oh God, it is unbelievable to know there are so many people who are hooked on marijuana, and it is unbelievable to know people are not committed to put their trust in Jesus Christ and ask God to forgive their sins. Jesus Christ loves you just as you are; I pray that you will surrender your soul to the Almighty God, who has the power to take your sins and leave them at the foot of the cross. Jesus will wash your soul in the blood of the lamb. He will set you free; Jesus Christ is standing at your door knocking. Jesus has given me these words to write, that someone may be led to Christ or ask God to clean their sinful heart, or come to receive their salvation. The word of God is God and He wanted these words to make a difference in your life.

Jonah 2:7-9 say, "When my soul fainted within me I remembered the Lord: and my prayer came in unto thee, into thine holy temple. They that observe lying vanities forsake their own mercy. But I will sacrifice unto thee with the voice of thanksgiving; I will pray that that I have vowed. Salvation is of the Lord."

Don't Give Up on God's People

In 1973, God led me to join the Army National Guard. In 1981, He led me back on Army active duty. While there more incredible things were happening. There was a sergeant who did not know Christ as his savior. He knew the Old Testament but hated the New Testament. I asked him what was wrong in the New Testament; he replied that he did not believe in the things Jesus did and he didn't believe Jesus was a true God. He loved the Old Testament because there were scriptures he could use against other soldiers. If he did not like a person, he would use one of the verses in the Old Testament to work for him against me, by destroying one of my important papers (DD-214), so I could not get promoted. I remember telling him you are not going to stop me, so. I wrote to St. Louis to send me a new DD214 and they did.

I hand-carried my package up to headquarters and I got promoted, even after his deliberate attempts to stop me. It is written in **Psalm 57** says, "Be merciful unto me O God: be merciful unto me: for my soul trusteth in thee: yea, in the shadow of thy wings will I make my refuge, until these calamities be overpast." In God I will praise his word, in God I have put my trust; and I will not fear what flesh can do unto me. I did not hate him for what he did to me; I keep on explaining the Bible to him.

Five years later, he got very sick and was admitted to the hospital. Some soldiers and I went to see him and I carried my Bible with me to pray for him. He saw me coming and asked one of the soldier to throw that (Odom) out. He said I don't want to see him because I am not dying and I don't need him to read the Bible or pray for me. "We were able to convince him to let us pray for him and he got well." Four years later he retired from the service. A year later I went to a church and I saw him standing at the front door. I asked him, "What are you doing here?" And he said he said God had saved him through the blood of Jesus Christ as his savior and had joined the church and was on the usher board. My heart was glad to know he had accepted Christ as his Lord and savior. Our God is not a fallen God; he said let your light shine and it shall overcome darkness. Plant a seed and God will make it grow. Every believer is to let his or her light shine, because Jesus Christ is the light of the world and saves us to spread His Good News of what he has done for us. Our testimonies will become a blessing to the lost soul; it will let them know there is a way they can turn their lives around.

I hate to say this, but it true we who are called Christians are afraid and ashamed to spread the Good News of Jesus Christ. We go to church on Sunday, and through the week our mouths are sealed about Christ. Oh Heavenly Father, I pray that you will help us to overcome our fear and shame of you, Lord. Change our hearts to be more Christ-like each day and give us confidence to spread your Good News. **Romans 1:16** says, "For I am not ashamed of the gospel of Christ: for it is the power of God unto salvation to every one that believeth; to the Jew first, and also to the Greek." It will be a blessing to my heart, to see your people doing the will of God. Lord I will praise and bless the Holy name of Jesus Christ.

Continue to Let God's Light Shine and It Will Overcome Darkness

THERE WAS a female soldier sent to my unit to work with me. She was an atheist and did not believe in the Bible. When other soldiers would come into my office and start talking about the Lord. She would immediately leave to avoid hearing the Lord's name. I asked her how she became an atheist and she said that her mother and their family did not believe in God at all. I told her, "You don't have to believe what they believe. I told her, "If you know Jesus Christ, He will change your life completely." but she did not want to change. She wanted to believe what her mother believed.

I went on talking to other soldiers, as they would come into my office. After about six months, she started listening to what was being said about the Lord. About three months later, she was able to talk to about Christ. She said she would not accept Jesus as her Lord and savior. She was moved from my unit to another unit, and I did not see much of her for about three years. One day, she sent me a book about Christ and shared how God had saved her soul through the blood of Jesus as her Lord and savior. Don't ever give up on God's people; plant a seed and the Lord will water it and make it grow up. You know there was a time when I was ashamed to spread the Good News of Christ, but when I really found out who he was and what he had done for me, I started talking to other Christians.

The next thing I knew I was spreading the Good News of Christ to Christians and non-Christians. The more I tell others about the love of Jesus Christ, the more I begin to grow by strengthening my faith in Christ Jesus with confidence and courage to talk to anyone about Christ. I tell you, there is no better feeling than to tell someone about Jesus Christ by blessing him or her with the inspiration power of God's word, his people are hurting and dying because of lack of God knowledge. God, churches, pastors are preaching His word to Christians in the house of God. Although there are problems in His house, the real problem is on the battlefields on the outside of His church. This is where the lost, hurting, and dying are. Preachers need to tell

Christians to go out on the battlefield and bring lost soul into the house of God. In **Ezekiel 34:11-16** say, For thus said the Lord God Behold, I, even I, will both search my sheep, and seek them out. As a shepherd seeketh out his flock in the day that he is among his sheep that are scattered; so will I seek out my sheep, and will deliver them out of all places where they have been scattered in the cloudy and dark day. And I will bring them out from the people, and gather them from the mountains, and will bring them to their own land, and feed them upon the mountains of Israel by the rivers, and in all the inhabited places of the country. I will feed them in a good pasture. I will seek that which was lost, and bring again that which was driven away, and will bind up that which was broken, and will strengthen that which was sick: but I will destroy the fat and the strong; I will feed them with judgment.

Give Your Troubles to God; He Will Answer Your Prayers

I WAS taking a correspondence course and my position was operations sergeant. This position included responsibilities to supervise and prepare operational training of six units. I failed my second test. I had to study hard to take the test over again and I had to study for the next one coming up. My commander would not give me time to study. I would study very late at night. I asked if he could make time for me to study like other soldiers have time, then I could prioritize my work. He replied, "No! You have a responsibility and you must perform it to standards." My performance got a little better. They scheduled me for another school during the same time I was taking the correspondence course. It seemed as if the whole world was crashing down upon my shoulders. I would ask, "God where are you?" My enemies are trying to destroy my soul, I need your help; my strength is weak and I can't do anything to stop them, Oh God I'm going to give my problems to you; I am not strong enough to carry this load."

Before I departed for school, my immediate supervisor wrote me a poor performance letter and my supervisor wrote me a poor evaluation report. I went off to school with a heavy burdened heart. I began praying day and night for those people. I prayed God would release this flame of fire which has trying to destroy my soul. Oh Lord, I pray you will lift my head above mine enemies round about me then, Lord, I will offer sacrifices unto the Lord. "Oh Lord, I pray you will forgive them and create in them a new and pure heart and bless them, that they may see you. Help them Oh Lord to become Christ like with your holy hand." When the course was over I returned back to my unit. The performance letters didn't go on my record. The evaluation report was rewritten with a superior report. I thanked God for answering my prayers. Prayer is one of the most powerful weapons we have to fight our enemies with, so I am glad God has given me the wisdom, knowledge, and understanding to stand on the prayers of God. What He has given me He has given every true believe of Jesus Christ the same. All you have to do is put your trust in Him and seek His will and be obedient and then ask Him to teach you how to pray. Read your Bible; there are examples how to pray.

When you learn to pray, put your trust in God. Pray and give your troubles to Him because God is all-powerful and he can do anything you ask of His will. This is one reason why so many of God's Christian are having troubles today, they don't know how to prayer. I pray you will find Jesus Christ as a prayer answering God, so give your troubles to him, take your hand off it, trust and believe in God, and every thing will be all right. My supervisor who wrote that bad evaluation report, than change it; six month later became a child of God. What a mighty God we serve. I praise, I bless the name of Jesus because there is no other God like the God of heaven and earth. **Daniel 9:3-4** says, "And I set my face unto the Lord God, to seek by prayer and supplications, with fasting, and sackcloth, and ashes; And I prayer unto the Lord my God, and make my confession, and said, O Lord, the great and dreadful God, keeping the covenant and mercy to them that love him, and to them that keep his commandments."

Love and Mercy Will Overcome Sin

DURING ANOTHER period in the service, there was an officer in the army who heard me talking about the Lord, and it did not seem to bother him. There were times we would discuss the Bible together. We went out to lunch and as we sat down to eat, I started a conservation about Jesus love for everyone. I was commenting on how God hates sin and how sin causes God's people to disobey Him. We left the restaurant and headed to the parking lot, when're he let me know that he didn't like what I was saying about sin and wanted to fight. I walked away. I didn't see him anymore until about two months later. We talked as friends, conservation continues about God. Six months later one day, another friend told me he had been saved. I went to see him. It was a blessing to know that God had saved him by redeeming through the blood of Jesus as his Lord and savior. Lord Jesus Christ, there is nothing in my power, nothing in myself; God was using me as a rod, to spread His Good News. God said all we have to do spread God's seed on good ground and he will give it water and increase the growth. This is all God asks us to do, to plant his seed and He will do all the work. I pray that Christian will become witnesses for Jesus Christ.

As it is written in **Luke 8:15** says, "But that on good ground are they, which in an honest and good heart, having heard the word, keep it, and bring forth fruit with patience." I prayed to the Lord the eyes of your understanding being enlightened; that you may know what is the hope of his calling, and what the riches of the glory of his inheritance in the saints, and what is the exceeding greatness of his power toward us that believes, according to the work of his mighty power, which he wrought in Christ when he raised him from the dead, and set him at his own right hand in the heavenly places?

I Thank God I Was Able to Help Someone

MY SECOND tour in the service was the most rewarding time of my life. It was a joy working with other soldiers, One day, God brought back to my mind all the soldiers that He used me to touch. I was a rod from His Holy hand to His people. I thank Jesus for giving me the ability to help those in need. They would come to me with their problems, and I would always encourage them to tell me what was on their heart. My question was always, "Are you a Christian?" "Depending on their answer, I would know how God would allow me to help them. I would always explain them according to the regulation and other guidance set forth by the military or unit guidance to help correct the problem. Pray and ask God to change the heart of those who have wrong us, and I would say, if you want me to talk to that soldier who wronged you to know his/her story, or I could talk to your supervisor and find out how and why this problem came about. If you can find the root of a problem, most time the problem can be corrected. Talking to someone with anger will not solve problems, but God wants us to speak with love and care to solve the situation. Jesus Christ will always work and make our problems right so put your trust in Him and have faith and be patience.

There were so many young soldiers who would say to me, "When I grow up, I want to be just like you." I would tell them, "With a clean hand and pure heart with wholesome living by the Holy Hand of God, obey His commandment and fear the Lord, stay out of trouble and let God guide your life, and being obedient to your superiors for they will help lead and guide you in the right direction."

Jesus Christ says we should let our light shine everywhere we go. It was a blessing to my heart to have helped and touched so many soldiers along the way. I thank God for soldiers who helped me to grow stronger in my knowledge and understanding. I thank God for leading my back in the army to become a better person. It was God's guidance for me to become a high ranking leader to give direction, leadership and guidance to soldiers under my command, to encourage young soldiers to go on and become top ranking enlisted soldiers and officers.

During my whole tour of service there was something keeping me away from large crow, whenever I would be around large crows I would feel uncomfortable. It was the language they used, and oftentimes the negative things they would say about others, with no respect for their fellow soldiers. Growing up, I was never in this type of environment. It seemed if God had other plans for my life to be around two or three soldiers who had something constructive to talk about and a goal in life. We would help strengthen each other in knowledge and understand the true meaning of life. This kept me away from idle minded people who didn't have a plan in life. You can be the problem or you can become part of the problem. Oh God, I pray you will lead them away from idle minded people. Soldier I know how you like to join together; I pray you will find a friend who has a clear view of life and join with them to become friends with the same goal in mind. God is looking for people who are committed to separate themselves apart. My friends, we ask you to be thoughtful of you leaders who work hard and tell you how to live for the Lord. Show them great respect and love because of their work. Try to get along with each other. Encourage anyone who feels left out. Help all who are week, and be patient with everyone. Don't be hateful to people, just because they are hateful to you. Rather, be good to each other and over come evil mined.

Young people, after high school, I tell you the military is a good place to start your career in life. In today's world there is no better place to receive the best training, discipline, morals, ethics, leadership, and courage. It a great opportunity to be in the service to serve your country and to continue your education through college. In many cases the service will pay part of your fee. You will get the opportunity to choose what career you want, travel all over the world meeting other people of other countries, see how they live, and what they like. You can make a career, or when your time is up, you may chose to go into a career field outside the military. You will have a better chance getting a higher paid job because of your experience and education from the military. The military was there and God gave me the ability to make a career. I can say it was God that gave me this opportunity in life and I thank Him.

When I left the service and started to work in the civilian world, it was amazing what I saw and heard. "And God was nowhere to be found" no moral, ethics, standard and discipline, I hate to say this; but it was almost like the world of Satan had taken control. And the church was silent; in the military those words stand to make a difference. Oh God what has happen to your people? There is not much difference between the Christian and the non-Christian, and Lord I don't understand.

Oh Lord, may God, I pray for every soldier in this country and those who are stationed around the world, Lord you will lay your Holy Hand upon their soul. Lord, I pray you will comfort their hearts with peace and love down in their souls. Soldiers, you are going to face situations beyond your control. When the enemies come, I pray you will look up to the mighty hand of God and ask Him to take control and clear a new pathway of righteousness. Soldiers I know the power of the Lord because He has always made a way for me. He treats all with blessing who love and believe in Him. Being a child of God, it will make your life a whole lot better. I pray you will lean on Him, put your trust in Him, give Him your entire problem, and have faith in Him. He will give you confidence, and strengthen your heart. The Lord is my rock, and my fortress, and my deliverer; my God, my strength, in whom I will trust; my buckler, and the horn of my salvation, and my high tower. I will call upon the Lord, who is worthy to be praised: so shall I be saved from mine enemies. The sorrows of death compassed me, and the floods of ungodly men make me afraid. The sorrows of hell compassed me about: the snares of death prevented me. In my distress I called upon the Lord, and cried unto my God: he heard my voice out of His temple, and my cry came before Him, even into His ears.

Two Great Soldiers Who Inspired My Life

THERE WERE two soldiers, "enlisted and officer" who were a blessing and an inspiration to my life. CSM Mitchell direction, leadership, and guidance helped shape and mold my life. She was one of the most knowledgeable and understanding soldiers I have ever known during my entire military career. I thank God I was able to have crossed her path, I praise God for her, and I thank God that she overcame all adversity and became the best State Command Sergeant Major for District of Columbia National Guard. I was so proud, when she was selected to hold the highest position of a non-commissioned officer. I thank God for her because she had that God-given gift to work and help all soldiers with the right guidance, knowledge, and understanding to service those in need. She has such great knowledge; she not only helped enlisted soldier, she also provided knowledge and guidance to officers. I thank God for giving me the opportunity to have been in her presence, a person with such a great wealth of knowledge.

There one other person in my life during my tour of service who helped shaped my life of becoming a Command sergeant major. Colonel Bolden who is held to the highest standard of the U.S. Army. She has such amazing knowledge involving operational planning and training along with coordination, development, and execution of the overall plan. She is dedicated and highly motivational in all her work. I was fortuitous to have worked for her as her operation sergeant. If you have ever heard of going from nothing to something, she took me to such a great high, I never knew I could have gain such great knowledge and understanding from one person. I thank God for her helping me become the best operation sergeant I could have ever been. I thank Colonel Bolden for her leadership and guidance. This is the way God wants his people to work for him; dedicated and motivated. If you fail to please your employer with the performance of work, you are cheating your employer and God is not pleased with you because you are cheating Him also.

Exodus 31:3 says, "I have filled him with the spirit of God, in wisdom, and in understanding, and in knowledge, and all manner of workmanship." **Proverbs 4:5-7** says, "Get wisdom, get understanding; forget it not; nether decline from the words of my mouth. Forsake her not, and she shall preserve thee: love her, and she shall keep thee. Wisdom is the principal thing; therefore get wisdom: and with all thy getting get understanding." **Proverbs 9:9-10** says, "Give instructions to a wise man, and he will be yet wiser: teach a just man, and he will increase in learning. The fear of the Lord is the beginning of wisdom: and the knowledge of the Holy Ghost is understanding."

When my retirement was near, I wanted to retire without a retirement ceremony. But my Commander Colonel Bolden and CSM Mitchell saw that I deserved more than just leave; they wanted me to have the best ceremony and that ever been conducted in this organization. It was more than I can ever thank them for. I never knew I had made such an impression and impact on so many people in my life. I thank God in heaven for His blessed people who have helped me. People know more about you than you know about yourself, and God provided for those who love him. After all second commandment "thou shall love thy neighbor as thyself." I am glad they thought enough of me to do this, because I would have never known what love is all about. We should always thank those who do good for you, for God will bless you. Lord God, their were so many other soldiers and officers who were involved in my life during my tour of service who meant so much to me by helping me along the way. It was the love of God that kept us together during the war, conducting operation training over sea and all over United State. Of all the schools I attended and friends I met, I thank God for letting me be a friend to them. I thank the Lord for their friendship also. I pray Lord that you will bless each one, one by one, and continue to cover them with your Holy hand. Grace and peace be multiplied unto you all through the knowledge of God, and of Jesus our Lord.

Do Good and You Will Be Blessed

THIS IS from the State Command Sergeant Major Mitchell: Consistently, I hear in the news about someone being nominated for the Hall of Fame. Our Commanding General had indicated that he would dedicate an area in the District of Columbia National Guard Armory to be dedicated to the Enlisted Soldiers. That area should be our Hall of Fame with you being our first nominee. Why? Because You, Command Sergeant Major have set the precedence for all Non-commissioned Officers.

I may not be with you tonight physically, but believe me I am with you spiritually. How could I not be? You have been my mentor. Sometimes, I think you talk to me like a father, other times as a brother, and sometimes as a friend. But you have always spoken to me as a leader. Sometimes you were in the lead and other times, you had to follow my lead. But always there was a mutual respect. That is what makes you a dynamite leader. You were never selfish in sharing your knowledge and experience. You always encouraged me to look at the entire picture. As a matter of fact, when I went to the resident phase of the Sergeants Major Academy, it was your teaching about the importance of understanding doctrine that assisted me in doing well in our battle exercise. Just think about all the other Sergeants Major you have assisted in graduating from the Academy. I remember one time you made me so angry. I decided to move out of our office and downstairs to Sergeant Abraham's office. We use to call SFC Abraham 'Honest Abe.' So when you questioned me about a work project, I told you I had completed it and you could ask SFC Abraham. You indicated to me that SFC Abraham may be referred to as Honest Abe but his word was not a prayer book, you wanted to see the evidence of my project. We laughed; acknowledging that there was not much you could get past the Sergeant Major. I moved my things back to our office. You worried us to death when I was a readiness NCO about suspense. I couldn't wait to get your job. I figured it couldn't be as much work as it appeared to be. I thought I was pretty good in what I did. My report card spoke for itself. However, when I did get your job, which you encouraged me to seek, I quickly realized that I needed your help. It was easy for me to make all the decisions in one unit. It was different to supervise the personalities of all the leaders in the different units, meet the suspense, and conquer the rigorous demands of the S-3. You never really let me fall. You took the time to teach me, guide me and discuss with me the errors of my way when necessary.

I know a great number of officers you encouraged to go to OCS and helped then to achieve their goals. Sometimes, you saw things in us we didn't know we had. You brought those things out, with your constant frustration, when we didn't do it right. Troops used to laugh because I could imitate what you would probably say about an issue, but we all knew we did not want to cross the Sergeant Major. Sergeant Major, you were always so personal, business, sensitive, firm and possessed all the attributes of a true leader. Right now you are probably saying when will Sheila stop talking. But we all knew it wouldn't be if this letter had been short. Finally, I would like for everyone to know, how you came to me and told me that you wanted me to be the State Command Sergeant Major. You talked to me about the things I should do to prepare for that position. You acknowledged that you were looking towards retirement and felt I was the best choice. I had not thought about the position at that time, but I was not surprised at your guidance and words of encouragement. You indicated after I got the position that you would be there for me, and you lived up to that promise.

I sincerely, hope that I can live up to your expectations. I pray that you and your family enjoy a great retirement. One that is definitely well deserved.

Command Sergeant Major Henry Odom, YOU ARE MY HERO.

During My Second Tour of War

DURING MY second tour of service I was assigned with the163rd M.P. Battalion. You see how God work; in the Vietnam war I was assigned with the 163rd assault helicopter company. In the Gulf war I was assigned with the 372nd MP Battalion, all through my life I being involved with three; because it is an important number in the Trinity of Christ.

We were preparing for Saudi Arabia War. There was a soldier who refused to go because of his religious beliefs. The chaplain and command sergeant major had talked to him, but they were unable to convince him. So they asked me to talk with him. I took him into the back roomed and said tell me the real reason why you don't want to go and he said his religion and that it is not right to kill. I said Is your religion involved in a God who take care those who love him? He said yes.

I said, Let me tell you about my God. He took me through the

Vietnam war, He saved me, I was a Christian, and God said it is not my time to die. There are Christians all over the service. Yes it is true God said we are not to kill, if you are afraid of dying or killing someone, You don't have to go to war to die, if God is ready for you, driving on the highway, your life can be taken or someone else's. Don't worry about killing someone; I pray God will lead you away from a killing zone. God knows our hearts. You made an oath to the U.S. Army and you made an oath to God. I am not afraid, so you should not be afraid nor worry about your religion. We service the same God Almighty. He will take care of you. **Psalms 27**:1 says, "The Lord is my light and my salvation; whom shall I fear? The Lord is the strength of my life; of whom shall I be afraid." The soldier did go to Saudi Arabia with no problem. God says, I will not forsake you nor will I leave you. Put your trust and have faith in me, and I will stay right by your side, and cover you with my outstretched arm. We arrived in Saudi Arabia. I saw him a month later, he was doing just fine and he said I thank you. The word got out that I knew Jesus Christ and I didn't have any fear but I was willing to help others soldiers. That came to me for advice, so I thanked God I was there to calm their fears. They would ask me what going to happen and how long would the war last, and how much longer would they have to stay or how involved would they be in the Gulf War?

These questions and many more, some were afraid because of the skull attack; I would explain only God could answer these questions. All I can do is offer pray, comfort, encouragement, and the understanding of God's love He has for all, to wait and put your trust in Him. I pray God will give you peace in your heart, with insurance and understanding of His love. Don't worry, I would say, God will watch over you. Continue to carry out your mission; everything will be all right. I would tell them God brought you over here, and I pray He will take you home alive with no harm. Put your faith and trust in Him. Don't let what happened to someone else worry you; God will take care of you. I would inform them that because we were in a war did not mean God was not with us. God is everywhere; He lives in our hearts, and He will protect us.

My unit moved up into Iraq, and one day I saw the soldier who didn't want to come over. He was driving a large fuel tanker. I asked him who was riding with him, and he said, no one. I found out he had been going up near the front line to deliver fuel for vehicles. You are not afraid; you are up there where fighting is going on. And you are not afraid of being killed or shooting the enemies? He said no, I don't have any fear; blessed is that man that maketh the Lord his trust. I went with him, and it was amazing how God had changed his heart. What was so amazing was, we went so far out, it was late, we tried a short cut back to the base before it got dark, but we didn't make it. It was at night. When it gets dark over there it gets so black you can't see anything in front of you. We were driving across a field, and we drove up on all kinds of ammunition, rockets, mortars, fuel cans full of fuel there were so many other army supplies and equipment, we could not identify who they belong to. The area was so large, we could not go around it. There was no one guarding the area, so we were afraid that someone had booby trap the area. We looked around the best we could and found no one. We had to drive straight through; we used night ground guide to lead us through and it took about a half hours. It was a scary time and we were afraid of setting off the ammunition or fuel cans, or stepped on a mine.

Oh God, I thank you with my whole heart for saving us that night, by leading us through that awesome dangerous place. What a loving and peaceful God I serve. Nevertheless, I shall abide in confidence with joy of faith more abundant through the righteousness of His grace, peace, and knowledge according to His divine power through the precious blood that saved our soul. **Psalm 32:7** say, "Thou art my hiding place; thou shalt perserve me from trouble; thou shalt compass me about with songs of deliverance Selah." While I was in the war during my job as the operation sergeant, there were time someone tried to make me look bad, or someone would say something behind my back or say I didn't do something right. To their surprise, I would not get upset I stays focus on my mission, remained at peace with God. I pray to my heavenly Father that every soldier who reads these words of God will find comfort, peace, courage, and confidence to hold onto what knowledge God has given them. Stay strong and do not let your enemies destroy your faith. Before departing all my enemies; God change their hearts to show love, I pray all saints will know the same God I service.

Blessing from the Powerful Hand of God

LAST MAY of, 2002, God spoke to me: Christians, God has given all of us salvation, grace, and mercy, along with His Holy Spirit. His Spirit, which is connected to our hearts, should be filled with love for our brothers and sisters by spreading God's word and helping those who are in need. This is my God given-gift, for me to do His will of my Heavenly Father to glorify my Lord and savior. God is showing me this was my purpose in the war as the sergeant major to carry out my assigned duties not only as the operation sergeant but also to bring comfort and relief to the soldiers who were concerned about their lives during the war. I am telling you this because of the blessing I received from my heavenly Father to write these words is beyond my understanding.

Before my unit departed for Desert Storm War, I was a Master Sergeant, on the MTOE I was in a sergeant major position, during which time I would receive the rank of Sergeant Major. After the war I would revert back to my original position. Sometimes I don't understand how God works, but all I could say was, we who love the Lord and work for Him will be rewarded. During the war I received a call from my state headquarter, informing me that the Bureau granted me the right to retain my rank after the war. All other solders had to revert back to their formal rank. I didn't understand why I was singled out. As time passed, I forgot all about it. Well, the last of May, 2002, God brought all of this to my mind, and I felt the presence of God all over with tears running down my face and they were tears of joy and happiness over what God had done in my life, and the obedience to do His will. God spoke and said it was made possible by God Himself, I was thanking and praising Him for blessing my soul. Oh Lord, I don't deserve any of this because I have not been good to you, Lord; I am a sinful person. Lord, I try to measure up to your standard, but I always fall short. How can I thank you?

During my time in service I was hoping to retire with the rank Master Sergeant and I was happy just where I was as a master sergeant. To go higher than this I could not even imagine. Christians, put your gifts to work for the Lord and He will reward you with a bundle of blessings. God is telling us how to be like Him. **Act 5:32** says, "And we are His witnesses of these things; and so is also the Holy Ghost, whom God hath given to them that obey Him." He is teaching us in **Act 20:35** say, "I have showned you all things, how that so laboring ye ought to support the weak, and to remember the words the Lord Jesus, how He said, It is more blessed to give than to receive."

In July of, 1996, my second wife and I were on vacation traveling through Ft Bragg, North Carolina. I received a phone call to call my unit. My commander asked me to return and prepare my package to send to the Bureau to be selected for command sergeant major. What an awesome feeling to know I might make the highest rank in the Army on the enlisted side. I harried back and prepared my package and sent it forward. The selecting process was from most of the fifty states; I was told by the sergeant major my package had credited the highest number point of all. God brought all of this back to my mind to let me know His hand was in the whole process of all the schools God had sent me to. All the training, perpetration involving operation mission, over sea deployment mission and in country training and letters of award for outstanding performance, this was help shaping my life for God will. As these things was unfolding in my life, I never thought of myself. I was there to please my commander and maintaining our unit's position in a highest state of readiness as possible, looking out for the training and welfare of all soldiers under battalion. maintaining command/control headquarters command. As I was involved in all of this God was preparing my life for the future of what was to come. Nowhere in my mind, I never thought my life would turn out this way, but God showed me if Christians follow His command and are committed to work on their job or position, and do their work to please their boss and God, and not be concerned about themselves, their heavenly Father would make sure they got what they desired. There are times you are going to feel unjust, stepped on, misused, but remember that God sees everything and He knows everything. Don't worry about yourself; hold fast to God's unchanged hand. Remember what your heavenly Father face while on this earth. He said we are to suffer as He suffered. When it gets beyond your control, call on God and pray for your enemies; God will hear you cry. Give it to Him; He will fight your battle. Never get angry with your boss. Or commander it will never solve your problem; it will make your day longer. Lord, I pray Christians will put their trust in you and have strong belief and faith that You are in the midst working on their behalf. Can you see what He has done in my life? What He did for me He will do for you. **Psalm 28:7-8** says, "Lord is my strength and my shield; my heart trusted in him, and I am helped: therefore my heart greatly rejoiceth; and with my song will I praise him. The Lord is their strength, and he is the saving strength of his anointed."

Two Years Remaining God Still Working

FIRST OF June, 2002, God informed me of another event in my life, that I had less than two years before retiring. The state command sergeant major asked me if I would like a change in position. She said that it would require losing my rank to Sergeant Major, but I would retain my rank when I retired. I said let me think about this. I will let you know the next day. She told me there were going to be major changes, and there would be a new change of command in the units, which I am current, assign, and that command want to bring his sergeant major with him. I thought yes, but I didn't have much experience as a security manger. To take you back to the start of my second tour of service, every unit I was assigned to, I would replace anywhere from two enlisted and a officer who were originally signed there already. Most of the time I had to work in all those positions to maintain units function. One position I was assigned to as the Command Operation Sergeant, as the Law and Order Enforcement NCO, I was the budget program activity director, managing close to half million dollars per year. Inputted order for entire Battalion and Command

Headquarter maintain Command/Control of seven units. Oversee all units Status Report of personnel and equipment to maintain oversea deployment level of readiness, plus assist units in making correction, input into USP computer system and forward it to the next Higher Headquarter. I was also the Headquarter Command Sergeant Major. I never complained or grumbled because it was a job and it had to be done. I never took break in most of the time I worked through lunch and I never felt over burdened. It was the strength of the Lord working through my soul. I could never master these positions; if it were not for the power of the Almighty God's strength, confidence and love He had for my soul. I was able to overcome all adversity and problems. To me; it was just another day at work, because I had the joy of the Lord down in my soul. He said we could do all things through Christ who strengthened us. This is one example of God working through me.

Christians, whatever workload your boss puts upon you, don't worry, God will be right there to see you through. He will lighten your load and make it easy. When He brought all this to my mind, I felt the pressure of His glorious hand upon my soul. God was telling me this was all a test of my life to see if I would fall down or stand, and as the tears were running down my face I felt His love, comfort, and joy, and gladness that He was well pleased. As I write these words the glory and divine power of His spirit is upon my soul. At time I would bring a peanut jelly sandwich to eat and keep on working. There are times when we are not busy and our time is wasted, our minds wander off into areas that cause problems. God and all His disciples keep busy doing His will; God's Bible is our guide and example of how we should live our lives. God ask me to write this book to show the reflection of His will, so we all must do to please our savior. I pray for every soul to get to know the Lord the way I know Him, or in your own way. I pray you will receive the glorious feeling that the spirit is upon you every day leading and guiding your every step.

The Powerful Glorious Hand of God Was With Me

IT WAS time to move over to DRC as the security manager and en-charge of all security personnel, when God brought this to my mind to write, I started thinking, "Where did all this power come from, and what was God trying to tell me." When you read these words you are going to wonder who is this God? Is this the God of the heaven and earth? This is the same God I met at twelve years old, and not a day in my life has He failed my soul. When I arrived in the position as the State Head Quarter as the security manager, there were two officers and an NCO working on a security system for the entire installation for about three years. They had great plans, and a great vision for how the security system should be installed. But it had stalled for lack of funds, and some of the equipment was just sitting, collecting dust and becoming outdated. God showed me those individual problems. They had their own plan, but they didn't know how to connect God's plans and blueprint, and they didn't have the master key to activate God's plan. They were only allowed fifty thousand per year for security requirement. I am talking about a plan costing close to a million dollars. With me being one NCO. My command told me that she wants and to contact the Department of the Army, and ask them to come in and give D.C Army National Guard a complete evaluation report of all security areas requirement of, two installation.

After two month it was completed, and my commander presented it to the commanding General. We had to do something about the deficiency. I received the report and determined how much it would cost to purchase the remaining equipment. I had a year and four months to get this project operational. There were people who didn't care much about me because I wasn't as bright as they were and I didn't hang around with them. My farther told me long ago; "Son, you must work twice as hard to compete with others. I knew I wasn't real smart, so I had to rely on what my father told me. I never had time to associate with others. I always carried out my assign duties to standards, never complained, never felt overloaded with work. I always got the job done. There were soldiers, who did not have confidence in me, but yet they were always trying to overcome their problems, but I never let that bother me. I would pray for them, that God would show them the light of His glorious power, and open up their hearts and their eyes to see God and understand His will. During my time in service my units never failed an inspection due to the grace of God and other soldiers.

I know this was a large, major, complex task to complete all, I mastered it one day at a time, through the strength of the Lord. Through all my years I have called upon the Lord to see me through. You know it is good to have a heavenly Father who will keep you focus on Him. When you put your trust in God you never fail or stall out. For the remaining year I was to focus on getting the money to purchase the remaining equipment. I contacted the Bureau to set up an appointment to visit them, I visited them carried the security report and the amount I needed to purchase the equipment. I met face to face and told them what we needed. I asked God to bless them with love and peace in their hearts. They had funds left from the end of the year, they told me to submit my request, I said, thank you, Lord. I went back and told my commander that I requested one hundred fifty thousand dollars. They sent one hundred twenty thousand dollars; I thanked the holy hand of God for opening up the door for me to order the remaining equipments.

When I arrived there, God showed me what the problem was, and I said, God help me to make this possible. He gave me the blue print and the master key to activate the plan. The secret to all problems and plans is in the hands of Jesus Christ. He is the one who sends His angels to go before us and make thing happen for us. There is nothing about me; I can't do any more then my Father tells me. **Proverbs 8:32-35** say, "Hearken unto me, O ye children: blessed are they that keep my ways. Hear instruction, and be wise, and refuse it not. Blessed is the man that heareth me, watching daily at my gate, waiting at the posts of my doors. For whoso findeth me findeth life and shall obtain favour of the Lord." God say I will give you understanding, I will make you wise, I will teach you, I will increase your learning, and I will give you knowledge of the My wisdom.

They had ordered a security badge system that no one could operate, but with the key from God, there is nothing too hard for Christ. He used me and another soldier to set it up and install all soft-wear, and in less than one month it was in operational, so I issued out badges for the entire installation. Taking nothing from the soldiers who thought of this plan, they did a great job, as you know in Acts the apostle Paul on trial and King Agrippa was there and he said to Paul "you almost made me a Christian." You see, "almost" is the same as having a plan and not following through for completion.

On the next project, the Department of the Army has sent forty high tech electronic security locks to be installed on all security safes. They were sitting because no one knew how to install them. There were soldiers who were school trained, no disrespect toward them, but they only did what they could do. If I didn't have God on my side, there would be nothing I could have done also. Christians, this is why it is so important to believe in God that all things are possible through Him. I looked at them and they did look complicated. I looked at a tape and read the book. That's all it took for God to give me the master key. There were a total of twenty five safes needed changing, Ft Belvoir, Naval Air Station, and District of Columbia Armory National Guard installation. I had to removed the old locks, installed the new high tech computerize locks and set the codes. There were high security rooms through the building, and my commander wanted security door locks installed.

The next project I had to tackle, so I contacted a security company to come in to make an estimation to install cards operating locks. In lest than six months remaining I was sent out to California for a security conference also was sent to school in West Virginia for security training.

In my last year, I completed the security budget plan for all security areas, of Ft Belvoir, Anacost Naval Air Station, and the District of Columbia, Army National Guard Armory. The budget I needed to complete and install the project was close to a million dollars. I submitted the request to the National Guard Headquarter Bureau. Then my commander sent me to a security conference in Kansas City, Mo. There I met a security representative. I explained to him what types of units we had and the side of installation, what type of security system we needed to install. They were out of South Carolina, so they agreed to come up to visit our installation and meet with the commander to have a security briefing on installing security. They made a survey and gave us a price.

The budget request was approved, and funds were available for installing the equipment. All this was due to the power of the Almighty God. I thank God for honor the budget request. It all about how you introduce yourself to people by showing love and making friends. Before I retired all equipments were available, and contract has been approved for installing and the work had began.

A year and half later, I visited the unit and felt great to see that the project was nearly completed. The prayer of God has power to overcome anything standing before you, and you must believe in your heart everything you do is for the glory of Lord. Without the true belief of God your life will never be complete; you will always face struggles, you will face hard times, because you believe in your own strength and knowledge. God said in **John 15** says, "Without me ye can do nothing. He that abideth in me and I in him, the same bringeth forth much fruit." With your strength, Satan will defeat you every time because he doesn't want to see you win. Once you put your trust in God and lean on His understanding, He will make everything all right. Another project was on my plate to install other security locks on all doors with high sensory equipment. also Order and set up a parking lot badge system and issue to all who own automobiles. During the last year and a half what was accomplished only by the grace of God working through my soul. For this last mission there wasn't a moment of time wasted. My mind was focused on what I had to do to please God and my commander. Most of my time in service was the reflection of this and I enjoyed every moment.

I thank the graceful hand of the merciful Christ Jesus for giving me strength and knowledge to do such awesome and complex jobs. **Colossians 1:11** say, "Strengthened with all might, according to his glorious power, unto all patience and longsuffering with joyfulness." Christians, this is an act of faith and knowing. God is with us always once we find our place in His will. He will unlock our blueprint and activate the master key, that we may glorify Him. Once Christ opens up our knowledge and gives us the understanding of His mystery, we will live for Him the rest of our lives and never turn back. I pray no matter what may come your way, let no one stop your plan of God; I pray you may never lose the sight of Christ Jesus. **Colossians 1:27** says, "To whom God would make known what is the riches of the glory of this mystery among the Christians; which is Christ in you the hope of glory." It was the power of God who made all of this possible. May we look up to heaven and say Oh Lord, give me strength, faith, hope, and understanding to unlock the mystery of my blueprint that I may walk in your footstep and do what you call me to do. Oh Lord, who am I to do your will to please you in every way by glorifying your name? There is nothing in my power or strength. I am not worthy to accept credit. I was only there to please my Heavenly Father and my commander.

God Led Christians accordance to His Will

IN MAY of, 1999, God led me to move to North Carolina. I found out there was a VA hospital located in Salisbury North Carolina. Every time I wanted to go, something would delay me. The second week in March 2001, God spoke to me to go see about my people. I told my wife I was going to Salisbury for a weekend. I left early that Saturday morning and headed to Salisbury. When I arrived there, I parked and started walking toward the enter door. I saw three men sitting out on a bench; I walked over and spoke to them. One of the men's hands that I shock had a bandage on his arm with the name Odom. I said "Odom, I am Odom also," and he said you know Blue Moon Odom he is my cousin. I said Yes, he is my distend cousin also. After talking with him, I found out he was a cousin I never knew. God is an amazing God. I find out that God is all about timing; God waited until the right time to send me to Salisbury VA Hospital.

While I was there, my cousins took me all around and introduced me to a lot of veterans. Many of them were from the Vietnam War. I was amazed to see so many Vietnam veterans there in the VA hospital. After talking to the veteran, I found many of them are there because of the drugs they took and had being wounded while in Vietnam. I spoke to many of them saying Gods love you, and I love you with my whole heart. Put your hope and trust in Christ Jesus. He wants to heal you and bring you out. He knows all your problems, and he will forgive you of your sins. God can heal all your sicknesses, hurt and pains. He wants you to get out this hospital to tell your testimonies to someone how the mighty hand of God can overcome our problems. **Luke 9:6** says, "And they departed, and went through the towns, preaching the gospel, and healing every where." **Luke 9:1** says, "Then he called his twelve disciples together, and gave them power and authority over all devils, and to cure diseases" Oh God we need to know the hope of your knowledge and understanding of your power in healing your people. They need the older generation to tell their testimonies about their story, how God brought them through the storm, to the young generation. I thank God for taking me there so I could speak to them and tell them I am a living testimony of all the things I went through. It was the grace and love of God that saved me. He needs our help to tell someone else about the love of Christ Jesus. I was there with them two days and it was sad to see them still there, but I was glad to tell the Good News of Jesus Christ, and they were glad to hear about the love of Jesus Christ. They asked me to come back and talk to them more about Christ Jesus.

The most amazing and incredible thing happened to me at work on that Monday. To take you back ever since I departed Vietnam, twenty-five years, I question God why did you save me and all the other you let die, and those left in the hospital. I would say God I don't understand you. I would say, God who am I, what do you have for my life, I was a trustee, I sang in the choirs, and I was a deacon. None of these were God's calling for me, but God used all of this to help shape and mold my soul. I was told I was going to be a pastor, but God never called me to be a pastor, then God put me through a crisis with my wife, during the crisis I went on a fast and pray to ask God what was the purpose he had for me. That Monday morning, the Holy Spirit came on me, and then God came to my mind telling me my purpose was at the VA Hospital. He came to me and said "This is why I saved you so you; can minister to my people and help deliver them out of the hospital by telling them about Christ, and prayed that they may be healed." Twice a month I will visit them to bring the Good News. I thanked my Almighty God for the love He has given me to tell people about Jesus true words and His living water. If you only could see the joy and peace on their faces and in their eyes, when the word of God is speaks to them. Sometimes I would speak to them and the Holy Spirit would touch both of us. I know right then God brought me here for a specific reason. They always ask me to pray for them. They always ask me back. Sometime I leave with tears in my eyes because of the love I have for them down in my heart. Lord, it is a blessing and a rewarding experience to be among your veterans to bring the gospel to them. All I could do was to praise and thank the Almighty God. Oh God, I love you with my whole heart. I have been waiting over thirty years, but you know everything is about the right timing of God. This is why God told me to work, wait, be patient and have faith, and God will see me through.

My prayer is that may the peace of God, which passeth all understanding, will keep you in perfect peace and understanding with your mind stayed on Him. May the God of love be merciful unto your soul, with abundance of joy. May the grace of God supply all your needs according to his riches in glory, as long you stay in his will. **Philippians 1:16** says "The one preach Christ of contention, not sincerely, supposing to add affiction to my bonds. But the other of love, knowledge that I am set for the defence of the gospel."

Only God Knows Where Our Futures Will Take Us

LORD GOD, you brought all these things to my sight, to understanding, my heart, mind, and soul in correspondent to my life. And you said to write my life story to go out to the entire world. These are the words of God, as I am only a servant and a messenger to write what He tells me. Thirty-one years of service have all been done for one reason, to glorify my heavenly Father,

Lord, and savior. You have equipped me to face my enemy; you have taught me to stand strong in times of trouble; you have taught me to stand on God's morals, discipline, and principal for my beliefs, to live in the kingdom of God. I am standing on His holy word, on the covenant He made with my wife and me to stand fast and wait on His promises. I will never give in to what the world will offer, because God gives me enough wisdom, knowledge, and understanding to stand on His principal and will to show others the righteousness of God's love. **II Peter 1: 3-4** says, "According as His divine power hath given unto me all things that pertain unto life and godliness, through the knowledge of him that hath called us to glory and virtue. Whereby are given unto us exceeding great and precious promises, that by these ye might be partakers of the divine nature having escaped the corruption of the world through lust." Lord, you knew what kind of life I would face in the future, for those things you took me through, for thirty-one years of service. They were to equip me for the future of your purpose. Whatever I'm going through at the present, I can say the trials and tribulations I have endured in the past year with all the pain, envy, strife, and suffering, without this I wouldn't have been able to face the awesome task You have set before me. Lord, I pour out my whole heart, mind, and soul, for leading me through despised of affliction, through the wicked and him that loveth violence his soul hateth. The wicked shall rain snares, fire and brimstone and horrible tempest: this shall be the portion of their cup, but my God has the upper hand and He is bringing me safely and sound through because He said the righteous the Lord loveth righteousness His countenance doth behold the upright.

Lord you told me to study your words, and tell the testimonies you sent me through. Lord I am doing my best to please you. You sent me to college to study your words; you called me to enter all your churches to tell your testimonies you gave me. Lord, I thank you for equipping my soul by, molding me, and shaping me, and making me more Christ-like each and every day. Lord, I have cast all my care and trouble unto your hand; now I am free to do your will. Lord, I am totally committed to be a servant of the Most High God, what ever you ask of my soul I am total committed to go all the way. Lord, I don't know what my future hold, but one thing I can say I will take it one day at a time, and leave my future in the hands of Christ Jesus.

God said stay true to His word, you will bring forth fruit from your labor to draw someone closer to Christ or brighten up someone's life with the consolation of the glory, grace, and peace of God with His true love in His divine power. This is how He has translated my soul into the kingdom of His eternal life. God wants us to be faithful down deep in our soul and not be moved from the hope of His calling to spread the Good News. He wants us to establish a pure heart with a loving relationship in holiness before Christ Jesus. He wants us to walk in a way pleasing unto Him. I will pray and glorify in the name of my Lord for His abundance of love, peace, and grace. I pray that I may keep in the knowledge and understanding of the truth of His word and be led into a quiet and peaceable life in godliness and honesty that I may be acceptable in the sight of my God and savior. Lord, your heavenly kingdom is my future resting place. But first, my foundation must be built upon nothing less than solid rock, a building made by the hand of God. I must be obedient, honest, and love my neighbors as I love myself, and be patient. I will dwell in the house of righteousness all the days of my life. I will be a witness; I will suffer for your gospel. I will continue to be a partaker of your glory, and the fullness of your spirit with a mind of Christ. I thank the Lord for making me strong with a right mind, body, and soul, and I ask the Lord to look into my whole heart. If you shall find anything not pleasing to your sight, Lord, I pray you take it to the foot of your cross and wash my sins in the blood of the lamb. Lord, I pray you will make me as white as snow, that I will be pleasing in your eye sight. Lord, helps our marriage to be a light to the world. Lord, I love you, I praise you, Lord; I worship you because you are an amazing and incredible God. I thank you, my Lord, for sending your Son to give himself for my sins; that He delivered my soul from this present evil world, and set my soul according to the will of God my Heavenly Father.

Be a Disciple For Your Heavenly Father

THE LAST weekend of July, 2001, God sent me on a mission to the Salisbury, North Carolina VA hospital to visit the Veteran , to bring the Good News to His people. On this mission I took my little five-year old grandson with me. I was outside talking about God's love to all people. It gives me such a great feeling and compassion to speak the knowledge and the love of Christ to His people. I love to pray for them, because I love them with my whole heart. I wanted to go into another building, and my grandson wanted to go in another building, I said no, he went anyway, so I followed him as he led me down the hall where there were two men talking about Christ. I stopped there and started talking with them. You know God wants us to fellowship with our brothers or sisters in Christ. Shortly, the other person departed and we were two left talking. After talking for while, I knew God used my grandson to lead me to this person. He told me why he was there. Come to find out, his problem with his wife was almost the same as mine. His wife had left him and taken everything. He said he entered himself into hospital because his lack of trust in God and confidence, worrying, and suffering in pain, he thought the hospital would solve his problems. The Holy Spirit came upon me to tell him to put your trust in God, go down on your knee and pray to the Almighty God asking for forgiveness of your sins and to forgive your wife. God wants to shape and mold you by sending you through the fire through the storm to clean you up, for His will. He wants you to study his words and tell your story to help someone in needs. God is rising up men to put back in His church, and one way is by, taking marriages apart to get to the one he wants to used to further His kingdom. While God is preparing you He will use your spouse against you, hold on because He will be in control.

Hold on, put all your faith and trust in God because He is going to restore your marriage. He said I believe you because I feel the Holy Spirit come upon me and I can't hold back the tears. I could feel the presence of God upon my soul; tears were running. I knew

God sent me to minister to him. Oh what a mighty God I serve. God spoke to me about three month ago saying you will touch my people wherever I send you, and it is so true. It is amazing but I can't explain how God leads me to so many needed people.

Each time I Go there, God will lead me to someone, they is in need of His help and all the problem they are facing. They will tell me their problem and ask for pray, many times they will till me they been praying to God to send someone to help them. He directed me right to them to answer their request by God. They are looking for love, a savior, and the true word of God. Every Sunday after church God led me to visit nursing homes to spread the Good News of Jesus among His people, to pray for them and show love to them. If you ever want to be blessed, visiting nursing homes, and hospital where God's people need to hear about His love, joy, and peace of Christ Jesus, and they will bless your heart by looking into their eyes and seeing their faces with peace and joy.

God will really bless you. Christians, we are called by God to be a witness and servant of God, and our fellow laborer in the gospel toward His people. God is speaking to us in **1 Thessalonians 2:10-12** says, "Ye are witnesses, and God also, how holily and justly and unblamelessly we behaved ourselves among you that believe. As ye know how we exhorted and comforted and charged every one of you, as a father doth his children. That ye would walk worthy of God, who hath called you into his kingdom and glory."

My prayer to all ministers of God, that you will teach the congregation their responsibilities as children of God to go and shear their faith of the Good News. The fields are white, the fruits are falling off the vine, they are thirsty for living water, and they are hungry for living bread. Who will go and work for their heavenly Father today?

God's in Charge of Marriage

On July, 3, 2000, a dramatic thing happened to my life. It was early in the evening about 7:00 p. m. My wife arrived home from work. I asked why were you so late? "She went off! You are not my father I don't have to answer you." I was in shock because I didn't know what was going on. Her job hours were from 5:00 a. m. to 1: 30 p. m. She normally arrive home around 2:15 p. m. She has been late the last three days. She never gave me an explanation why she was late. I thought she was out shopping. She still would not give me an answer. Instead she raised her voice at me and replied but she didn't have to tell me anything." I asked ,Were you out with someone else? this was heavy on my heart She said, You have judged me. I said, "Oh Lord, I was only trying to find out some information."

"I really got up set because she would not tell me the truth. I grabbed her by her arm and she got really upset and said turn me lose I am leaving; I won't stay here anymore."

She went out that night and stayed in a hotel across from where she works. After two days she returned.

I tried to have a conversation with her and she said this is the third time you have judged me of doing something wrong. I told her I was only trying to find the truth but she would not say anything. I said I only wanted to know why she was acting this way. She said, "You have judged me for the last time and I am leaving you." "There is nothing you can do to make me change my mind." "You are not my father; I will go and come as I please." If I want to stay out all night, I will. I don't have any children to look after anymore. "Oh Lord I was facing a situation I had no control over." I asked her to forgiveness of me sin that I committed against her. I said I would do anything you ask of me. Give me one more chance. Nothing I could say would make any difference.

I fell on my knees and cried out to the Almighty God, Oh Lord "What is going on? Why is this happening to me? Why is this coming upon me this way, Oh Lord? Where did I go wrong? What did I do to bring this on? Oh God help me. Oh Lord, you gave me a beautiful wife; I love her with my whole heart. She has been a blessing to me. Oh God, what did I do to drive her away from me so quickly? I really don't understand why is this happening I am in real trouble Satan is somewhere working in the mist trying to destroying our marriage.

Oh God is you preparing to send me on another incredible journey? The next day I spoke to her about going out I said, "You told the children not to stay out late and call when they were on their way home. These things you told our children not to do." I don't understand you now say you have the right to do what you told them not to do. As time past, things would not get any better.

Two weeks before this happened I went to church, and she didn't go. When I arrived I didn't see the pastor; later I found that he had departed after twenty-five years of service. After the service I went home and told my wife. The next Sunday she went and another pastor was preaching. There was someone in the congregation who got up to voice her opinion about what went wrong, but the trustee and deacon remove her and the service went on. When we returned home, we had a conversation about the young lady who got up. My wife said they should let her speak; I told her no that would have been wrong. What she should have done was waited until the service was over and goes to the deacon to have a meeting to discuss what she had to say. You never stop God's work when it is in progress for something like this. But my wife didn't agree with me. That same week the church had a meeting about the pastor leaving. My wife and I went to hear the meeting and during the meeting I noted that she got really up set. A lot of things were said; it was really amazing what had been going on according to those who were speaking. After the meeting we left I was talking to her, but there was a change in her; I could tell in her voice and by the way she was acting. Something had happened, but I didn't know what it was.

Oh God, I love all of your people. Father, we need help; your church have become divided among the body of Christ. We need to search our hearts and souls to see the sin we have committed, Oh God we are not qualified to judge anyone of their wrongdoing. But father, we have cast the first stone upon our brother. Lord God forgive us of our sin; we are no better than the Jews who crucified Jesus Christ on the cross. Oh God, we are standing in need of your prayers of forgiveness Lord God, these same problems are happening, in many of our churches today.

Lord God, we have brought the world's system into the churches of God. **John 8:7** says**,** "So when they continued asking him, he lifted up himself, and said unto them, He that is without sin among you, let him first cast a stone at her." Lord God, we have lost fellowship with the true body of Christ, and a loving relationship with our first love. Oh God, come unto Your churches; help us go down on our knees, and ask the Almighty God to forgive us of our sin. Lord God, give us a clear direction in the way we must go and what we must do, Oh Lord. And Oh God help us to worship You back into the house of God. We need you Lord; we can't do anything right on our own. The churches belong to Christ and Christians are the body of the Church and Jesus Christ is the head of the body. **Cl Corinthians 3: 16-17** says, "Know ye not that ye are the temple of God, and that the Spirit of God dwelleth in you? If any man defile the temple of God, him shall God destroy: for the temple of God is holy, which temple ye are."

The power of Christ Jesus, Holy Spirit inspired me to tell the world about our marriage, also to teach marriage how to have faith and understand the love, mercy, and power of the living Christ Jesus. He is the one who joined all marriages together in heaven, not man. He wants all marriage to last. He wants to strengthen, to build confidence, and to give us courage to look unto Jesus Christ to maintain a strong and healthy marriage relationship under the anointing power of Jesus Christ. Also Christ is raising up disciples within marriages. We made a covenant with God for better or worth. During our bad time God use it to strength our faith in marriage. So when God calls and sets us apart, our spouses may not understand the power of the true living God. He wants to anoint you with His Holy Spirit like you never felt before. Then you will know He has set you apart for His special purpose.

Conflict will arrive, trial, temptation, and tribulations, will come, fires and storms will rage. Call on God to give you strength, courage and confidence to go on. In **Matthew 19:6** God is speaking to marriage, "What therefore I hath joined together, let not man put asunder." Have strong faith, be patient and wait on the Lord. Because the other spouse is not anointed by the power of the living Lord the way you are, God will use your spouse as an evil spirit against you to test your faith. While you being molded, shaped, and prepared for the work of the Lord, he/she will be covered by His Holy hand to ensure that he/she want go to far over to the dark side of Satan. When the Lord finishes, He will reunite both together as one in the eyes of the Lord to carry out His will and purpose.

God will change the other spouse's heart; He will strengthening you with the power of His Holy Spirit; building you both up in love, and teaching you the knowledge of His true word.

My Heavenly Farther said write this story to give marriage a clear understanding of the true living Christ Jesus whom we serve. Give your trouble to Him and put your faith and trust in the Holy hand of the Almighty God, and do just what He said. **Jeremiah 17:13-15** says, "O Lord, the hope of Israel, all that forsake thee shall be ashamed, and they that depart from me shall be written in the earth, because they have forsaken the Lord, the fountain of living waters. Hear me, O Lord, and I shall be healed; save me, and I shall be saved: for thou art my praise. Behold, they say unto me, where is the word of the Lord? Let it come now."

God Sent Me on a Journey to Witness to His People

THE FIRST week of September, 2000, as our trouble continued. I told my wife I needed to get away to clear my mind and talk to God. I went away for a week to visit my relatives. I visited my sister in Richmond, Virginia and. my nephew in Petersburg, Virginia. There Christ were the center of our conversation. I was told the pastors had departed the churches there also. Then I visited my relative's in Norfolk, Virginia. It was a blessing to see one of my relative's who had been changed from the darkness of his sin. I thought he would not make it out of the hand of Satan. But you know God is the only one who knows how our lives will turn out. Oh God, you have set him free from the bondage of Satan and redeemed him through the blood, the forgiveness of sin, according to the riches of His grace, by the true living Lamb of God. My heart rejoiced, and I was glad for what the Lord has done in his life. It was a blessing to have had a conversation with him about Jesus Christ. The last two days of the week I visited my hometown in Emporia, Virginia. I went to my sister's home and one of my brother was there; we had a good time talking about the Lord discussing His word.

During our conversation my sister told me the pastor of the church where God saved me had left and the church down the road their pastor had left also. I asked what was going on with pastors? It is not so much the pastor's fault; it is the congregation and the leaders that have problems also. She said the church was having revival service this week. I went the next two nights. The first night I was sitting by a man I didn't know; I spoke to him and he spoke to me. Later in the service I was looking through my Bible, and he said turn to. **Psalms 27**, "I didn't tell him anything about my problem or anyone else's." I looked at it briefly and then waited until I returned home in North Carolina; then I opened my Bible and read it. Oh God, I thank You for that man. What a blessing from God. This was just what I needed to give me courage, strength, and confidence. If you have a problem or adversity in your life, I pray God will encourage you to read this chapter.

Psalms 27 Gave Me Strength

V1. "IT IS my light and my salvation; whom shall I fear? The Lord is the strength of my life; of whom shall I be afraid?" **V2**. "When the wicked, even mine enemies and my foes, came upon me to eat up my flesh, they stumbled and fell" **V3**."Though an hot should encamp against me, my heart shall not fear: though war should rise against me, in this will I be confident." **V4**. "One thing hive I desired of the Lord, that will I seek after; that I may dwell in the house of the Lord all the days of my life. To behold the beauty of the Lord and to inquire in the temple." **V5. "**For in the time of trouble he shall hide me in his pavilion: in the secret of his tabernacle shall he hide me; he shall set me up upon a rock." **V6. "**And now shall mine head be lifted up above mine enemies round me: therefore will I offer in his tabernacle sacrifices of joy: I will sing, yes I will sing praises unto the Lord."

V7. "Hear, O Lord, when I cry with my voice: have mercy also upon me, and answer me." **V8**. "When thou sadist, Seek ye my face; my heart said unto thee, Thy face, Lord, will I seek." **V9**. "Hide not thy face far from me; put not thy servant away in anger: thou hast been my help; leave me not, neither forsakes me, O God of my salvation." **V10**. "When my father and my mother forsake me, then the Lord will take me up." **V11**. "Teach me thy way, O Lord, and lead me in a plan path, because of mine enemies." **V12**. "Deliver me not over unto the will of mine enemies: for false witnesses are raised up against me, and such as breathe out cruelty." **V13**. "I had fainted, unless I had believed to see the goodness of the Lord in the land of the living." **V14**. "Wait on the Lord: be of good courage, and he shall strengthen thine heart: wait, I say on the Lord. This chapter I read it ever day night and God gave me confidence, courage, and strengthen to overcome whatever troubles my enemies confronted me with He gave me peace and joy to continue in His work.

The last night of service, after it was over, I was outside talking to some of my old friends. After about ten minutes there were only two vehicles left on the parking lot, which was a Deacon with his family, my sister, my brother, and me. Before I got in my car I overheard a conversation about locking keys in the car; I walked over and asked. "Is there any thing I can do to help." The deacon said; "My keys are locked in the car." I had my key in my hand; I was driving a Toyota Camry and he had a Ford. We tried the key and God opened the door. I could not believe this. My sister was praising the Lord and I was saying what an amazing God we serve.

I returned home to North Carolina. Early during that week I asked my wife to go and see a counselor and she said it wouldn't make any difference. I asked "Why not?" "I told you there is nothing going to make me change my mind." I said, "Let's try it anyway." So she agrees to go. That next night I called a pastor; he agreed to see us that Friday night.

That night I got on my knees and I prayed to the Almighty God as hard and long as I could. That was the only thing I could do. I asked God to overcome the darkness in my wife's heart. The moment I said that, "I felt the power of God's Holy Spirit come upon me, like never before, as if to say, "My son, it is done." I thanked and praised Jesus; that was the most correct thing to do. Her mind was set and not going to change, but I felt the power of God He was going to do something. But it was not clear. As I continued to pray, the Holy Spirit came upon me against like an electric shock. Then something strange happened to me that night, I was asleep, about 3:00 a. m, and God took my body and made me light as a feather. I could not feel anything; I was half asleep and half awake. I felt my body floating in the air. I felt as if I were in heaven, I felt so calm, so at peace. I felt the glorious hand of God holding me up.

That next morning, I was on my knees praising, thanking, and glorifying God for His glorious hand, I asked Him to help me face my problem. Also I was praying for my wife's sin, and the Holy Spirit came upon me as if an electric shock had hit me again. I went to brush my teeth and the Holy Spirit came upon me again. I could not stand up; I felt if I had fire shoot up in my bones. **Jeremiah 20:9b** says, "But his word was in mine heart as a burning fire shut up in my bones." I went down on my knees praising and thanking the all-loving God. At this time I did not know what all this meant. As time pasted God would reveal all this to me.

That Friday night my wife and I went to counseling. The pastor said a prayer before he started to speak to us. He gave us information from the Bible and he explained it from his knowledge. I **Corinthians 7:14,** says, **"**For the unbelieving husband are sanctified by the wife, and the unbelieving wife is sanctified by the husband: else were your children unclean; but now are they holy." **Ephesians 5: 21-27** says, **"**Submitting yourselves one to another in the fear of God. Wives, submit yourselves unto your own husbands, as unto the Lord. For the husband is the head of the wife, even as Christ is the head of the church: and he is the savior of the body. Therefore as the Church is subject unto Christ, so let the wives be to their own husbands in every thing. Husband, love your wives, even as Christ also loved the Church, and gave himself for it. That he might sanctify and cleanse it: with the washing of water, by the word, That he might present it to himself a glorious Church, not having spot or wrinkle, or any such thing: but that it should be holy and without blemish." **V33** says, "Nevertheless, let every one of you in particular, so love his wife even as himself, and the wife see that she reverence her husband" **V30** says, "For we are members of his body, of his flesh, and of his bones. For this cause shall a man leave his father and mother, and shall be joined unto his wife, and they two shall be one flesh."

During the counseling the pastor asked her; "Do you love him" and she said no. "This was the first time I heard her say this." I started thanking to myself, "What did I do to her that was so damaging that she would stop loving me all of a sudden?" Later the pastor asked her; "Can you foresee any changes. Her answer was No, I never will."

We returned home and she said, "I am going away for the weekend," I didn't say anything. The next week she wanted me to leave and she would stay and take over the house. I told her, "God didn't take me from Maryland and bring us to North Carolina to have me to leave home for no reason. I don't understand why you want me to move out of our house?"

Later during that week she asked for a separation and divorce. That night I prayed to God and asking "What are you doing to me? I know you didn't give us twenty-four good years of marriage and now you are going to let the devil take us apart. You kept us together as one in the eyes of You. Oh Lord, after all the years you have never failed me; why are you failing me now? And why did you wait until I retired from the U.S. Army to let this happen to me? Lord, I don't understand why she wants to leave me; she told me she was not in love with none else."

II Corinthians 2:4 says, "For out of much affiction and anguish of heart I wrote unto you with many tears; not that ye should be grieved, but that ye might know the love which I have more abundantly unto you."

God Spoke and Said, "Your Marriage Is Safe"

THE DAY **of October, 2000,** at work I asked my coworkers if they knew of a church in Greensboro that had Bible study on Wednesday nights. They told me about Mount Zion Baptist Church. That Wednesday night I went to Bible study, and an amazing thing happened. The instructor that was teaching the

Bible study and God's word that spoke that night was the same thing that was happening in our marriage. The instructor also said that I should thank my wife for what God was doing in our marriage was that God would separate marriage, and take the one that has the stronger faith in God, because He wants to prepare me to carry His message. I felt the spirit of the Lord, but I didn't understand what all this meant.

I left the church and on my way home, the Holy Spirit came over me so strong I almost had to stop. Tears of joy were coming from my eyes so fast my handkerchief was wet. God has spoken to my heart that night. God was informing me, that what that instructor was teaching was the true word for my marriage. I started thanking and praising Christ Jesus. I was beginning to see clearly and to understanding what God was doing in our lives, and my faith was growing stronger in Him. I went home and told my wife; and I thanked her for what God was doing in our lives. She didn't say anything, because I don't think she understood what was saying, I said "May God bless you."

That great day of October 3, 2000, the awesome power of the amazing hand of God answered my prayer. God spoke to my heart and in my ear and said. Go tell your story to the Church how I saved you out of the war. Study my word and your marriage is safe. I felt the power of God releasing the burden off my shoulder; I felt at peace like I never felt before. I pray you will wait on the Lord before you make the wrong dissection and destroy your marriage.

Matthew 11:28-30 says, "Come unto me, all ye that labour and are heavy laden, and I will give you rest. Take my yoke upon you, and learn of me; for I am meek and lowly in heart: and ye shall fine rest unto your souls, for my yoke is easy, and my burden is light." I began to thank and praise the holy hand of the Almighty God who is in heaven and upon all the earth, and in every heart of those who love Him. Thursday evening I told her what the Lord had told me. She acted as if she didn't want to hear what I was saying. I would say, "I love you; I pray God will continue to bless you my darling."

That weekend she went to Maryland. She left a note saying. "Maybe this was meant to be, and nothing can be done about it." For a while I felt she was right. I stayed focused on the Lord and His church. I told the church leaders about my problem, and they prayed for me. God told us to confess our problems to one other and pray. **James 5: 16** says," Confess your faults one to another, and pray one for another, that ye may be healed. The effectual fervent prayer of a righteous man availeth much."

Every day and night I will pray and ask God to pour out His blessing upon all of my coworkers one by one, the students and the whole staff. I continued attend Bible study, I found out, the same student from North Carolina A&T State University attend the same church where I attended Bible study to gain knowledge and strength from my Heavenly Father. Thursday nights from 9:00 p m until 11:30 p m, they conducted praise and worshipped service. What a blessing to be among these young students; they gave me such encouragement and inspiration to go on. I praised and thanked the Almighty God for leading me among these young people. Their souls were on fire for the Lord. And they had a mighty man who is full of God's Holy Spirit; he knew how to rightly divide the Word of God to real life situations among the students.

The students also conducted Bible study on the campus on Saturdays from 8:00 p m to 12:00 midnight. I attended Bible study with the students with brother Price who is a man who followed God and had been touched by the hand of God. He has been a real inspirational to my spiritual life. So one night at the end of Bible study brother Price knew of my problem; he walked with me out to my vehicle. He prayed for me. He also told me that, by my praying, spreading God's word, and blessing students, a young female student that heard God's word and it saved her from committing suicide. Oh I thank God and His awesome power in His word and prayer. It a blessing to know His word is working in someone's life to make a difference. His word is all-powerful, it is God, and only God can do this. Nobody else can do this work but the Lord Christ Jesus. He said my word will go out, it will not return empty. **Proverbs 18: 4,** say, "The words of a man's mouth are as deep waters, and the wellspring of wisdom as a flowing brook." Oh I thank Him for using me as a rod to do his will; He is more than I can explain. You must pray and study His word every day; then you will come to know and understand the real power of His word. If you have something going on in your life, I pray you will find the true word of God, because His word will convince your heart, and led you into a loving relationship with Jesus Christ.

I pray whatever you are going through God will answer your prayer and comfort your heart; but most of all stay strong in His word, and continue to show love.

Isaiah 42:12-14 says, "Let them give glory unto the Lord. And declare his praise in the islands. The Lord shall go forth as a mighty man, he shall stir up jealousy like a man of war: he shall cry, yea, roar; he shall prevail against his enemies. I have long time hold my peace; I have been still, and refrained myself: now will I cry like a travailing women; I will destroy and devour at once."

Hold to God's Unchanging Hand for It's Going to Get Rough

THAT NEXT week after my wife returned home, the storm was raging, the journey was getting rougher, and the race was getting harder to run and she said she wanted a divorce I am going to get a lawyer. "The week before God came to me and said your marriage is safe". For the next three weeks I was like Paul on the racked ship out on the high sea not knowing how to come to shore. I spoke to other people; the conversation would come up about divorce. Some were going through divorce or the divorce was over. I spoke to ministers and they would tell me they were going through counseling with couples. I would hear it on television, and the radio. For three weeks God used Satan to take me down in his pit. It was the darkest three weeks of my life. All I could see were people getting divorced. It was as if man had turned his back completely on God. And there were more marriages breaking up in the church than in the world. And God knew what going on and He is not pleased with what man is doing.

There is no respect and don't fear God, no respect to the churches body of Christ, no respect to their children or family. Oh God when are we going to wake up and recognize our failure to maintain unity in the family and in the church? Oh God, we need your help. Oh Lord, I pray you will come and see about us.

I don't understand why we have given ourselves over to Satan to destroy what you have put together. It seemed as if the world was caving in all around my soul. I never knew people were getting divorced this rapidly. I said, "Oh God, what is happening to your marriages today." Everybody is getting separated and divorced, running looking for something better. Oh God, please brings me up from Satan's pit, that I may see the light. God was showing me the dark side of life. This was hard, because I was beginning to lose my faith and hope in God. I was really down; I felt God has abandoned me.

There was no one I could speak to about the light of God. No one I could find any comfort, no release and no encouragement the desolation of my soul was in the depths of my fear. Those were three weeks and distress and darkness in my life. I felt all darkness were upon my shoulder. I said to myself, "I will give her what she wants; divorce her and sell the house. You go your way and I will go my way." I was at a point I just didn't care anymore. I knew what God said, but my faith and belief were getting weaker day by day. Because Satan was telling me there is no hope, give in; don't believe your marriage is safe. I wanted to give up and give in. I felt I was alone and no one was around who cared anything about my problem. I felt God had departed my life, and He was not speaking to me. I have took my eyes off God and was focused on what my wife had asked for.

The Holy Spirit of God was driving me to continue to attending church. They said, "We will pray for your marriage," but I felt I had lost my last friend. We had gone through trial and tribulations in our marriage before, but nothing like this, I knew God said our marriage is safe. I had abandoned my faith in God, and taken on the old natural body of my flesh, and Satan was filling my mind with all kinds of darkness. For three weeks I felt I was burning in hell, and there was nothing I could do about it, Satan wanted to destroy our marriage, Satan was telling me there was no hope for me. God was with me all along, yet I did not recognize Him. He said in **Isaiah 43:2** say, "When thou passest through the water, I will be with: and through the rivers, they shall not overflow thee: when thou walkest through the fire, thou shalt not be burned: neither shall the flame kindle upon thee." I went down on my knees thanking and praising God Almighty, asking Him to forgive my lack of faith and hope in the Lord, Oh Lord, you know

I am weak; I am not strong; I can't walk alone; I need you every hour, every day, and every night to hold my hand. I pray, Lord, you will give me strength, and give me courage that I may grow stronger in the divine power of You confidence.

In Psalms these are God's words that give me strength and courage to hold on and to fight on until the end. "For the Lord God is a sun and shield: the Lord will give me grace and glory: no good thing will He withhold from me if I will walk upright. Truth shall spring out of the earth; and righteousness shall look down from heaven upon my soul. Teach me thy ways, Oh Lord; I will walk in thy truth: unite my heart to fear thy name. I will praise thee, Oh Lord my God, with all my heart: and I will glorify thy name for evermore. Oh Lord God of Hosts, hear my prayer: give ear, Oh God of heaven and earth. He shall call upon me, and I will answer him: I will deliver him, and honour him. Let the beauty of the Lord my God Be upon my soul for ever and ever."

Isaiah 40:29-31 say, "He give power to the faint; and to them that have no might he increaseth strength. Even the youths shall fait and be weary, and the young men shall rtterly fall and make mistake. But they that wait upon the Lord shall renew their strength; they shall mount up with wings as eagles; they shall run, and not be weary; and they shall walk and not fait."

At the end of November 2000, one night I went to Bible study and they asked who needed prayer. I went forward, and one of the pastors took me into a back room. I told him my trouble and he shared with me that he had two close calls with divorce with his wife. He said I prayed and prayed to God to forgive me and He healed my marriage. That made me feel good to know somebody 's marriage had been saved by God grace. It gave me confidence and encouragement to go on. He prayed for me. As I departed for home that night and I was talking to God. If You saved his marriage, I know you can save my marriage. God had already told me my marriage was safe. You know Satan and my wife were trying in every way to derail our marriage and have me give in and say yes. I said, "I will never sign any paper involving separation or divorce. **Deuteronomy 32:4** say, "He is the rock, his work is perfect: for all his ways are judgment: a God of truth and without iniquity, just and right is he."

God's Direction for Marriage

(1) WHEN GOD speaks to us about His will for our life. Satan becomes stronger, because he does not want God to take away what he has. So there is going to be a spiritual war taking place in our life. Remember our Heavenly Father is there to fight our battle. Let Him handle it; don't take on your battle. We are not strong enough; we don't know the right words to say. Our mouths could be our worst enemy. It can bring on hate and anger toward each other. In **James 3:16** say, "For where envying and strife is, there is confusion and every evil work." Show love, stay humble, be patient and wait on the Lord, and He will see you through.

(2) Sometime we don't understand the truth of what God says and what plans or purposes He has for our lives. We begin to wonder, will He do what He said? Satan will say focus on the dark side and blame the other person. Stay in the will of the Lord, study your Bible, and let Jesus speak to your heart, fellowship with positive speaking friends. When the other person says worldly things against you, stay focused on the Lord's promise. In **Titus 2:12-13** says, "God will teach us that, denying ungodliness and worldly lust, we should live soberly, righteously, and godly in this present world. Looking for that blessed hope, and the glorious appearing of the great God and our Saviour Jesus Christ"

(3) We made a covenant with God at the beginning of our marriage; when we face problems or hard times we are ready to abandon what God joined together. This is not the will of God, but the will of Satan. Saints we made a covenant with God for better or worth, don't use negative words toward each other. Have a positive attitude involving your conversation between each other with all truth and love. Sure there are going to be hard times, but hard time won't last always. God use hard times for His purpose to strengthen our hearts to draw us closer to Him **II Timothy 1:13-14** say, "Hold fast the form of sound words, which thou hast heard of me, in faith and love which is in Christ Jesus. That good thing which was committed unto the keep by the Holy Ghost which dwelleth in us."

(4) Today we have become a people who feel we have the power to change each other lifestyle. At birth God made every

man and women different, so how do we believe we have the right to change what God has made, only God can change a person. Whether we believe it or not, every marriage is made in heaven because God has His hand involved all marriage, both non-church and church. Because He is the author of life, no man or women have the power to undo the work of the Lord. There is no perfect match or marriage. Remember what we were before He change us. God changed us into His salvation of righteousness to be more Christ-like serving the Lord, by the spiritual power of Christ. The stronger spiritual spouse will humble him/herself with patient to help the weak spouse to grow stronger in the Lord, and let weaker spouse see the love of Christ through you.

Men and women must be committed to come together and discuss their shortfall and call on God to work their problems. Our job is to show love, be patient with each other, and be kind to one other, be tenderhearted; and be forgiving of one another as Christ's sake hath forgiven us. These are God's word. We are to help build each other up in the strength of the true living God, that we may submit ourselves one to another in the fear of God. What ever one spouse are weak in, the other spouse are to help strength and build him/her up. Drew closer to God in love for each other, complement each other with Joy and peace, don't deny the other because of their weakness, but teach each other to do well. This is why there is no perfect marriage; marriage is an arrangement to come together as one. Each has a responsibility to help each other grow strong with the love of God. Make sure every things line up according to the will of God. He wants us to come to understand each other and not find fault with each other. If we truly a child of God, this is the kind of loving hearts we should have toward each other.

What we must know and understand when we first became a child of God is that everything from that point becomes new to your life. The first few years you feel the joy, peace, and you are worshipping and praising Jesus Christ. Then you begin to lose that feeling and your Christian life begins to get a little harder, read the Bible, stay in church, and assemble around strong saints and fellowship with each other to grow stronger. By the grace and mercy of God, He will help your marriage stay strong in His will. Marriages must be agreed for better or worth, stay strong in the eternal power as Christ had united us together as one. What hurts my heart so badly that are so many church members who don't understand the love of Christ Jesus involving their marriage. They have set themselves up to be the judge over each others life. No marriage will work this way, and they are doing just what Satan wants them to do, destroy God's plan for marriage.

(5) **1Timothy 4:10,16** say, "For therefore we both labour we trust in the living God, who is the Saviour of all men/women, especially of those that believe. Take heed unto thyself, and unto the doctrine: continue in them: for in during this thou shalt both save thyself, and them that hear thee."

(6) When problems come we fail to seek God for answer. We fail to hear His calling, or we disobey His call by doing things our way. Saints, are we being Christ-like? Or do we feel we should do things our own way, and blame the other, and feel we are always right, and we can't make mistakes. We are perfect in our own eyes; we shut the other person completely out of our lives, and take control. The other person tries with all their strength to fight back, but he/she is fighting a losing cause. This is a marriage ready to explode. Saints, where is God in your life? Listen to what God has to say about this **I Timothy 6:11-12,** says, "But thou, O man of God, flee these things; and follow after righteousness, godliness, faith, love, patience, meekness. Fight the good fight of faith, lay hold on eternal life whereunto thou are also called, and hast a good profession marriage before many witnesses."

(7) We don't understand that God is the head of every marriage. We want to be in charge and in control of everything and disobey Him. Churches, the older men and women are to be a teacher unto young marriages. **Titus 2:4**.says, "That they may teach the young women to be sober, to love their husbands to love their children. To be discreet, chaste, keepers at home, good, obedient to they're own husbands. Young men likewise exhort to be sobering minded. In all things shewing thyself a pattern of good works: sound speech. Having no evil thing to say of each other." Saint of God holds true to these word of your Heavenly Father."

John 6:45 says, It is written in the prophets, and they shall be all taught of God. Every man therefore that hath heard, and hath learned of the Father, cometh unto me."

(8) God is calling on marriage for the stronger one to be set apart for His purpose. Many times we don't recognize God is working in the midst to bring about His will and purpose in our

marriage. Hold on; put your trust and faith in Him, He will speak to your heart; be patient and wait. Saints, God is at our mercy to stay together. We must talk to find out about each back ground, to receive a clear understanding of each other family life, and let there be no hidden secret that may reveal itself in a damaging way, that will up set marriage. When problems accrue in his/her lives, talk to each about it, don't let it build up to become a conflict between each other. Marriage will face many problem, also remember God's is always there if you abide in His will, He will abide in you, call on Him and He will lighten you burden. The most damaging things in a marriage are to fight back. You will never win, humble your self unto mighty hand of God and stay faithful to His will and pray for your enemies and show the love of Christ through your action.

(9) The other spouse; God will use her/him to bring darkness against you to test your faith and make you grow strong in the Lord. Remember, God will not destroy your marriage. He will cover your spouse with His holy hand and no harm will come against your spouse or you. It is the responsibility of the church/family to teach the people before they become married, and continue teaching them during their early stage in life.

(10) Most important thing we must understand is why this is happens. I pray this book of God will open up your knowledge and understanding to all marriages to let you all know God is working in marriage to bring His church back in line with the glory and divine power of the true living God. Because we are going to suffer pain, hurt, rejected, being lied on and hate will come upon you. These things are there to strengthen us, so be patient with each other, call on the Lord, Jesus Christ will you comfort our hearts, and will you give us strength and peace of mind. He will show you how to work together to overcome these problems. Remember saints it is God's job to help us through hard and difficult times. Stay strong in your faith and all ways trust in the Lord. He is there to see you through. He is speaking to us. **1 Peter 2:20-21** says, "For what glory is it, if when ye be buffeted for your faults, ye shall take it patiently? But if, when ye do well, and suffer for it, ye take it patiently, this is acceptable with God. For even hereunto were ye called: because Christ also suffered for us, leaving us an example, that ye should follow His steps". **II Timothy 2:12** says, "If we suffer, we shall also reign

with him: if we deny him he also will deny us." Let your mind be at ease and listen and hear what God tells you. We must go through suffering. He wants to strengthen us, to build us up in courage, knowledge and understanding of His purpose He has for our lives. We all have a purpose in the life of Christ. Let us hear His voice when He speaks. Have patience and wait on Him; humble ourselves and obey His calling. I pray these words of God will answer your problem and prayer. Remember man doesn't destroy marriage; it is Satan who destroys marriages, because we are control by two spirit, one of God and the other of Satan. Satan desire disruptions, God desire peace. Christ wants to see marriage to grow stronger in the knowledge and understanding of our Heavenly Father. God is beginning to rebuild His church, and Satan will not win or stop the work of the Lord. God spoke and said I am coming back for My church, get ready.

There Is Power in the Faith of God

THE SECOND week in October, 2000, I went to church that Sunday and there were three pastors. I was sitting in the front row with the deacon. After preaching, one of the pastor pointed his finger right at me and said "your prayer is answered." Oh God, what a blessing! Lord, I thank You and praise Your Holy Name. He asked me to stand up and put my hand in the air. He touched my forehead and I fell back and the deacon caught me. When there is a problem in your life, and you know the Lord as your personal savior and you have a sincere heart to call on your heavenly Father, He will hear your prayer. There are many ways He will give you an answer to your prayer. That pastor, knew my prayer because God used him as a shepherd to inform me that my prayer has been answered. One things God will not always give us is the timing. In heaven the problem is solved, but on earth sometime God wait until He finishes preparing us for His calling before releasing it. This is where many saints fail God, because they don't have strong faith and patience to wait on the Lord. This is the time we need to assemble ourselves around strong saints of God to help strengthen us with all might according to His glorious power, unto all patience and longsuffering with joyfulness in the spiritual knowledge and understanding of Christ Jesus.

I pray you will seek the will of the all-true, living God's. Stay strong and commit your whole life to serving His will. I pray He will pour out His Holy Spirit upon your soul, and give you the understanding of His wisdom and the riches of His knowledge. I pray that your faith will be rooted, grounded and settled, and not moved away from the hope of the gospel. We all need to feel the power of the Almighty hand of God. I have found out what He is, how He is, who He is, and what He can do. I will never leave Him, because nobody can do for me what the Lord Jesus is doing. God has changed my heart to tell the Good News to His people because they are hurting for His true word, and to help us to understand His calling.

Psalm 55:22 say, "Cast thy burden upon the Lord, and he shall sustain thee: he shall never suffer the righteous to be moved."

That third week of October, 2000, there was a student at A.T. University where I work. who was very much concerned about the Old Testament. Each day I saw her I would teach and explain it to her; also she would complain about her wrist hurting. One day I said, "Might I pray that God will heal you? She said yes so I held her wrist and prays to God. Immediately she said, something went through her arm and she didn't feel no pain." The awesome powerful hand of God healed her wrist. Oh what a joy to know the Power of the Almighty God. She said "Oh thank You Lord." Do you believe God has the power to heal you?

She had faith in God. He healed her according to her faith. In **Mark 5:34** says, "Jesus speak "daughter, thy faith hath made thee whole; go in peace, and be whole." We need the faith of God to remain and being stead fast in His will. Through righteousness we being justified by faith we have peace with God also we have access by faith into this grace wherein we stand. God said I created you to have faith and a true living testimony of my word, My word must be a seed planted so it may grow and produce good fruit; it must be a word planted down in your heart, that you may be pleasing unto the Lord's eyesight and hold on to your faith in God.

What Do You Do When You Are Angry?

THE FOURTH week of October, 2000, I went to Bible study at Mount Zion Baptist Church This time God has giving me a better understanding of why this was happening in my life. God was telling me this was His plan he had for my life and me alone. But He has to mold, shape, teach and train me for His purpose and His will, first. I had to go through the fire to be reshaped, remolded, purified and sanctified through the blood of the Lamb. For purification of my heart, mind, and soul to carry out God's plan and the will he had for my life, God would split us up and have her show no love toward me. I remember one day we were talking and she said, "Your problem is, and you are letting those people at church run your life." I knew right then God has released her to see the darkness of the world. "I told her God is the head of my life. The church or no one else runs my life." After I knew this was God's plan, I felt relieved and the peace of joy was showered down in my heart, mind, and soul.

But there are other problems in my life; anger. I didn't know just how bad it was. I was trying to speak to her one day, and she stormed out of the house so she would not hear what I had to say. "I got angry and threw a lamp against the wall, broke the lamp knocked a hole in the wall". "Another time I got angry with her and I threw a glass and broke some dishes." Another time, I had stopped drinking for more than twenty five years. I was mad at God; because the fire was getting so hot, I felt that God had forgotten about my soul. I went to the store, I bought a quart of beer, and in my old days I used to drink a half-quart and it would put me out. I drank the whole quart in a half hour, I could get drunk but I would feel nothing. God has his hand upon me all the time. He never left me; my faith was not strong enough to wait and trust Him. I went down on my knees and confessed my sins, asking Oh Lord to take my anger away from my soul. Oh God, I never knew how bad my anger problem were until I got upset, and God healed my anger. Instead of anger, God placed love down in my heart, my mind, and my soul. Now when she tried to upset me I would say, "May the grace of God bless you, with peace and love down in your heart and," It worked every time. Lord, I thank you for taking care of my problem and blessing me with the love of God. What a mighty God I serve.

Matthew 5:22a says, "But I say unto you that whosoever is angry with his brother without a cause shall be in danger of the judgment." **Proverbs.15: 1,** "says, "A soft answer turneth away wrath: but grievous words stir up anger." **Ephesians 4:26** says, "Be ye angry, and sin not; let not the sun go down upon your wrath." Displeasure sin is entirely righteous. When ascribed to God, anger is not to be understood as a tumultuous human passion, but a righteous aversion to sin and wrongdoing. Sinful anger often exists in man, as a work of the flesh or as a result of pride; it may often lead to the commission of even greater sins. Anger was a problem I knew I had to get rid of it and fast. I had to pray, asking God to take away my anger. One morning God led me to turn on the television and there was a pastor teaching on anger, Oh what a blessing from God. I recorded it on audiotape, and when I would driving to work I would listen to this tape and God healed my anger. It is hard to explain what God is doing in my life. The Holy Spirit has placed His glorious love down in my soul so greatly. As my wife turned up the fire, if God had not taken away my anger, I would have hurt her. Now there was no anger in my heart; all I have for her is love no matter what say or do. I would say; may the mighty holy hand of God bless you with love, peace, and joy down in your heart, mind, and soul." You know when the fire is high; you use these words of God and it is like pouring water on the fire. Blessed be the Lord; God, You are my everlasting God. Anger is something most men struggle with; it will come out when you become upset or someone upsets you, then it becomes hard to control; it is something you can't control. It is the evil spirit of Satan and it will not go away. The longer you hold on to, the worse it becomes. It is that old nature which is control by Satan. I will pray that you will call on God to remove the anger out of your heart. The only way it can be released is by the power of God. **I John 1:8-9** says, "If we say that we have no sin, we deceive ourselves, and the truth is not in us. If we confess our sins, He is faithful and just to forgive us our sins and to cleanse us from all unrighteousness." **Psalms 103:8-9** says, "The Lord is merciful and gracious, slow to anger, and plenteous in mercy. He will not always chide; neither will he keep his anger forever."

Isaiah 51:16 says, "I have put my word in his mouth, I have covered him in the shadow of mine hand, that I may plant the heavens, and lay the foundations of the earth, and say unto Zion, thou art my son."

Being under Control in the Heat of the Battle

LATE OCTOBER, 2000, my wife got a lawyer and had separation papers ready for me to sign; and God has given me confidence that every thing would be all right. Two days before she turned up the fire upon my soul, I was at work one night when the Lord came to me in my mind and said "My son everything is going to be all right." So when she asked me to sign, I said; the Lord told me everything would be alright and God has said our marriage is safe I would not sign. "She said if you don't sign, you are going to pay a lot of money." "You are going to hear from my lawyer." "The Lord is with me and He is my lawyer and has already won my case. Your lawyer can't overturn my God's case, because my lawyer never lost a case. You and your lawyer will not win, you see my lawyer has all power, and victory is won. I have strong faith and I trust in Him, therefore I am not worried about anything. My lawyer is in control of my life each and every day." There was not anything she could have said or done to upset my soul. **Isaiah 33:22** say, "For the Lord is our judge, the Lord is our lawgiver, the Lord is our king; he will save us."

Trust him; commit your life to the Lord Jesus Christ. Storms may come, winds may blow, enemies may attack, Satan may oppose, things may seem impossible, but as long as you stay in the hand of Almighty God, everything is going to be all right. He will never leave or forsake you. God is the rock and my salvation. He didn't promised me that life would not be easy. He said your marriage is safe and be strong, My son. In the Bible God said you will face trails and tribulations, in your lifetime, and they surely will come. But with Him on your side, there are no enemy in the world who can defeat the power of the true living God. No hurt, no pain, or sickness will overcome me. No darkness of Satan will come upon my soul. No disappointment will upset my heart. The wicked shall rain snares of fire and brimstone and horrible to tempest me, I shall not be moved, because I'm standing upon the solid rock of my Heavenly Father. **Psalm 27:1** says, "The Lord is my light and my salvation; whom shall I fear? The Lord is the strength of my life; of whom shall I be afraid." My God has already established a place in heaven for my soul. **V14** the victory is already won," wait on the Lord: be of good courage, and he shall strengthen thine heart: wait, I say, on the Lord." Because He is my lawyer when I' m in trouble He is always there. **Colossians Chap1:9b-12** says, "Pray for you, and to desire that ye might be filled with the knowledge of His will in all wisdom and spiritual understanding. That I might walk worthy of the Lord unto all pleasing, being fruitful in every good work, and increasing in the knowledge of God. Strengthened with all might according to His glorious power, unto all patience and longsuffering with joyfulness. Giving thanks unto the Father, which had made us meet to be partakers of the inheritance of the saint in light."

I pray you will have faith in God and let Him be your lawyer in time of troubles; I pray you will stay strong and in His will and let Him be in control at all time. He will fight your battle.

Isaiah 47:3 say, "Her nakedness shall be uncovered, yet her shame shall be seen: I will take vengeance, and I will not meet her as a man. As for our redeemer, the Lord of host is his name, the Holy One of church." **48:15** says, "I have spoken; yea I have called him; I have brought him, and he shall make his way prosperous. I have not spoken in secret from the beginning; from the time that it was, there and I now the Lord God, and his spirit hath sent me."

Show Love and Let God Work Out Your Problems

During September and October I tried to show love and affection by buying her gifts; she would accept them, but her cold affection was still there. So I stopped, but a strange thing happened. On her birthday in September, I had bought her a gift and my son and I had decided to take her out for dinner. My son had picked out a place, I told her what we were going to do, she agreed. Around 1:00 p m. she starting getting dressed, and said "I don't want you and our son to take me to dinner; I am going out with my friends to a club." This was about 2:00 p m. on a Sunday; she shocked me, and I thought about those evil sinful people she worked with. Were the same people who helped her turn to sin. I prayed to God that He would take away all of their sin and bring her back to me and to the house of God. She had also told me she would never go to church again. She was also preparing to move, since she could not get me to leave This was her whole plan, to run me away, and she would bring her friends over. You see this still was all a shock to me; what could I have done so badly to her, in such a short period of time, that she wanted to do this to me? So she went out looking for apartment; She had told me what she was going to take from the house and started packing. During the month of November the first week the fire was really burning; she had not given up on separation. She would ask me to sign; I would say no. God had everything under control and He told me our marriage was safe and I believed and trusted Him. When you finally give your problem unto the Lord, and take your hand off of it and pray to God, you need to stop worrying. Believe, have faith, trust, be obedient, study His word, and He will give you the comfort of your heart. **Psalm 31:14-15** says, "But I trusted in thee, O Lord: I said, Thou art my God. My times are in thy hand: deliver me from the hand of my enemies, and from them that persecute my soul." Be of good courage, and he shall strengthen your heart, be penitence and wait on God.

I pray your love will not depart your heart when problems are trying to get you down; pray and ask your Heavenly Father to give you the strength to carry on.

Isaiah 42:16 says, "I will bring her blinded by a way that she know not; I will lead her in paths that she have not known; I will make darkness light before her, and crooked things straight. These things will I do unto her, and not forsake her." O thank you Lord God Almighty.

The Fire Is Burning; God is My Rock and Salvation

THE SECOND week of November, 2000, I went to church and I was sitting up front, during the time of collection I saw her come around. I said "Oh God thank you. What a mighty blessing hand of God to have sent her there". I thought, "God, this is one thing she said she was not going to do," God change her mind. That week my son's car needed repair work. He needed a way to college and work. So I told my wife I would go to work early so he would not miss class, and he could take my vehicle. So she said she would pick me up. Later at work I called and gave her directions on how to get to my job and what time to pick me up. I worked at the college; she had been there before. She came there a little early, really upset. "You gave me the wrong direction." There was only two turns onto the campus; how could she get turned around? She was on fire so I did not say anything else. I was praying to God calm her down. I had to work a little later and she got upset again and the fire from her tongue was really blazing, I said calm down; it wouldn't be long. Also this was my birthday. So we left for home and she turned the fire up so hot, I asked God to pour water on her to cool her off and not let me get burned. I did everything I could to stay calm, and let her talk. **Psalm 61:1-3** says, "Hear my cry, O God; attend unto my prayer. From the end of the earth will I cry unto thee, when my heart is overwhelmed: lead me to the rock that is higher than I. For thou hast been a shelter for me, and a strong tower from the enemy." I knew my God was right with me to control my mouth, she said;

I should not have to wait for you. I don't care what happens the next time. I will not pick you up." After all, God didn't let me get burned. We came home and she was rushing "to go to dinner with her friends. My birthday didn't mean anything to her." I stayed home, read the Bible, and prayed to God to work on my wife's heart and take away her sin and bring love and peace into her heart and to overcome the fire from her tongue. Oh God, I pray you will wrap You loving arms around me and cover my soul with your holy hand of salvation and keep me under your wing and don't let Satan destroy my soul.

In **Psalm 57** says, "Be merciful unto me, O God be merciful unto me; for my soul trusteth in thee: in the shadow of thy wings will I make my refuge, until these calamities be over past. I will cry unto God most high; unto God that performeth all things for me." It is hard to hold on to God's hand. It is also hard; seeing those things happening right in front of my eyes, and there is nothing I can do about it. At times I would ask God, "Where are you Lord?" Are you still with me? Deep down my heart I knew He was right there, I knew He have not abandoned me. Later on the Holy Spirit would come upon me, and give me courage and confidence and not to worry. God is still in control. When God gives me this feeling, it doesn't matter what she says or what she does. I know God is in control and I have strong confidence, courage and faith in Him. He will make everything all right. Have confidence and put your trust in God. He is speaking to us II **Corinthians 1:3-4** says, "Blessed be God, even, the Father of our Lord Jesus Christ, Father of mercies, and the God of all comfort: Who comfort us in all tribulation, that we may be able to comfort wherewith we any trouble, by the comforted of God."

Isaiah 41:10 says "Fear thou not my son; for I am with thee: be not dismayed; for I am thy God; I will strengthen thee; yea, I will help thee; yet I will uphold thee with the right hand of my righteousness."

II Thessalonians 1:7 say, "And to you who are troubled, rest with us, when the Lord Jesus shall be revealed from heaven, with his mighty angels, in flaming fire, taking vengeance on them that know not God and the obey not the Gospel of our Lord Jesus Christ."

You May Run But You Can't Hide

October, November, and December my wife had acquired a strong personality for going out with her friends every night of the week. And on Friday night through Sunday night she would stay out real late. One night I arrived home from work around 7:30 p m she had left me a note saying, not to wait me. I would stay up late anyway reading my Bible or typing God's story, when she comes home, she would ask me, "Why are you up spying on me?" I would say No, you told me way back you would go and come when you got ready. I am not worried about you; I just hate what you are doing to yourself. "If she came home early, she would turn right around and go right back out. God would often remind me He was watching over her and not to worry."

During the last week of November I was watching a Christians program on television, called the Liberty Institute of Biblical Studies. Three days later God came to me in my mind, and said; Order this course. That same day I called and ordered it. Now I am taking this course. It is amazing, At the beginning of my problem, God said, "Study my word." Every since God has provided me a way to study his word. He is an incredible and amazing God. When I am at work or somewhere away from her, He would warn me, by His Holy Spirit, and comfort my soul with peace, when I arrived home, nothing she will say could dampen my spirit, because my Lord warned me ahead of time. God is an amazing and an incredible God; He has yet to fail me. Oh God, I thank You with my whole heart, mind, and soul for making a way for me. You are an Almighty God. When God tells you to do something, He will not fail you; He will stand right by you. He will walk with you, lead, guide, and direct you along the way. O what a mighty God I serve. Who ever reads this book of Jesus Christ, I pray you will never go through anything like this. Take care of your marriage by the Holy hand of God. Always put Him first in everything, and most of all believe in His will of what He has called you out for. And the Holy Hand of God will richly bless your heart. Away continue to have a clear communication between husband and wife. Ensure the family life is going according to God's plan. The husband is the spiritual head leader of the family, the wife is to submit herself unto the husband, and they become one and Christ become the overall head. Oh God I pray, husband, its their privilege and duty to maintain the family household responsibility being the spiritual leader as the head of household, teaching his family love, direction and guidance. They will be blessing by the Holy Spirit of the powerful hand of the Almighty God if they follow God's plan. In **Colossians 3:18-19** says, "Wives, submit yourselves, as it is fit in the Lord. Husbands, love your wives, and not bitter against them. **V15-16** say, "And let the peace of God rule in your hearts, to which also ye are called in one body; and be ye thankful. Let the word of Christ dwell in you richly in all wisdom; teaching and admonishing one another in psalms and hymns and spiritual song, singing with grace in your hearts to the Lord."

Isaiah 46:9 says "Remember the former things of old: for I am God, and there is none else; I am God, and there is none like me. I have spoken it, I will also bring it to pass; I have purposed it I will also do it."

You Must Have Strong Confidence in the Lord

ONE DAY I asked my wife, may I go with you to meet some of your friends? She said you are not good enough to meet my friends. I felt as if I had been shot with a gun; I had not felt this low in a long time. I felt bad for a little while. Then I asked God to forgive her and her friend's sins. You know people can be cold toward other, if you don't have God on your side to give you confidence to overcome those evil things, they will hurt your soul by really getting you down, and lead to real problems. Hurting from sin will stay with some people all their lives, until they come to know the love of Jesus Christ. Confess your faults one to another and pray one for another and ask Jesus for forgiveness. **James 5:15** says, "And the prayer of faith shall save the sick, and the

Lord shall raise him up; and if have committed sin, they be forgive him." I thank God who is my savior. God said love those who heat or persecute you in **Matthew 5:44-45,48** say, "God is speaking to us, but I say unto you, love your enemies, bless them that curse you, do good to them that hate you, and pray for them which despitefully you, and persecute you. God send rain on the just and on the unjust. Be ye therefore perfect, even as you Father which is in heaven is perfect."

The storm and fire I was going through to tell you the truth was hurting experience. Every time I would go through a critical situation. God was right there to pull me out or He will stand right by my side to comfort and strengthen my soul. You know when you have a friend like Jesus Christ; there is no need to worry. Because Jesus is the only friend you need in times of trouble. My wife still rejected me, when I would tell her about the Good News of Jesus Christ, what He had done through me or what God had told me to tell His people. She would look at me as if I had lost my mined. She said I was losing my mind and going crazy and I should have you put away in the crazy home. These things would hurt my heart, but with God on my side nothing she could say would get me upset with her. I tell you I am living in two worlds; I am living on the bright life of God, and living on the dark side of life with my wife. I tell you this is not an easy life to live this way. I often tell God I don't understand what is going on. Lord You split my wife and I up so you can work on my soul. Then God took me to **1 Samuel** as He place an evil spirit upon Saul against David. Now He had place an evil spirit upon my wife heart against my soul to test my faith in what God wanted to do in my life, and make me who He wanted me to be. He had anointed me with His Holy Spirit down in my soul. Lord, You have given me strength you give me confidence and you given me courage to overcome any problems that confront me. I won't let anything stop me now from going and telling peoples the Good News of Jesus Christ.

Every day I will do just what you ask of me. You told me to study your word; I am doing that. With the help of you, Lord, you said my marriage is safe. But I don't understand why you let her continue to reject you and me Lord. I know, Lord. I am not suppose to question you, but Lord you know my heart; look upon me and have mercy on my soul. Oh Lord, I am nobody in Your presence I am not worthy to bow down before your presence. Lord, I am asking you; bring my wife out of darkness and back into a right understanding of You, I will praise your name every day, Lord. You know, Lord, my love for her is just as strong as the love I have for you. You say love your wife the way you love the Lord. Oh Lord, God, you have given me a loving heart, with such a strong compassion for everyone. I love her despite what she has said or the thing she is doing to me. God, you have taught me not to hate anyone, despite who committed sin against me. Lord, I pray to your Holy Name forgive my wife and my sins. Help us do and say the right thing that we may be pleasing unto your Holy Spirit Lord. My wife has going so far as to turn my son against me with her rejecting anger. She has caused him to reject God. I am an unwanted person in our house. In **Mark 6:4** says, "but Jesus said unto them A prophet is not without honor, among his own kin, and in his own house." I pray, Oh Lord, every day and night, release her from the darkness of the world, and return her to the light side of Jesus Christ. I know, Lord, if I continue to pray, the door will open one day. She continues to introduce him to the way, of the world. I pray whoever reads this book of God; it will help head off problems before they become under controllable. Don't let anything turn you back, because you are under the control of the living Almighty God. The Lord will never lead your life in the wrong direction. I have totally given myself up to God. I spoke to my Heavenly Father; I will be committed to die and take to heaven, if He would bring my wife back to a saving grace of Christ Jesus. That's how bad I want to see her return from darkness and back to the miraculous light of God.

Colossians 3:12-20 say, "Put on therefore, as the elect of God, holy and beloved, bowels of mercies, kindness, humbleness of mind, meekness, longsuffering. Forbering one another, and forgiving one another, if any man has a quarrel against any even as Christ forgave you, so also do ye. And above all these things put on charity, which is the bond of perfectness. And let the peace of God rule in your heart, to the also ye are called in one body; and be ye thinkful. Let the word of Christ dwell in you richly in all wisdom teaching and admonishing one another in psalms and hymus and spiritual songs your hearts to the Lord. Wives, submit yourselves unto your own husbands, as it is fit in the Lord. Husbands, love your wives, be not bitter against each other. Children, obey your parents in all things; for this is well pleasing unto your Heavenly Father."

God Will Lead You to Help Others Overcome Problems

ON NOVEMBER 13, 2000, my daughter called from Maryland, and asked me to come and have Thanksgiving dinner, I said I don't know; I was thinking about going away for Thanksgiving. My wife came home that night, and she called my daughter, who told her what she had ask me. I told her I would have to think about it, and she told me her friends have invited her to dinner, so she was not cooking Thanksgiving dinner for our son and me. That night I prayed, asking God what shall I do. The next morning I felt God leading me to go, so I told her I would go.

I visited my daughter, and the morning of Thanksgiving. I was up writing God's story. After about one hour, something told me to go out. I was not hungry, but I went out, I stopped at McDonalds and they were closed. There were something leading me down the street. I saw Denny's, I stopped there, and the waitress seated me in a seat behind a man and a lady with a baby. I was sitting there waiting, and God's Holy Spirit came upon me, and I asked God what is going on? Then the lady in front started saying real bad abusive language. There was a lady sitting in front of them. When she heard those sinful words she got up, looked back, and departed. I rebuked her sin in the name of the Holy Spirit of the Almighty God. I heard her say something that touched me. She stopped using abusive language. Oh Lord, what a mighty powerful hand of God. I praise your holy name. **Isaiah 50:4-5** says, "The Lord God hath given me the tongue of the learned, that I should know how to speak a word in season to him that is weary (speak evil) he wakeneth morning by morning he wakeneth mine ear to hear as the learned. The Lord God hath opened mine ear, and I was not rebellious neither turned away back." Lord you know how to used your Christians peoples to touch other in time of trouble, and bright upon their life. We all, who study the word of God, should have faith and be committed to take up the cross daily and follow Christ and have personal fellowship with him. You will have the anointed power of God blessing with the Holy Spirit of Jesus Christ to heal and cure for the sin and sickness.

The Almighty God has placed these things in my heart, mind, and soul. Whenever the spirits come upon my soul, I know there is something God wants me to do or someone in need of healing or whatever the problem may be. As I was eating my meal there was peace not abusive language. When I got up to leave I said my the mighty holy hand of God bless you all. They said May God bless you too, and I said think you.

Isaiah 66:15-16 says, "For beholds, the Lord will come with fire, and with his chariots like a whirlwind, to render his anger with fury, and his rebuke with flames of fire. For by fire and by his sword will the Lord plead with all flesh; and the slain of the Lord shall be many."

I Serve a God Who Answers Prayer

Late November, 2000, I prayed every day for all of my co-workers, students and staff. There were two ladies who asked me to pray for their problems. One had serious leg and knee problems and the other had a son seriously involved with drugs, who slept in abandoned buildings and alleys, she was afraid he might be killed. That night I fell on my knees praying to God Almighty asking the Lord to heard my prayed and answer these ladies requests. Let your mighty hand touch them with your healing power. Three days later, I was on my way to work, when the Holy Spirit came upon my soul and God came to my mind and said the lady with leg, and knee problems was being held. The lady son on drug was going to be all right, so hold on and have faith. I started singing praises to the Almighty God. When you pray with a sincere heart, and have faith, God will deliver according to His will. I pray you will have faith, and confidence to hold on to God's unchanged hand. When I arrived at work, the lady with the son told me her son was picked up by the police. It was a great blessing to hear this. He is in jail but he is safe. And while he was there, they would clean him up and feed him. I told her God is at work upon his soul; I will continue to pray that God will led him back to the grace and mercy of Jesus Christ. Two year later I saw her, she said God had save her son; and wash him through the blood, and he is working during find, prayer navel fail. Think the Almighty God, have faith and believe in Him. The next day, I saw the lady with leg and knee problems. I told her God said You will be heal by the Holy Hand of God, because You request had been answer according to your faith. In the middle of December I asked about her condition, and she said "My leg and knees are healed; I don't feel any pain; I feel fine." Oh what a blessing from God Almighty. **Psalm 138** say, "I will praise thee with my whole heart; before the gods will I sing praise unto thee. I will worship toward thy holy temple, and praise thy name for, thy loving kindness and for thy truth: for thou hast magnified thy word above all thy name." Why don't Christians people believe the power of God's prayer and have faith that God will heal them and others? What a power for hand of God I serve! He said all my people could be free from problems, if only they put their faith, truth, and confidence in His all-powerful Hand; there is no change in Him from the beginning. We Christians must go out with the love of Christ Jesus in our hearts to tell the lost and hurting. Come unto the Lord's house. He will give you rest and relief; He will heal your pain. He will give you the living water. He will feed you the true living bread of His word. He will give you salvation along with His Holy Spirit. He will build you a new kingdom in Heaven. Oh God, we need more followers of Christ who are committed to go and work for you.

Oh Lord God, you have given me such compassion, and feeling for your people. With a loving heart, I want to see all peoples come to a loving relationship with Him. When I see people, I look past their sin and see only the love of Christ in them. We are all God's children made in the image of God and created in the likeness of Him. God has placed a strong, loving compassion in my heart, with a powerful understanding of how to care for Christians and non-Christians. I would tell pastor/leaders and other believer of what God had told me to tell them. Some will look at me with a strange look, and some will look at me not understanding what I am saying. And some will think I'm false prophet. I, praise and thank the Almighty God. **Psalm 119:169,172** say, "Let my cry come near before thee, O Lord: give me understanding according to thy word. My tongue shall speak of thy word: for all thy commandment are righteousness." I must wait, be patient, and obey His calling.

Sometimes I would ask God what all this meant? Things are so amazing. When I would buy something, the Holy Spirit would come upon me telling me what to buy. I remember one time I went to buy something, and the Spirit came upon me telling me what to buy. I disobeyed God by buying something else. I was so disappointed when I arrived home; I did like it. Another day I went to buy an item, and there was several items the same. The Spirit told me which one to buy, and when I arrived at the cash register, the price was a lot less than what was posted. I will never disobey God again. Whenever I will have a pain on my body, I will lay my hand on the place of the pain and immediately it will depart. Again these thing I don't understand, but I do understand it is God's power working in and through me, not of myself, I have no power to do anything, except what my Heavenly Father tell me.

Acts 3:16 say, "And his name through faith in his name hath made this man strong, whom ye see and know; yea, the faith, which is by Him, hath given him this perfect soundness in the presence of you all." Things like this, I can't find enough praise to praise God or how He is using me. Oh, you are one awesome powerful God; you are amazing God; you are an incredible God. I am afraid to tell my wife of these things anymore; early I have told her about these things God has done through me and she said I am going crazy and losing my mind. **Exodus 31:3** says, "And I have filled him with the spirit of God, in wisdom, and in understanding, and in knowledge, and in all manner of workmanship." **Isaiah 61:1-2** says, "And the Spirit of the Lord shall rest upon him, the Spirit of wisdom and understanding, the spirit of counsel and night, the Spirit of knowledge and of the fear of the Lord. The Spirit of the Lord God is upon me; because the Lord hath anointed me to preach good tidings unto the meek; he hath sent me to bind up the brokenhearted, to proclaim liberty to the captives. And the opening of the prison to them that are bound; to proclaim the acceptable year of the Lord, and the day of vengeance of our God; to comfort all that mourn."

My Wife Has Been a Blessing to My Heart

AFTER ALL these trials and tribulations I am going through, whatever the outcome, I will continue to hold on to God's un-changing hand. Before all of this started, my wife meant more to me than anything in the world, because she had stood right by me all twenty four years. She had been a blessing to me heart, while I was in the service, away from home. She took control of the household, and she conducted all administrative requirements. She raised our two children up with love, peace and how to be respectable children of God. She gave them good guidance and direction. She entered them into Girl and Boy Scout; She made sure they maintained good behavior. Good grades in school; she attended most school functions. She took them to church; she led them to the glory of God they received their salvation through the blood of Jesus Christ. She had been a blessing to my heart. I can't thank her enough for what she had done for me, and God. She had been a faithful wife. She was more involved in raising our children than I was. I had not been a good husband; I was not always there for them. "My God knew it." I was not always there to provide the necessary support, direction, and guidance. I had asked her forgiveness; that's hard for a person who did most of the work.

I was there but the army took up most of my time. Sometimes being a husband and a provider is not enough to keep a family together. God's plan is for man to be the breadwinner, head of the household and the spiritual leader with God love. The wife is the administrator roll of the family and God is the head over all, because He is the center of every godly family. God know I tried but it never seemed to be enough, I thank God she was able to carry on. She meant a great deal to my life. So you see how much I miss her. My prayer goes out to every husband. Love your wife with your whole heart, your mind, and soul. Put God in the center of everything. Be there for her all the time if possible. Keep her happy; take care of her as she is the most important, beautiful and precious woman in the world. Look upon her as if you are looking at her through the eyes of Christ Jesus. Thank God for her being my wife.

Ephesians 5 20-21,23 say, "Giving thinks always for all things unto God and the Father in the name of our Lord Jesus Christ, Submitting you one to another in the fear of God. For the husband is the head of the wife, even as Christ is the head of the church."

During our marriage God allow us to do the right thing by letting my wife stay home and take care the children, providing for them with the right guidance and direction in their up bring until they were older enough to attend school at a responsible age. I thank God for her during the right thing, and I thank God I was making enough money to support my family with no problem.

I Was a Judge Against God and My Wife

OH LORD God, I have sinned against you and my wife. I prays, Oh Lord, forgive me for I have committed these awful sins. Lord redeem, me through the blood and clean me and create in me a clean hand, a pure heart, and righteousness mind, Oh Lord. I was committing these sins but I was not aware, not until later **February1, 2001,** than the Lord show me my mistake. While I was living in Maryland attending church, every time I would attend church, my wife was not there. It would always seem the message being preached, was for her and she should have been here to hear it. Also the same thing would happen when I attended other churches without her. I had become her judge knowing what she needed to hear. On my way home, in my mind, I would tell her what was preached to let her know what God wanted her to know and do. By the time I arrived home, I will always forgotten all about it. When God brought this back to my mind, I thought it was strange. Whenever we would attend church together, I would never think this way.

God was telling me all the time; this message was for me, not my wife. He brought it to light; I had been trying to equip you with my word all the time, but you refuse to hear me. I felt so bad. All those years I was blaming my wife about what she needed. Satan was controlling my heart, mind, and soul all that time. "You don't need these words in your heart." "Find someone else and tell them what they should hear." Satan's job is to deceive you by crossing up your mind to keep God's word from your heart. **1 Peter 5:6-8** says, "Humble yourselves therefore under the mighty hand of God, that He may exalt you in due time: casting all your care upon Him; for He careth for you. Be sober, be vigilant; because your adversary the devil roaring lion, walketh about, seeking whom he may devour." This was a real problem I had, about telling other people in my mind what they needed. When we do this, we are committing sin against God and the other person. We sit ourselves up as a judge, and jury to bring judgment upon others people. This is the work of Satan, not of God. Only He knows our every needs. In **Roman 14:10** say, "But why dost thou judge thy brother? For we shall all stand before the judgment set of Christ?" Oh Lord, I bow before your presence asking the Master hand of Jesus Christ to forgive me for my awful sin I have committed against You and my wife. I pray you will take my sins to the foot of the cross and wash me in the blood of the lamb, and set my soul free. God is calling upon us to overcome our sin. For it is written, as I love, saith the Lord, every knee shall bow to me, and every tongue shall confess to God. So then every one of us shall give account of himself to God. Let us not therefore judge one another any more. This is His will, to provide his people with their needs. Oh God I thank you with my whole heart, you had set my soul free from my sin, and only God can change our heart and clean us from all unrighteousness.

II Chronicles 19:6-7 say, "And said to the judges, take heed what ye do; for ye judge not for man, but for the Lord who is with you in the judgment." Wherefore now let the fear of the Lord be upon you; take heed and do it for there is no iniquity with the Lord our God not respect of persons, nor take of gifts."

Lord God, I know enough about you now, to know your voice from the voice of Satan. I will hear you when you speak; I believe in your true word; you have taught me to know and understand when you speak to me. You speak by the Holy Spirit, through the Bible, prayer, circumstances, church and anyway ways He reveals His purposes for my life. When we do the will of God, by spreading His Good News among His poor and lost people and glorifying Him in heaven, then He will teach us to hear and know when God is speaking. God said we are to equip ourselves with the word and find out where He is working and join him in His will. Once you experience the work of God, you will come to know him by obeying him, and let Him performing His work through you, let Christ Jesus teach you of your needs that you may be pleasing in His eyes sight of the true living God.

This is the Most Amazing and Incredible Journey of My Life

THE LAST **week of January, 22-28, 2001,** every morning on my way to work and at work I had a feeling something was going to happen. Will On Thursday night when I arrived home from work my wife had left a note on my desk, which had several items listed on it. One item was that my sister was in the hospital in Emporia. Virginia. That night I got down on my knees and I prayed Oh God overcome her problem by defeating and destroying whatever was affecting her body, and granting her peace and healing power to sitting her soul free. That Friday at work, my sister and my niece were on my mind about healing. The Holy Spirit came upon me so strong tear were running from my eyes. One of the students saw me, and came over and asked if I was all right, I said "Yes, the Holy Spirit just spoke to me". I could not hold back my tears, and he ask me to pray for him. When the Holy Spirit comes upon my soul, God has already taking care of the problem. It is an amazing feeling to know the power of God is answering prayer. After the Spirit departed, peace and joy come upon my soul, as it to say your prayer is answered. Everything is all right; your sister is healed. Oh God I pray that every believer would feel the awesome power and glorious hand of Your Holy Spirit: it is like nothing you're ever felt before.

That Friday at work I was providing security for the dining facility. There was one group of students acting up, making all kinds of noise. Everyone else was calm and I love them all from the bottom of my heart. It seemed as if that group was trying to provoke me by getting me upset with them. God has already given me peace and joy, and I was not going to let the devil take away what God has given me. They went on for one hour and half. I would walk around, asks God to bless them, and remove the evil spirit from their hearts. I didn't let them bother me I say calm thanking and praising God Almighty. In **Philippians 2:1-3,5** says, "If there be therefore any consolation in Christ, if any comfort of love, if any fellowship of the Spirit, if any bowels and mercies. Fulfill ye my joy that ye be like-minded, having the same love, being of one accord, of one mind. Let nothing be done through strife or vainglory; but in lowliness of mind let each esteem other better than themselves. Let this mind be in you, which was also in Christ Jesus."

When I arrived home, I asked my wife if she would like to go with me to see my sister. She said no she had something to do. She was still rejecting me, but I didn't let it bother me anymore. I am about my Father's work, I prayed for her, and put it in the hands of the Lord. There is nothing in my power to bring her back; I know one day God will make a way.

A mouth ago a strange thing happened I was in bed about ready to go to sleep and God showed me a vision of my sister sitting in a rocking chair just as clear as day. I didn't know what this meant later on I found out something was going to happen to her. He was warning me what was to come.

That Friday at work, also something elf strange happened, God showed me a vision, and I saw my sister daughter, brother; husband, and I standing by her bedside praying for her in the hospital.

That day, Saturday morning, I left headed to Emporia. On my way there the Holy Spirit kept coming upon my soul, and I asked God what were going on "Lord, what do you want of me? Lord, I don't understand why this continues to come upon me for so long? It was two a and half, drive, and it kept happening for about fourth five minus. I arrived in Emporia at 11:10 a. m, and I went to my other sister's house. She called over to the hospital, and my niece and husband were there. I went to the hospital and the same people God showed me Friday were their. I asked them what time did they arrive; they said 11:10 a. m. I didn't think anything about it. I said God told me who all would be here. My cousin said, You are here to pray for us. I said to myself "How did he know?" So we all did what He had showed me to prayer. I told my sister "God say you are healed by the holy hand of the true living God," and "she said Hallelujah! Thank you, Lord Jesus." We were praising His Holy Name that He would continue to bless her and overcome her problem. "Thank you, Lord Jesus, for all you have done, and what you are going to do."

I left out for a while. On my way back I was talking with my cousin's husband. There was someone coming out of the hospital; I knew him a long time ago. He said his wife was in the hospital really sick. The doctor didn't expect her to live; my heart went out for her. I said I would like to pray for her, and he gave me her room number. I went up to see her; she didn't know me. I told her who I was, a longtime friend of her husband's and I would like to pray for her. I asked, do you know the Lord? She said yes, I said you believe God can heal you? "She said yes. Then the Holy Spirit came upon me, I grabbed her hand, and said, let's pray." When I finished praying, she acted as if she didn't want let go of my hand. The Holy Spirit was moving upon both of us.

I left the hospital and went back to my sister's house. She said I wanted to talk to you, I needed some spiritual advice. During our conversation, it seemed as if God sent me to minister to her. What she was going through. I had already faced, and was still going through. God has given me such confidence and courage through faith to help other overcome problems through the spirit of Christ Jesus. I told her God was preparing her for something, but first she must go through the storm. He wanted to mold and shape her for his purpose. The storm was going to get rough; she must have strong faith, and study His word and continue to show love and, most of all, be patient and wait on the Lord, and He will see you through. As we were talking the Holy Spirit came upon both of us. We knew God was speaking through me to her, giving her the assurance in the knowledge of the Lord to strengthen her with all power and understanding of his word along with, longsuffering, and joyfulness of God leading her through the valley of the shadow of death. In **Hebrews 10:36** says, "For ye have need of patience, that, after ye have done the will of God, ye might receive the promise." In **James 1:3-4** says, "Knowing this, that the trying of your faith worketh patience. But let patience have her perfect work, that ye may be perfect and entire, wanting nothing."

That Sunday morning I was explaining to my sister that God is pouring out his Spirit upon all flesh, your sons and your daughters shall prophesy. She said she had a gift for kids; I said He may be getting you ready for that. She asked. How can you bring young people up today in a world of materialism, and the corrupt environment we are living in. I said you must bring them up in the nurture and admonition of the Lord, and train them to be a light to the world. If they want to get involved with worldly activity, you must have a plan, and have guidelines, discipline, and control, and with the love and help of the Lord, they should be all right. My sister was watching television, she called me, and said. Look, they are explaining the same answer you gave me. I said this is a confirmation from God, Oh I praise the Almighty holy name of Jesus Christ what a mighty God we serve!

Last summer while in Emporia, I visited my niece. She had been given tainted blood about twenty years before while living in Washington, DC, There were other problems; there were two lumps on her breast, one large and a small one. God led me pray for her. Friday when the Holy Spirit came upon me letting me know her problem was healed, I saw her that Saturday at the hospital. She said she went to the doctor and the doctor found no lump. I said Hallelujah to Almighty God! thank you, Lord, for what you have done. Prayer is a powerful weapon; I wish every child of God would believe in the power of prayer. I thank God for using me as a vessel to bless his people and bring glory unto Jesus Christ.

Sunday on route back home to North Carolina was a strange and amazing journey, every thing was so calm, and the scenery all around me was so peaceful. I stopped to get fuel. As I was getting out of my vehicle, a man walked over to me, and started talking about churches and God, This was on my mind all the time. We talk as if we new each other, but he was a stranger and I was a stranger in the world's eyesight. But to God's people there is no stranger; it is a great blessing to fellowship with His people. Then we departed. I continued on my journey home, everything remained the same, and it was an amazing and incredible feeling from the glorious hand of Christ Jesus.

All of a sudden the Holy Spirit came upon me with an incredible feeling. I felt the presence of God inside the vehicle with me

It was so strong tears of glory were running from my eyes, and I had to stop on the side of the highway so I could see. The Spirit was telling me something incredible. Friday at work, God showed me who I would meet at the hospital to pray for my sister. They were there as God said. But the most amazing thing was that we both arrived there at the same time at 11:10 a. m. They came from Maryland and I was from North Carolina. This is only the work of Christ Jesus. He brought this to my mind; that's why I had to stop. Also, the lady I prayed for who was scheduled not to live, the Spirit was upon me telling me that lady would be healed. What an incredible feeling of God's Holy Spirit that was upon my soul for about five minutes before the tears would stop. I felt at peace that passes all understanding. What a mighty God in heaven and earth. This was the most incredible journey; I can't find words to describe it. All I can say is this God I know is all powerful, He is Holy, be loving, merciful, from the bowels of kindness, humbleness of mind, with meekness, patience, and longsuffering. He is the healing Lamb of heaven, an everlasting, and understanding God. He is faithful, all knowledgeable, and Almighty. **Colossians 1:16-20** says, "For by Him were all things created, that are in heaven, and that are in earth, visible and invisible, whether they be thrones, or dominions, or principalities, or power; all things were created by Him, and for Him. And He is before all things, and by Him all things consist. And He is the head of the body of the church; who is the beginning, the firstborn from the dead that in all things He might have the preeminence. For it pleased the Father that in Him should all fullness dwell. For, having made peace through the blood of his cross, by Him to reconcile all things unto himself; by Him, I say, whether they are thing in earth, or thing in heaven." Oh Lord, I pray these true words of the true living God will open up the hearts of every reader of this book of God. He said this book will go out to the entire world and they will be blessed by the knowledge of God.

Isaiah 35:1-2 says, "The wilderness and the solitary place shall be glad for them; and the desert shall rejoice, and blossom as the rose. They shall blossom abundantly, and rejoice even with joy and singing the glory of churches shall be given unto it, the excellency of they shall see the glory of the Lord and the excellency of our God."

Fire from Heaven

THE POWER of God is amazing and incredible. **The first of February, 2001,** I was at work providing security for the cafeteria students. That day they were making lots of noise. I was praying to God, "Oh Lord, please calm these students down," and then the Holy Spirit came upon me. I really didn't know what was going on until later. The Holy Spirit was saying all God's children would be quiet. For about three minute, it was real calm, and then the rest of that day they were quiet and calm. I had stretched out my arm. I said, "Oh Lord God, let your Holy Spirit fall from heaven upon every soul on this campus and touch every heart, and let the glorious fire from heaven touch us all." I could see in their faces that every believer of Christ has been touched by the Spirit of God. In the past they would sit in the cafeteria late talking, but now they ate got up, and left. I thank the Lord that I served. He is a powerful and incredible God. I thank God every day for placing me among these students, they are a blessing to my heart, and I love them all. I will pray to the Almighty God to send more praying worriers to pray that the darkness of Satan's spirit will release his hand off of God people, so the brightness of God's light will shine, and the Holy Spirit will open up every heart and soul.

That even I left and went to open the door of my vehicle; fire came out of my finger. I didn't think much about it until I arrived home, and everything I would touch, fire would come from my finger; I was so afraid, I didn't know what was happen to my soul. It was long red flashes coming from my finger at first I thought my hand was on fire. I was looking in my wallet to find a phone number to call a pastor to help me or tell me what was happening to me. I was so nervous, I couldn't find it, my wallet fell on the floor, I Fall Unto a chair, saying "Oh Lord, what is happening to me, why is fire coming out of my finger? Lord, please help me." Then it stopped and I was praising and thanking the Almighty God. It was amazing what God was doing. Fire was coming from my hand, but the fire was not burning my finger. It was incredible what was happening to me that night. **Ezekiel 10** says, "I stretched forth my hand unto the fire, because this was the living creature I felt unto God."

Jeremiah 23:29 says, "Is not my word like a fire? Said the Lord; and like a hammer that breaketh the rock in pieces?" **Psalm 97:3-4** says, "A fire goeth before him, and burneth up his enemies round about. His lightning's enlightened the world: the earth saw, and trembled."

That same month I would continue to bless the students as they come into the cafeteria, and one day a student came up to me and said he given my life to the Christ Jesus. I felt the Holy Spirit come upon me "Hallelujah!" Thank you, God, what a blessing to see one more come unto your kingdom. God wants all of His children to spread the Good News to His people who are hurting and waiting for someone to tell them about the love of Jesus Christ. He is standing by, waiting for you. **Revelation 3:20** says, "Behold, I stand at the door, and knock: if any man hear my voice, and open the door, I will come in to him and will sup with him, and he with me." Oh Lord God, I pray, somebody will do something to turn this world around to overcome the darkness that you Lord will bring your bright light back into this old world. Lord raise up an Abraham, Joseph, Moses or a David to turn this world around.

Exodus 3:2 say, "And the angel of the Lord appeared unto him in a flame of fire out of the midst of a bush; and he looked, and, behold, the bush burned with fire, and the bush was not consumed."

Don't Let Money Become a Problem

THE SECOND **week of February, 2001,** I told my wife I needed money to send to the book publisher. I arrived home that evening and on my desk was a note saying you are taking all the money out of the saving account so when we separated there would not be any left. And she still wanted a separation because we could-n't continue to live this way, and she want to buy a new car. After reading her note, I spoke to my Heavenly Father. You haven touched her heart yet, the way her mind is set, Lord, God, I can't bow down to her wants, and Lord, she is in your hands. And I am in your hand, all I can do is pray and wait, and be patient. In **James 5:7** says, "James is speaking be patient therefore, brethren, unto the coming of the Lord. Behold, the husbandman waiteh for the precious fruit of the earth, and hath long patience for it, until I receive the early and latter rain."

This is not an easy road to travel. Lord, I pray you will overcome the darkness of her life, and release me from her oppression. Then I thought, some people go through trouble all their lives, they are not complaining. Lord, if I have to go through this problem all my life, I will; this is how much I love You and her. Oh, Lord forgives my soul for complaining. Lord some time it get hard to live in the light and she with darkness all around my soul. Lord I know you are working on your time, and when you get ready you will bring her back into your church. Then we shall be one in the eyes of the Lord. I asked her to write the check. She said "did you read the note," I said yes. She said, "What are you going to do about it." I told her I could worry about that. This was the work of the Lord, and everything we have belong to Him. If it wasn't for the Lord we would not have been bless with this. She wrote the check. You can't fight against God, when He speaks and gives you a mission there is nothing anyone can do to stop His progress.

Have faith and stand firm upon His solid rock. Be patient; you will be all right. In **Hebrews 10:23-24** says, "Paul is speaking, "let us hold fast the profession of our faith without wavering; for he is faithful that promised; And let us consider one another to provoke unto love and to good work."

That same week my daughter and her friend came down from Maryland, and said they were going with me to church on Sunday. I thought to myself, my wife may go, but it didn't happen. They did go and they enjoyed the worship service with the congregation. Well it is automatic now every weekend she is out of town. God has place a comfort in my heart. Don't worry; be strong. I just pray that the Holy Hand of God will bless her and keep her safe and sound from all hurt and danger from wherever she may go. While I was at church last Sunday; God came to me in my mind saying pray for her friends. That night I prayed for her friends that God would turn their lives around and led them to call on Him. I prayed that He would take away their sin, so they would see the light of Jesus Christ and become a light to my wife that would bring her and her friends from out of darkness. While I was praying; I felt God's Spirit come upon me letting me, know he would save them. Oh God, I thank you for your power and glory; you are an amazing God. I know you have the power to turn people's lives around.

You know, when we start to grow stronger in Him, picking up our cross. He says come and follow Him. He will walk with you and you will walk with Him. This is when Satan becomes the stronger; he will try his best to win your soul back. God said put on the whole Armour of God for protection. He will be with you because you have been called out to do My will.

Hebrews 10:22 say, "Let us drew near with a true heart in full assurance of faith, having our heart sprinkled from an evil conscience, and our bodies washed with pure water."

You see the masterwork must go on. I pray to God Almighty you will know and understand that what you have, doesn't belong to you. Everything you calm to own belongs to the Lord. If you don't give back what he asks. The world will take it from you. In Malachi God is saying will a man rob God. He is saying if you do, you are cursed with a curse. Don't let our downfall become like of God's knowledge. I pray for all saints; they will learn to believe and have faith and patience to stand firm when times are beginning to get rough. Do not jump out of the ship or bow down to pressures; stay in the hand of God Almighty Lord Jesus.

Fellowship with God's People

THE THIRD week of February, 2001, was an amazing week. One day at work I meet a man we had a conversation about the Lord' I found out he is going through the same problem as I was facing. God was using me to minister to him because of the thing I had already experienced. It was God's blessing because he could shed some light on my situation also. During our conversation he asked me to read **1Conrinthins 7:1-15** and I told him to read **Psalms 27**. You know God is the only one who can bring his people together in times of trouble to receive comfort. God; I thank you for your mighty hand.

That same day God led me to someone else who was going through the same problem, again God using me to minister to him. Give him courage and confidence and the understanding of God's mystery of His word. I explained what God was doing in his life; his marriage would not be destroyed. He wanted to mold and shape your life, because the Lord has work for you, and you and your wife will become one in the eyes of the Lord when He finish shaping your lives. The next day I was blessing someone with the love of Christ and a student heard me, and asked me to explain the Holy Spirit to him, and he asked if Jesus Christ was so intelligent why didn't He write the Bible? I told him the Holy Spirit is a gift from God. I "asked are you a Christian?" "He said", I think so. I said" "You are not sure." I explained to him how to be saved, and he said "Yes, I am saved". "don't say I think so you need to be sure and say Yes I am saved." I said ever child of God received the Holy Spirit in their heart, and his Spirit will give you power and knowledge to understanding of God word. Yes God is intelligence with the Holy Spirit from His Father in heaven, do you remember His disciple and prophets of God, He use these individual to write His holy word in His Bible; by His empowers them with the intelligence of His Holy Spirit. I told him I would bring him some scripture that I hope and pray will help him, the next day I did.

That next day I was talking to a man about God's church. During our conversation he was telling me he had an experience with God, told him to go and tell the churches to removed the world system out of My house, and he said God led him to a church and he told the congregation. I informed him God told me the exact same message. All I can say God has an incredible mind and he knows how to bring his people together whom He has given the same message, for a clear confirmation. Oh God, I don't understand it; this is why you are God and I am; who I am, all I can do is what you tell me. Lord God, there is no other like you. In **Ephesians 1:17-18** says, "That the God of our Lord, Jesus Christ, the Father of glory, may give unto you the spirit of wisdom and revelation in the knowledge of Him. The eyes of your understanding being enlightened; that ye may know what is the hope of His calling, and what the riches of the glory of his inheritance in the saints." Saints of God, I pray your hearts will grow stronger in the Lord your God, I pray He will enlighten your eyes to see the love and knowledge to fellowship with each other in Christ Jesus.

A Problem That Would Not Go Away

ON FIRST March, 2001, God said, tell your whole life story and all your problems, in our marriage from the past. When I would do something not to her liking, she would start an argument and sometimes it would turn into a conflict. The bitter anger of Satan would come out of us, but I was not aware this was a problem. I would try to talk to her about it, some how it would get out of control, and another conflict would accrue. I would try to work out my problems by my own knowledge, and not saying anything to her, hoping it would get better. It got so bad I would say, "I want a divorce from you because you think you are so perfect, and never make a mistake, Satan on his job. But yet I can't do anything right in your eyes." At times it would seem things would get better, and they did for a while. Then Satan would allow something else to come up, and another conflict would accrue. Before we moved, things were working out all right; it seems as to be going just fine, Satan was asleep.

Then we moved to North Carolina, and my wife invited her family and my family down for Christmas dinner in December 1999. Christmas morning Oh my God, it seemed, as if all hell had broken loose. Satan was awake and in full control. I was cooking breakfast and according to her I didn't cook the right food. Her anger (Satan) was so bad, she didn't show any respect for me, her family, or my family, that was the darkest Christmas of my life, Satan have no fear. Her family and mine felt so bad what was taken place. In my own house there was nothing I could do, but stay humble and pray to God. {When Satan on the lose, humble and pray} If I had tried to fight back or take control, there would have been a great conflict. In this situation, good spirit and evil spirit will never work out, if you fight back there be no winner. Humble yourself and pray to God. **1Colossians4:2-3** says, "Continue in prayer, and watch in the same with thanksgiving; withal praying also for us, that God would open unto us a door of utterance, to speak the mystery of Christ, for which I am also in bonds."

The remainder of the year things were going okay, against Satan was asleep again until **July, 3, 2000,** This was a major disruption that caught me complete by surprise. Before we moved to North Carolina, little did I know all this anger was building up inside of our heart? I was a deacon in the church, and these problems were at home and church. This was a bad example for my two children. The Most of all God was not please with me as a deacon in His house. I would not confess my sins because Satan; said I don't have a problem. Blame your wife she is the problem, Satan had me thinking I didn't have a problem, you are find it is always the other person fault. But little didn't know Satan was in full control in my life; he kept informing me I could work out my own problems by not praying to God for help.

1 John 1:9-10 says, "He is speaking not so, if we confess our sins, he is faithful and just to forgive us our sins, and to cleanse us from all unrighteousness. If we say that we have not sinned, we make him a liar, and his word is not in us." Again little did I know how bad Satan had been controlling my life. All along I thought I could make my problems right. As I write, God brought to my mind. "This is why you could not be a good deacon for me, and you cause sin in your home. You brought your sinful heart into the body of my house. I was not pleased with you; also I am not pleased because you didn't confess your sins unto me." This is a problem only God can fix, but I thought I could fix it. I though it would go away; this is why so many marriages are falling apart today. People think they can fix their problem themselves. I tell you the truth ;you are wrong;, you will lose every time. You must call on God to confess your problem by asking Him to clean your heart from all unrighteousness, and create in you a clean hand and pure heart. **1 Peter 3:11-12,14** says, "Let him eschew evil, and do good; let him seek peace, and ensure it. For the eyes of the Lord are over the righteous, and his ears are open unto their prayer: but the face of the Lord is against them that do evil. But and if ye suffer for righteousness sake, happy are ye: and be not afraid of the terror, neither be troubled."

Saints of God I pray you will understand that you can't fix your problem. I pray you will seek your Heavenly Father and ask Him to set your soul free. I tell you there is nothing like being set free from the hand of Satan. What peace of mind, to be in the glorious hand of God.

God Sees And Knows All Things

SECOND WEEK of March, 2001,God woke my up about 3:00 a. m in the morning and say these word "plagiarism." I didn't understand what He was trying to tell me, He started again saying "plagiarism, plagiarism." Than all of a sudden God brought to my mind "You have written someone else "material" and I had written some "false information about myself". All words written in this book will come from my lip unto your mind and heart for you to write this book; I call you to write the truth. I felt so bad I put my head back under the cover thinking I could hide from God. That upset my soul so bad I could not go back to sleep, I knew I had done wrong in the sight of the living God. I prayed and asked the Lord, Will you please forgive me of my evil sin, and set my soul, mind and heart free to do your will right. Lord I will never again do you wrong involving your holy word. Early that morning I went and deleted all that I had done wrong. Saints of God, we can't do anything that God doesn't see or know. Please don't do as I did stay, free from sins, because the Lord knows our hearts. I can truly say this writing is not from my mind; these are the true words of the true living Christ Jesus.

Don't Disobey God's Calling

THE THIRD week of March, 2001, I was at work one day and a student and I were discussing the Bible. He asked me a question and I explained God's word, but I couldn't remember the scripture or verse. I felt real bad. The next day I was talking to God why I'm so dumb and ignorant of Your word? I try to study Your word as best as I know how, but I can't seem to remember. Lord God, I don't understand please help me. Two days later I was at work and I overheard a co-worker say he was in school. God's Holy Spirit came upon me, informing me, go to school and study His word. That same day I asked my co-worker where are schools that teach Bible theology of God. I received a list of five schools. The next day I started calling. The third one was John Wesley College of theology. The Holy Spirit came upon me, and "said this is where I want you to go." I knew right then this was where God wanted me to be. I had just recently told someone I would not go to school again because I had enough while in the military. You know God; he is always in control. I asked the college to send me information.

A week before this my aunt had invited me to come to Branchville Virginia to help celebrate her birthday, the next weekend I visited them. That Sunday I went with them to church. During the service they asked to stand and tell where was you from. This was so embarrassing I could not remember the name of my church or pastor's name; I felt like crowding under the bench. I said, "Lord, what is wrong with me," and God would not answer. Then the chorus started singing that all God's creation is made beautiful and all men and women are created in the image of God. The power of God's Holy Spirit came upon me, saying I created you just the way you are, and you are not dumb. **Psalm 139:14,17** says, "I will praise thee; for I am fearfully and wonderfully made: marvelous are thy works; and that my soul knoweth right well. How precious also are thy thoughts unto me, O God! How great is the sun of them!" I have to praise my heavenly Father, asking for forgiveness of my soul.

That same day we went out to dinner. I was sharing with them what God was doing in my life and as I was talking the Holy

Spirit came upon them with tears coming from their eyes. My cousin asked me to pray for her back pain, and I prayed with her.

That Friday at work someone told me a student was preaching on campus. That week, I received the information from the college. This college was really expensive, so I asked are there other schools, not too expensive? They told me to check around and I found one. I started questing God, Why would you send me to a school that costs so much? I haven't been to a civilian school in more than thirty years; beside? I am not smart enough to compete with those young people at college level. Lord, you know I can't remember. I dropped out of high school in the eleventh grade. I complete the GED test while in Vietnam. I started looking for a school that was not so hard and not too expensive.

That Friday evening, I went to service on campus. In the service, the Spirit of God was moving like I never seen before. As the student began to preach, he spoke about the burning bush and God calling Moses to go and bring His people out of Egypt. But Moses begins to question God. In **Exodus 4:10** says, "Moses, said unto the Lord, O my Lord, I am not eloquent, neither heretofore, nor since thou hast spoken unto thy servant: but I am slow of speech and of a slow tongue." Every word he spoke was penetrating my heart. God was speaking to me, saying you are not dumb or ignorant. I made you in my own image and every thing I made was good and perfect and you are perfect in my eyes. I am in charge ;don't worry about the cost. I will give you knowledge and understanding to learn My word. You don't question me, I am your God; do as I command you. "I felt if God was whipping me with a belt," "I couldn't sit still, I felt so bad; every word said was convicting my heart with the strong power of His holy spirit." I couldn't hold back the tears; I was saying Oh Lord please forgive my sinful soul; I am sorry; I will never question you again. Oh Lord, I will never disobey you again, Lord help me. I left; I didn't have no dot in my mind what God wanted me to do. I went home and applied to John Wesley College, and on the first of June, 2001, I started summer school.

I prayed to the Almighty God to bring my wife back before I started school because I didn't want this on my mind while studying His word. On my first day before I left to attend school all hell broke loose. That night I fell on my knee calling on God to help me. The fire is burning all around, come and put it out and save my soul.

A week before I went to Richmond I was at my sister's house and I was talking to a man I had never seen before. I started a conversation about people seeking God. He told me he was the second biggest drug dealer in Richmond. He said; I got tired, and then I saw an old friend who was a pastor. He said I want to talk with you, and he told me to come to his church. I did and God changed my whole life. "The past ten years he has been working for the Lord. While we were talking he knew what I was going through. He said your life is going through a puzzler and you are going to face more problems. God spoke to me a month before and said my life is going through a puzzler. The Holy Spirit came upon me, and I said, "Lord, I didn't tell this man anything. How could he know what I am going through?"

On my way back home an awesome thing happened and it was real calm and peaceful. I was driving along the radio was off, I heard church songs in my ear, and then I head music playing. I start praising and thanking the Almighty Holy hand of God, what an incredible Christ Jesus I service.

The months of **April and May, 2001,**God has taken me through an incredible journey along with my wife. My life has been like a roller coaster. My wife continually pressuring me about signing papers for divorce, I told her I am not signing any paper. I told you God is my lawyer and He has everything under control. She got upset and said "you are going to sign or I am going to Mexico and get a divorce. And I am moving out." I told her God said our marriage is safe. "This is what you want. I can't stop you. Do whatever you think is right. My trust is in my God I'm not worried about anything everything is going to be all right."

In **1 Peter 4:12-13** says, "Behold, think it not strange concerning the fiery trial which is to try you, as through some strange thing happened unto you: But rejoice, inasmuch as ye are partakers of Christ's suffering; that when his glory shall be revealed, ye may be glad also with exceeding joy."

My God is in control and one day He will bring us together once again. Some days the journey is peaceful and other days I have to hold onto God's hand. I pray night and day God will take this bitter cup away from my lips and bring an end to our marriage situation. I pray there will be peace in this house once and for all. Oh Lord, I know this must as be just hard on her as it is on me.

That next week I went to the VA hospital for a rash on my foot. They checked my blood pressures and it was unbelievable 190/160. They asked Are you on medication? No, I feel fine. "Lord, I don't understand what is happening to my soul. A month ago it was 130/84. The doctor said most people will have a heart attack and die; you could have one. They wanted to admit me and give medication. I was thinking to myself, Oh God, you are my doctor. What is causing my blood pressure to go so high? What is happening to me?" What are you trying to tell me? I had just quit my job to go to school full time. Oh Lord, every time I draw closer to you, something comes along to destroy my soul. No Lord, this is not going to happen I will not do as the doctor said. I rebuke it in the name of the Lord. Satan departs from my soul. I plead the blood of Jesus against you. I will not take medication; nothing is going to stop me from doing the Lord's will. Satan is doing his best to stop me from drawing closer to the Lord. Jesus you will take me by your hand and don't let me fall. But led me closer to your promised land. Oh Lord, I want to meet you in heaven, don't let these things continue to oppress my soul. Give me strength and confidence to overcome my enemies. **Psalm 48:1-3** says, "Great is the Lord, and greatly to be praise in the city of our God, in the mountain of his holiness. Beautiful for situation, the joy of the whole earth is mount Zion, on the sides of the north, the city of the King. God is known in her palaces for a refuge." **Psalm 27:1-2** says, "The Lord is my light and my salvation; whom shall I fear? The Lord is the strength of my life; of whom shall I be afraid? When the wicked, even mine enemies and my foes, came upon me to eat up my flesh, they stumbled and fall." As time passed my blood pressure became normal. I praised and thanked the Almighty hand of the true living God, who is all knowing and all powerful. Will you put all trust and have strong faith in Him?

God Is Preparing Me to Tell His Good News

THE FIRST weekend of July, 2001, my aunt's family invited me to attend their reunion in Branchville, and Emporia Virginia. I thanked the Almighty God for bringing me to meet people I attended school with while growing up, and to see how God had changed their lives. It was a blessing to have met so many friends who love the Lord. One of God's precious gift is being able to fellowship with God's believing people who have a mind of Christ. This is one way our life can be enriching, and you can see and understand the mystery of God. He is speaking to us in **Ephesians 3:9** says, "And to make all men see what is the fellowship of the mystery, which from the beginning of the world hath been hid in God, who created all things by Jesus Christ."

I thank my God for allowing me to testify my life story while enjoying fellowship with other believers by telling the Good News of Jesus Christ.

I visited my aunt in Branchville. The last time I was in Emporia my cousin asked me to pray and asked God to heal her back. She said after I left she went to get in her car and noticed she didn't feel any pain. She said When you prayed you had your hand on my back "She said I felt something go down my back At that time she didn't know what was happening but God instantly healed her." She said she was so overwhelmed with joy, she called me. I didn't receive the message and she called her family, telling them of the Good News what God has done for her. Believe, have faith, and trust in the love of God, He said in **Philippians 1:5-6** says, "For you fellowship in the gospel from the first day until now; Being confident of this very thing, that he which hath begun a good work in you will perform it until the day of Jesus Christ." I thank Him for using me as His rod to pray and lay hands on the sick, and people with financial problems.

Christians, we are all called by God to work for Him. If we do half the work for the Lord we do for our job and ourselves, God will be pleased. Remember the job, house, car, and food on our table. Health and strength have all given to us by the grace and mercy of God, and then we tell Him we only can give two hours out of seven days? How can we say we love the Lord? These words are not from me; My Lord gave these words and said write this book to show my people you must love the Lord with your heart, mind, and soul. Give all ourselves unto Christ Jesus; you will begin to grow in His love. He will open your up to the mystery of His knowledge and give you understanding of His word He has for your life. What God has done for my life is no mystery. He can use anybody who is committed to carrier his/her cross.

God is saying to His saints, open up your hearts and feed my people; He said my people are destroyed for lack of knowledge. O Lord, I pray this prayer these words will go out to all saints of God, and fill them with Your Holy Spirit, and release your mighty Power that will enable to them go out where people are in needs of your blessing. Saints our purpose in life is to help feather the kingdom of God. I want to see all His people receive a home in heaven, specially the poor, the hungry, the under privileged, the helpless, and the lost. These are the ones I have such strong compassion to help bring them unto Christ Jesus.

Oh Lord, I pray you will rise up someone to help bring peace, healing power, and feed your people with your true living word. And be not ashamed, but be bold to proclaim the truth of your resurrection power.

Proceed to Help Built Up God's kingdom

THIS IS what the Lord has place on my heart, and I spoken to God of my heavenly Father and said all proceeds of His Book for my part, I will give it all to feather His kingdom in Heaven, except my wife and family are to be blessed. I want to see God's people blessed by the power of God. The poor, hungry, lost, hurting, and those who don't know where their next meal or don't have any place to lay their head. These

people are the one who have no means of helping themselves; mainly they are from other country. God has called me to go to African to plant churches and help the poor and lost. These people of God I have such greatest heart for. Because this book is not about me; it is about my Heavenly Father. All the glory and honor belong to Him. I am already blessed beyond the richest man in the world. To have such a glorious divine bless peace of mind down in my heart that pass all understanding that come from my Heavenly Father. The love and compassion I have for my Heavenly Father and all of His people. Don't misunderstand me; being rich is good, as long as you are feeding God's people accord to His plan. In **1 Timothy 6:17** "God is speaking. Charge them that are rich in this world, that they be not high-minded, nor trust in uncertain riches, but in the living God, who giveth us richly all things to enjoy. But to receive the true riches of Heaven." In **Colossians 2:2-3** "That their hearts might be comforted, being knit together in love, and unto all riches of the full assurance of understanding, to the acknowledgement of the mystery of God, and of the Father, and of Christ; In whom are hid all the treasures of wisdom and knowledge."

God has opened my mind, heart, and soul to receive all these blessings, and I thank my Heavenly Father. And Lord, I will pray every believer will receive the same blessing you have given my soul. Lord, I want them to have this and more, because we are your children.

Love from God to My Wife

THE SECOND week of July, 2001, while I was on my way down to Salisbury. North Carolina to visit the veterans in the VA hospital. I had my wife on my mind. Then God's Holy Spirit came to me and this is what He said. With tears in my eyes, I stopped on the side of the road. And said write these word about your wife. When you were in service in the war in Saudi Arabia and Iraq, You traveled for miles and miles; and, for days all you could see was sand and sandstorm. As you traveled from place to place onetime you saw a flower or a small green bush. Then I started wondering how could something so beautiful and lovely as this could grow in this heat? No rain, and sandstorm all the time. Then I would think only by the hand of God, who is the creator of every good and perfect thing. God was telling me this is the way I must look upon my wife. As a lovely beautiful flower the way I saw that plant. He was telling me all those things I was going through with my wife. I am not to look upon her as if these things are her fault. I'm using her to test your faith. All you see in her is a pure and beautiful woman as a flower. I have created her with My own hand I created her with love, she is like the brightness of the sunshine. She is beautiful as a cluster of tender grapes as it appears in the early morning. As God opened up the bright sunshine, she is like the sweetest of the golden apple that sparing with honey. As God's sunset in twilight of the evening. Deborah is more precious than pure silver and gold. She is as a precious stone in the eyes of the beholder that created her. My wife shall be a fruitful and lovely vine by the side of thine house: the children like olive plants round about thy table. Behold, that thou shall the man be blessed that fear the Lord; the Lord shall bless you all the day of thy life.

As I was writing this I received, a strange feeling. I felt His glorious love all around my soul.

God has changed my heart to see love through the eyes of my heavenly Father. Oh what an awesome feeling to know God is leading me to be more like Him each and every day of my life. Oh how I love my wife; I see her as a majestic child of God created in the image of Him. God said love your wife as you love Me.

She is like pure gold setting in precious stone with purple blue scarlet cover with embroidered girdles in miter. With the finest linen, embrace into her glorious beauty toward our love to be together, His greatest commandment is for us to love Him with our heart, mind and soul and to love your wife as she love you. Love come joy, with joy come peace, peace come happiness, with happiness come confidence, confidence come knowledge, with knowledge come wisdom, wisdom come understanding with understanding come the open mystery of God.

November 29, 2002, God showed me these verse to write unto my wife from the Song of Solomon: my beloved Deborah speak,

Rise up, my love, my fair one, and come away from out of the darkness into His marvelous light as the sun rise up high in the sky with the glory of thy kingdom. For, lo, the winter is past, the rain is over and gone; the flowers appear on the earth. the time of the singing of birds is come, and the voice of the turtle is heard. The fig tree putteth forth her green figs, and vines with the tender grapes give a good smell this is you my love, Arise, Deborah, my love, my fair one, we will go up to the temple and worship the Lord.

Oh Deborah my dove, that art in the clefts of the rock, in the secret places of the stairs, let me see thy countenance, let me hear thy voice of your words; for sweet is your voice, like the breaking of a new day with shadows of the breather blowing in the wind. Her hands are as gold rings set with the beryl; her belly is as bright ivory overlaid with sapphires. Her legs are as pillars of marble, set upon sockets of fine gold. Her mouth is most sweet; yea we is altogether lovely. This is my wife, my beloved, and she is my beautiful jewel. Oh God how can I thank you for such precious and beautiful wife with all blessing created by you Lord?. Oh Lord, I am not worthy to receive this blessing of such, beautiful wife. But he looked down from heaven and said Henry my Son, you done everything I commanded of you, I am your Father; I say yes, my son, you are more than worthy; you are who I have created, you are the one I set my eyes upon to go and bind up my marriages. **Psalm 96: 6-9** says, "Honour and majesty are before him strength and beauties are in his sanctuary. Give unto the Lord the glory due unto His name: bring an offering, and come into His courts. O worships the Lord in the beauty of holiness: fear before Him, all the earth."

Deborah my beloved God desire is toward us. Come, my beloved, let us go forth into the field; let us lodge in the villages. Let us get up early to the vineyards; let us see if the vine flourish, whether the tender grapes appear, and the pomegranates bud forth: there will I give thee my loves to teach and save God's people.

My love until the day brake and the shadows flee away, I will get me to the mountain of Zion, and to the hill of frankincense. That are fair my love Deborah, there is no spot in thee, come with me from far my wife to the top of the mountains which is the solid rock a foundation of love, salvation with living bread and living water. This is the Holy Mountain and the top shine glory all around us, my wife you are my crown of glorious.

Another Mission from God: Go Tell The Good News

THE FIRST week of August, 2001, God sent me on another incredible mission. The week before I departed I felt God's Spirit but it was not clear what I was to do. It was the middle of the week, and God spoke to me again and it was clear; I want you to go and tell the story of your marriage situation to her and your whole family and friends. In **Acts 9:15** say, "But the Lord said unto me Go they way: for you is a chosen vessel unto me, to bear my name before My people and kings and the children of Israel." Ever since it first started my wife didn't want anyone in the family to know what had happened involving our marriage. I had honored her request. Now God was telling me this was the right time to go tell our story and testimony.

This was during the summer college brake, and I had two weeks before fall class started. And my little grandson was down for the summer and I was to take him back up to Maryland to his mother. I was concerned about how should I tell my wife what God had said. I went down on my knees and asked God, "What I shall I say to her about our situation?" The Holy Spirit gave me the words to say to her. I told her God wanted me to go and tell our marriage situation to our family and friends. She did not say anything.

The next day she came to me and said, "You are going to be embarrasses. I am going to have my lawyer draw up the papers and have the police serve them to you." When she said this the Power of God's Spirit was very strong upon me. Nothing she could say or do upset me. It was like someone shooting arrows at me and they were falling short. God has cover my soul in the blood of the lamb for my protection. **Hebrews 10:19-20** says, "Having therefore, brethren, boldness to enter into the holiest by the blood of Jesus. By a new and living way, which he hath consecrated for us, through the veil that is to say, his flesh"

That same week I prayed for two students in my class. One have a long lasting back problem and the other have a real bad breathing problem for a long period of time. I said I would like to pray that God would heal them. That night I prayed to God for divine deliverance healing power of His Holy Hand that they be set free. That same night I could not go to sleep; the Spirit was upon me real strong telling me He was going to do something, but I didn't know what.

That Friday morning we departed on God's mission, and these are the words God wanted me to Tell you. In **Isaiah 55:11-12** say, "So shall my word be that goeth forth out of my mouth: it Shall not return unto me void, but it shall accomplish that which I please, and it shall proper in The thing whereto I sent it. For ye shall go out with joy, and be led forth with peace; the mountains and the hills shall break forth before you into singing, and all the trees of the field shall clap their hands." I stopped in Petersburg and Richmond. Virginia, as I spoke to my relatives about our marriage situation and that God had told me to write a book of my life to go out to the world and this book will be like His Bible. It was during this time that God let me know the purpose of my mission: till the story to strengthen other marriages family how God wants them to stay faithful, and stay in the word of God together with love in their hearts, and peace that will shower down upon their families, and keep them under the wing of the Holy Hand of the Almighty God. Give them confidence to stay in the house of God, and grow strong family foundations with tender love and care, to bring unity back into the family with the love of Christ.

Have a clear understanding of His knowledge to stand upon the rock of faith in God. Stay strong when trail, temptations, and suffering come Don't fight your battle, cast all your care upon Him and put your complete trust in Him. Humble yourselves therefore under the mighty hand of God. Always have a clear channel of communication with family and Jesus Christ. This is the message from God.

I told all my relatives and friends in Washington, Maryland, Virginia Beach, Emporia. and Branchville, During the work of God is amazing and incredible because as I spoke these words of God, so many people were touched by the Spirit of the Living Hand of God. As I was doing His work there was a powerful feeling I can't describe It was upon my soul all the time. All who believe in Christ Jesus, that have been called by God

I pray you will do just what He has been calling you for. If you do God's will, He will bless your heart in a way you won't be able to explain. This is one amazing and powerful God I serve. In every family God led me to, the husband and wife and some case the whole family was home. This was amazing. God led me to pray for the family. You know this is the work of the Lord. Since I devoted my whole life to Christ, there is nothing in this whole world, not gold or silver that, can separate me from the love of Christ Jesus. Oh how I love to do what ever He tells me. I love to praise His Holy Name each and every day. The Lord has given me the tongue of learning, that I should know how to speak a word in season to him that is weary. The Lord God has opened mine ear, and I was not rebellious, neither turned away back. I have set my face on the Lord and I will not be ashamed.

While I was in Norfolk I stayed with Sam and Eva. Eva is my cousin; these two people's lives have been touched by the hand of God and they are doing a mighty work for the Lord. Sam asked me to prayer for his mother. She was not able to feed herself. That day we went to midday service and she was there and after eating I said I would pray for her right now. So I called on the healing hands of the Almighty God to touch her with His anointing power and release whatever was defeating her and make her whole. About two mouths later I received the word. God had answered her prayer, she was around eight five year old. This was her strong faith in God. Who can deny the power of God? I thank Him, I praise Him, and I glorify His Holy name, for what He has done. It is the work of His power of the Holy Spirit. **Luke 4:18a** says, "The Spirit of the Lord is upon me, because He hath anointed me to preach the gospel and to heal the brokenhearted.

After returning home six months later, God spoke to me about my brother in Christ Sam.

God "said, I have chosen him to be My disciple for him to join this operation." He is calling saints all over the world to carry out God's great commission. I know him as a true man of God who loves to service His people by teaching them the true living word of God, and helping them to overcome the blindness from their eyes. And let the glory and divine power of God's light rule and rain in their hearts. **John 15:16-17** says, "God said I have chosen you Sam, and ordained you, that ye should go and bring forth fruit, and that your fruit should remain: that whatsoever ye shall ask of the Father in my name, He may give it to you. These things I command you to continue to love one another." Go and feed my sheep they are hunger for my true living word and thirst for my living water. I have known Sam for some time Lord, I, can say I have met a true friend who loves God people; he has such a great heart. Sam and his wife pray together every morning before departing their home, this keeps their family together in love with unity and to stay safe through their daily walks with the Lord. This is the kind of men God is looking for to build up His kingdom in heaven and church on earth. I thank God I have meet such true man of God.

In **April 16, 2003,** God spoke to me about his Eva to say she is a beautiful saint in Christ, and she has received the divine grace of His anointing power upon her soul. God showed me how beautiful and wonderful a marriage can be, when God taking control and be the head of a marriage who love the Lord with all their mind, heart, and soul. They pray together and God says you will stay together. The righteousness of their hearts has made them right in the eyes of the Lord. From the time I have known my cousin Eva she has been my favorite cousin; she always has such a warm kindness and tender loving hearted person, she always seen to be at peace with a loving heart for all people. She is a humble and faithful; God will increase the truth of His righteousness, and she will walk in the truth of the mighty hand of God, because she will glorify His name forever more.

There is something about her that has always been on my mind. God is beginning to bring it clearer. Whatever it is God has prepared it before the beginning of time. I do know she has been prepared to work in His vineyard. In **Psalm 85:10-13** say, "Mercy and truth are met together; righteousness and peace have kissed each other. Truth shall spring out of the earth and righteousness shall look down from heaven. Yea the Lord shall give that which is good; and our land shall yield her increase upon this marriage. Righteousness shall go before them; and shall set." Sam and Eva shell walk in the way of the Lord. These are the words God command me to write. I pray to the Almighty God He will keep you under His wing, and set you apart, that He will continue to prepare your hearts for His future plan.

I returned home to start my fall class on 15 August. I saw those two students I pray for; I asked how they were feeling. The female student told me she was find God has healed her completely. Oh I thank the Holy hand of the Almighty God; I praise and bless you, what a amazing God I service. Lord, I thank you for using me as a rod so you can heal your blessed people. Lord, there nothing in my power; it is all done by the grace of God. The other person, God is still working be patience and wait.

Called by God: Go, I Will Prepare You

IN SEPTEMBER 1998 I felt His calling, but I didn't understand the meaning, I was still in the service. As time pasted I forgot all about it until August 2003 His holy spirit brought this to my mind and said "Write what I informed you in 98." This time God gave me a clear understanding why He moved my wife and I to North Carolina after retiring from the service. God had spoke to me as He spoke to Abraham, in Genesis 12:1-3 "Henry, Get thee out from Maryland, from around your kindred, and from your friends, and unto a land that I will show you; And I will make you a great nation, and I will bless you, and make your name great; and you shalt be a blessing. And I will bless them that bless you, and curseth him that curseth you; and in you shall all families of the earth be blessed." "This is the message God spoke, pack up my family and departs, from Maryland, move to North Carolina." "After you arrive, I will come and tell you what I want you to do."

During my life growing up, I never knew God could take a nobody and make somebody and place him deep into the kingdom of God's glory. He did it by setting me apart from the world and placing me into the Holy Hand of glory of the divine love of God Almighty, which is my heavenly Father. I will praise, shouting hallelujah, singing praises of holy, holy and glorifying my Heavenly Father. My God has taken me through some amazing and incredible journeys this far. Along my journey He is preparing me for the future coming of Christ Jesus.

Jeremiah 26:12-13 say, "Then speak Henry unto all the princes (churches) and to all the people, saying, The Lord sent me as a (messenger) to prophesy against this world and against your city, and (churches) all the words that ye have heard. Therefore now amend your ways and your doings, and obey the voice of the Lord your God; and the Lord will repent him of the evil that he hath pronounced against you."

God Reveals His Purpose for My life

WHEN GOD called me to attend college, that was to let me know He wanted me to study His word to become knowledgeable to know who He is. To learn all about His disciples, property and receive a true understanding how they live their lives by been obedience, faithful and walking in the righteousness of His footsteps of the true Master. I am doing my best with the help of the Lord by studying His word, staying faithful every day of my life, to walk in my Master footstep. Lord I waited patiently for you to tell me my purpose for over forty years. May 2001 I was home watching a Christian program from Africa I saw how the needy were neglected, hurting, and dying. The Holy Spirit came upon my soul, and I was touched by the Holy Hand of God saying "This is where I want you to go and tell the Good News of the love of Christ Jesus." I understood right away He was trying to tell me something. But it was not clear what I would do there. While in army I always sent money to Africa to support the poor, I have a strong compassion for helping those people. Many church leaders had identified my calling, but not God.

My prayer goes out to every Christian called by God; they will listen and heard what He is saying. He never sends His people out unprepared. God want us to take one step at a time, don't rush or not let someone else talk you out of something God has already called you for.

Act chap 1-2 says, "When Christ told His disciples to go into an upper room at fifty day of Pentecost, they were with one accord in one place and suddenly from heaven rushing mighty wind, and filled all the house. And appeared unto them cloven tongues like fire and it set upon them and filled them with the Holy Ghost, and they went out to minister and heal the needy. This is what God wants us to do: wait until He prepares our hearts.

On August 20, 2001, I went to class. When I arrived, one of the staff personnel told me my class date was not until October. I said no one informed me and she said, "Would you like sit in on this missionary life & work class." There was another student there; she said Want you take this class it will be over before you're next class starts, "I said why not."

The instructor was teaching us how to become a missionary. Later we had cheaper service I was there the Holy Spirit spoke to me telling me my purpose, (missionary for Christ), I could not hold back my tears; it was amazing feeling, the Hand of God has touched me soul. That night an incredible thing happened I was not quite asleep and as clear as day God showed me maps of Africa, South America, Center American, North America, Europe, Asia, Middle East, Vietnam, Turkey, China, Japan, India, Germany, Russia, and many other countries. It was unbeliever, amazing and incredible what God showed me. When this first started back in October 2000 God spoke to me saying "You are going places all over the world. You are going to meet people you never seen. You are going to bring My people out of darkness. You are going to show them My light of forgive their sins and receive the salvation of Jesus Christ. And you will teaches them how to love Me with their whole hearts, minds, and souls, and love their neighbor."

I am beginning to receive a clear understanding of God's puzzle He has for my life; it is coming together. In **Act 2:16-17** says, **"**God is speaking to you and me, but this is that which was spoken by the prophet Joel. And it shall come to pass in the last days, said God, I will pour out of my Spirit upon all flash: and your sons and your daughters shall prophesy, and your young men shall see visions and your old men shell dream dreams."

God Spoke: Go to the Mountain Top

October 31, 2001, I rose up early that morning and I left for college. I arrived there at 7:20 a. m. I was sitting in my vehicle; the class didn't start until 8:00. At 7:30 God spoke to me and said "Go up on the mountain." I started thanking He keeps saying go to the mountain three times. All of a Sudden His Holy Sprit hit me with His holy power and with tears running down I could stop crying. It was tears of joy. His spirit was that strong. I didn't question why; all I could do was praise and glorify the Holy Name of my Almighty Heavenly Father. Oh Lord, I thank you with my whole heart. I don't know what this means but I will do just what you say because you are an amazing God. You are my Christ, with Your Powerful Hand.

I entered my classroom I told my professor and he said read **Mark 1:35** say, "And in the morning, rising up a great while before day, he went out, and departed into a solitary place, and there prayed." I had already spoken to God about going away for a weekend. I wanted to go somewhere peaceful and quiet. I needed to study for a test and I wanted to get away from the coldness of my wife heart. Also I wanted to talk to God. I had already made a reservation in Asheville, North Carolina, in a mountain area. That same weekend I journeyed there, God show me mountain Mitchell Mount on the map.

That Saturday morning I journeyed up toward the mountain. It was so high it was beyoung the clouds. I came to a station; I stopped and asked how much father, the man said about fifteen more miles. He said the driving was not easy because the clouds were so thick. He said to put my flasher on and drive slowly.

So I journeyed on as he said, but the clouds became so thick I couldn't see the road. I said Lord, I can't see; how can I go on. Immediately the clouds lifted up as if it were not there; I was praising and thanking the Holy Hand of the Almighty God. What an incerdable God I service; I felt the presence and power of God, I knew right than He was looking out for my soul.

My heavenly Father said He would always make a way for those who love Him and do His will. As I arrived up on top of the mountain the cloud started to return, but I was all right; I could see I found a solitary place I read His Bible and Psalm 27 which had brought me this far. I prayed, praised, and I thank the Almighty God. I gave Him my burden; I poured out my heart for this nations that God would rise up somebody to help turn this old sinful world around. In **II Chronicles 7:14** says, "If my people, which are call by my name, shall humble themselves, and pray, and seek my face, and turn from their wicked ways; and I will forgive their sin, and will heal their land." Now mine eyes shall be open, and mine ears attent unto the prayer that is made in this place.

As I was journeying down the mountain the Holy Spirit struck me again, saying, Go, write another book and bring my people together, Black, White and Jew and all other races coming together. He said they work together; shop together, eat together, and do other things together, but they go into separate churches. Some worship other gods. They are to worship the one true God and one Christianity Gospel. Said God, My people are to be one in My eyes. Tell them I will break down the barer that serprate them and join them together to worship the one true living God. There is only one church under God Almighty and that church must prepare itself for the coming of the Lord. The Lord said Go to Africa and build churches for my people; you are to teach them how to love and I will bring peace into their land and bring my people out of darkness. And let My light shine all over the world. Tell them the Good News of my holy word that I have taught you. He said, "When my word goes out it will not come back void, because my people are hungry for my living word and water. I want you to go and feed them all over the land." Then He gave me the title for the next book; **"You Are Rich, Yet You Are Poor".**

I am preparing you to be My disciple to evanglize my word. **Act 1:8** says, "But ye shall receive power, after that the Holy Ghost is come upon you: and ye shall be witnesses unto me both in Jerusalem, and in all Judara, and in Samaria, and unto the uttermost part of the earth."

Christian's if you want to feel the presence of the living God. I pray you will open up your heart and let Him come in and be the Master of your life. Let Him direct, lead, and guide your every step. He will change your life into such a peaceful, joyful, glorious blessing, you won't be able to describe it. All I can say is you don't know what you are missing. All these things my heavenly Father is putting me through is because of nothing special I have done. I just obey His calling as His disciples. As God called you, you have the same opportunity to obey Him the same way. Saints of God, I pray you will open up your eyes and hearts, because God is getting ready to do something in this world you have never seen or heard before except what is written in His word. I pray you will read and study His word and ask God to reveal His mysteries plan unto your heart. I tell you if you have ever been in the presence of God, it is an experience you will never forget, to feel the presence and know He is a true and real living God of all the whole universe.

Isaiah 40:9 says, "O Zion, that bring good tidings, get thee up into the high mountain; O Henry, that bring good tiding, lift up your voice with strength; lift it up, be not afraid; say unto the cities of the world, Behold your God!" Behold, the Lord God will come with strong hand, and his arm shall rule for him: behold, his reward is with him, and his work before him."

God Calls Us to Be a Witness to His People

In January, 2002, early in that month during my regual visit to the nursing home, I was sharing God's word with two ladies in their room when one of the employees came and sat down, listing to what I was saying. She said her back was hurting. I said; May I pray, and ask God to heal you, She said yes. A week later, I saw her and the amazing powerful God had healed her. That next week I went back God led me to talk to another girl who work their, she ask about salvation, God led me to lead her in the sinner pray and Christ Jesus save her soul, **John 3:15** "that whosoever believeth in him should not perish, but have eternal life." Praise be to God Almighty one more.

On that Friday when I was sitting on my bed I felt something move up and down in my stomach. I said "Oh God, what is wrong with me?" He spoke and said go on a fast three time and He said for fourteen days; the longest I had ever fasted was twenty-four hours. For fourteen days I prayed and fasted to my heavenly Father; all I had was water and I never was hungry; not one minute, I saw food and it didn't bother me. **1 Corinthians 7:5** says, "Defraud ye not one the other, except it be with consent for a time, that ye may give yourselves to fasting and prayer; and come together again, that Satan tempt you not for your incontinency."

The first week of my fast, my nephew and sister from Richmond called and saying they were coming down to visit the family and go to church with me.

That Sunday morning My sister and husband, my nephew and wife came. I asked my wife if she would like to come, I thought she would go, but it didn't happen.We went and had a great time in the Lord and fellowship with the saints of God. My sister said she felt is if something was wrong with me. I told her God has led me on a fast and I think it will be fourteen days. She said I much eat, and I said I must wait on the Lord, He is controlling my life. After church we all had a great time fellowship together; we prayed and they departed. After the fourteen days I felt hunger pains and I knew He has released me from the fast. My God is an awesome and incredible God; I thank Him for taking me on a fast for fourteen days, and cleaning all my un worthiness, unright-eousness, and the purifying of my heart, mind, and soul to be set free. Oh Lord, how can I ever thank your Holy Name?

That same week on Monday He spoke to me, saying "Go feed my people," I questioned God I didn't understand; I throught I was doing just that? "Lord I pray you will speak so I may know what you mean." No answer from Him. On my way to college on that Friday, He spoke and said go into all my churches in and all around North Carolina and I will tell you what to tell my people. They are hungry for my true living word and my living water; go and feed my people because they are hungry; looking for the true righteousness of God. Lord I thank you I praise your holy name for answer my prayer.

Job 36:2-7,10,11,12 says, "Suffers me a little, and I will shew thee that I have yet to speak on God behalf. I will fetch my knowl-edge from afar, and will ascribe righteousness to my Master, for truly my words shall not be false: he that is perfect in knowledge is with thee. Behold, God is mighty, and despiseth not any: he is mighty in strength and wisdom. He preserveth not the life of the wicked: but giveth right to the poor. He openeth also their ear to discipline, and commandeth that they return from iniquity. If they obey and serve him, they shall spend their days in prosperity, and their years in pleasures. But if they obey not, they shall perish by the sword. And they shall die without knowledge."

Will You Obey and Trust God When He Calls?

May, 2001, God led me to started summer semester classes, and then the fall semester came. No money from the government, I was five thousand dollars in debt from the college. All along the VA was not sure I was eligible to receive school benefits.They sent me a letter; it said I had to call and schedule a date, and go to Washington, D.C. they would provide a lawyer and present my case. I said Oh God what are these people doing to me, Please, Lord, helps me. I spent thirty one years in the service and fought in two wars. They really didn't know what I been through, but the Lord you knew.

When I first signed up for VA school benefits, I told them I was scheduled to attend college
that summer. It was April and they said if I were approved it would take ninety days. I said What if I start school and the fund not approves. They said they couldn't say. I said I would go, God would make a way. As time passed problems continued to mount. I said, Lord, you are my Lawyer and I appoint you to take my case, and win this battle. The college kept sending me reminders of my late payment. When God brought me off the mountain He gave me all these mission to accomplish. Now the college threatened to cut off my education, If I didn't pay this bill by the end of fall the semester, they were going to terminate me from college, and the payment must be paid. I said; Lord, I have faith in you, but Lord it is getting weaker by the day Lord, please come and help me. Lord, you know I am not strong.

I went down on own my knees talking and praying to God Almighty. How can I accomplish your work Lord if I cannot finish school? You ask my to accomplish these thing. If you will not open up the door, What am I to do? You sent me to college to learn about You. Lord you are my lawyer, yet Satan has closed the doors in every direction. Oh Lord, I have given myself unto You as a living sacrifice of my soul. I am in your hands, I am your child; and you are my Heavenly Father. I am depending on you to open up a door that I may receive Your knowledge and understanding.

Psalm 91:14-15 says "Because he hath set his love upon me, therefore will I deliver him: I will set him on high, because he hath known my name. He shall call upon me, and I will answer him: I will be with him in trouble; I will deliver him and honour him." Just as the fall semester ended, the college prepared my finial letter to be terminated.

That night I prayed to God. "Lord, I can't see my way out, and everything is closing in all around me. Lord, I need your help." The next day it was on my mind to I called VA The man said; I have a five thousand dollar check ready to send you. Oh Lord, you are the greatest and powerful lawyer; in the world, you have won my case. I thank You and I praise your Holy Name; you are amazing, God. You have opened up another door and now I can see a little clearly, Oh thank you, Lord. Your puzzle in my life is beginning to come together, but many more parts are still closed up. Oh Lord, I thank You for helping me along my journey. I know you are trying to teach me to walk along without you holding my hand I must have strong faith and committed to trust you all the days of my life. As I continue to stand upon your holy word and growing stronger, you will open up another door some day. You are teaching me to be patient and obedient, Lord I thank you for supplying my needs. **Jeremiah 17:7-8** says "Blessed is the man that trusteth in the Lord, and whose hope the Lord is. For he shall be as a tree planted by the waters, and that spreadeth out her roots by the river, and shall not see when heat commeth, but her leaf shall be green; and shall not be careful in the year of drought, neither shall cease from yielding fruit." In times of trouble, I pray to God Almighty that all believers will designate God as their lawyer to take on their case. Put your trust and faith in God knowing He will deliver.

God Spoke: Go Feed My People

February, 2002, my God is still opening up my heart with His knowledge and understanding of His word and will. I want to take you back to October 2001 God has been leading me to go to Salisbury, North Carolina to visit the veterans in the VA hospital. The college gave me a community service form to be completed and signed. Since I was spreading God's word among His people there, I thought I could get the minister to sign so I could earn credit. I went to him; he asked, who authorized me on this post I said "My God." He said "You are not authorized on this post." I said God wanted me to speak love and tender care of His word and pray for His people. I said I was in the service thirty-one years and some of them are from Vietnam when I was over there. He said he couldn't allow me to speak about God to the veterans and that I must leave. If I come again he will have me arrested. I said, I pray the Almighty God will bless you with peace and love down in your heart. I shook the dust off my feet and I departed. I asked God, Why is this happing, I was only doing what you asked me. "I felt the presence of His peace come over me tears and He said, Don't worry, my son everything is going to be all right."

The first week of **May 2002**, I felt a strange feeling come over me, Then God said Go back where I sent you, "My people need you to feed them." It came to my mind the VA hospital. This is God speaking to Paul and me **Act 18:9-11** says, "Then speak the Lord to Paul in the night by a vision, Be not afraid, but speak, and hold not the peace: for I am with thee, and no man shall set on thee to hurt thee: for I have much people in this city. And he continued there a year and six mouths teaching the word of God among them." My first time back a man was healed by the power of God; he told me his problem and I said Do you believe He can heal, he said yes. I said Let go to God in prayer. We prayed to the Almighty God for His awesome working power to heal this request, the man was immediately heal by the power of God.
In **Acts 4:22** says, "For the man was about forty years old, on whom this miracle of healing was shewed." Christians who going

through problem why don't we believe in the Heavenly Father and pray that He will heal and blessing you?"

Two weeks later God led me back. I met a man sitting down, I spoke, "How are you, my friend?" He told me his problem. First he said he was hungry, and second he needed money, to catch the bus. I gave him some money, and he said thanks. As I spoke to him about Christ, he said he knew Jesus Christ, I was just sharing God's word to the drug people in Ward four. I said where, and he said "I will take you there." When we arrived there they were eating; he went to eat. I started out, and I saw a big tall man. God Spirit was telling me to follow him. He went out and sat on a bench with four other men. I went over and started a conversation about how God has blessed us with such pleasant weather, and the conversation of Jesus Christ went on. That man kept looking at me as I was talking, so I stopped to see if there was something he wanted to say. He said, "could I tell you a story." I was amazing. He said his little girl and wife were both going to be with the Lord from an accident. It hurt him so bad, he broke down, and this is why he was in the hospital. As he was telling this story, I felt the power of God. I felt a strong compassion for him and my heart went out to him. He asked me "How can someone get saved?" I told him **Romans 10:9-10** says, **"**That if thou shalt confess with thy mouth the Lord Jesus, and shalt believe in thine heart that God hath raised him from the dead, thou shalt be saved. For with the heart man beliveth unto righteousness and with the mouth confession is made unto Salvation." He said I wanted to be saved.

There was another man sitting there and he said I wanted to be saved also "Let's go to God and pray" and the power of God's Holy Spirit was all over us, I felt His presence and they was shedding tears. I knew God's angels up in heaven were praising and thanking the Almighty God; two more soul were entering His Kingdom. What a mighty God I serve. He said "I was praying last night, asking God to send someone to help me, and God sent you?" Everything is about God's timing. Just about every time He led me there, someone has been praying and God will always led me to them. I don't understand how to explain it; it is like this everywhere He lead me. This is a true living God I serve. I pray God will teach you to help his people who are in need.

This is a great adventure from heaven; it is amazing and incredible doing the work of my Heavenly Father to carry out His will.

It's amazing to see the powerful hand of God at work through my life, this is just what He said He would do through those who love Himand hold fast to His true living word. I pray to the Heavenly Father that each soul who reads this book will be transformed by the renewing of your mind, that ye may prove what is that good, and acceptable, and perfect, will of God Almighty.

A Vision from God in Heaven

APRIL, 16, 2002, while at college. I was outside waiting for my next class. I was praising and thanking God. Then His Holy Spirit came upon my soul, speaking through my mind and God's showing me a vision in Emporia, Virginia. my hometown. He was showing me a large church. I asked "Who are the people who will fill your church." As I said that, I couldn't keep my eyes dry: tears were of joy running. It was amazing what I saw: people from all over Emporia and surrounding areas of all race's: white, black, and Spanish, and people rich and poor. They were all going into the house of God; they would come together to fellowship, praise, and worship the one true Christianity of God word. He said "My people are hungry and thirsty for the true living word and the true living water; they will never be hungry nor will they thirst again." It was one amazing and incredible seen I saw. He even shows my how He wanted it built. It would contain a day care center to teach kids the love of Christ Jesus for single parents. It would contain Bible College so the people would gain knowledge and understanding of My word. It would contain Sunday school classrooms. It would contain a large fellowship hall. It would contain three-pastor office. It would contain a pastor study room. It would contain a dentist's office to give free dental care. He said once it's built people will come and fill it up because they are hungry for My word. Build a recreation center for fellowship of large family gatherings, also to be used for basketball to bring young people together to teach them about Christ. Build a 24hr-feeding cafeteria to feed the poor, and build a Bible training center camp up near the mountain. God show me a vision young peoples will come from all over the world to attend this camp. It was amazing, He said I will bring pastors, teachers, I "will bring in a dental doctor to take care their dental needs." He was showing me who would be operating and managing the people and building. He said people would come from all over to study His word, and gain His knowledge of His word. They would be filled with His Holy Spirit of wisdom, to go and feed those in needed.

The Future of God's Presence Is Coming

First December, 2001, God spoke to me as His messenger to write His word. I told this story to His church people. They seemed in disbelief, and I began to dout if this realy was God speaking to me. They seemed so cold towards me as I spoke God's words. I began to lose faith and trust in God and myself, so I stopped telling people about what God told me to tell His people. I started thinking. "Could this be Satan and his tricks." Except one time I was sharing this message at a church, the pastor stopped me and said, just this morning I received this same message from England and ten other country are preparing for this same operation for God. Church God's word is on the move prepare yourselves for the coming of the Lord presence.

In **March 23, 2002,** on my way to Maryland, the powerful hand of God spoke to me with His Holy Spirit. His presence was so strong it filled the inside of my vehicle. This is what He said: I am speaking to you the second time. Don't worry, if they don't believe you; you are My messenger. Tell them I will open up their eyes and hearts. Saints of God what you are about to read is the truth of the real and true living God. If you don't have strong faith and belief, I pray to the Almighty God you will go down on your knees and ask the true living God to strengthen your faith beyond your understanding, and believe upon His understanding and believe in His everlasting word.

The first of December, 2001,God said I would gather His churches leaders all over the world, every nations to assemble themselves in Washington, D.C. to stop the killing of His babies. He reminded me by His Holy Spirit it was time to receive the fullness of His message. It would be the largest prayer meeting. in the history of the world **Numbers 20:6** says "Moses and Aaron assembly unto the door of the tabernacle of the congregation, and they fell upon their faces: and the glory of the LORD appeared unto them." Your pray will consisted of; stop destroying My babies, stop drugs from infesting and destroying My people, bring families back together under the leadership of God, put prayer back in schools. I will overcome AIDS, which is destroying my people. I will stop hunger and I will bring peace. I will overcome sickness. Every nation will come to know the true Christianity of Jesus Christ. Every form of idle worship will be destroyed from the face of this earth. Every nation will come to know and worship one true living God, the Father Lord Jesus, Christ by His glory of the Holy Spirit of wisdom, revelation, and the knowledge will fill their hearts.

Psalm 86:8-12 says, "Among the gods there is none like unto thee, Oh Lord; neither is their any word like unto thy works. All nations will come and worship before thee, Oh Lord; shall glorify thy name. For thou art great, and dost wondrous things: thou are God along. Teach us thy way, Oh Lord; we will walk in thy truth: united our heart to fear thy name. We will praise thee, Oh Lord my God, with all my heart: and we will glorify thy name for evermore." He is saying my saints (leaders) will come together for prayer, and they will come from every nation and they will bring their concerns, which is causing my people not to accept the true living word of God and other problems. He is saying my people have been living in fear too long; they are dying all over the world, which is controlled by the hand of Satan and his dominance, which is destroying my people and has overtaking my dominion that I have put man in charge of. Now Satan has taken charge.

All people will assemble and unified there hearts, minds, souls, and prayers to the one true living God to break down all strongholds, overcome dominate forces that have come amond God's people. God said to tell all His churches and families to prepare themselves, by teaching His people how to pray and what to pray for, so when this day come they will understand His requirement, He spoke to me and said His people have been living in darkness ever since the fall of Adam and many of His people have not learned His ways. Many have refused to learn of Him. Many have been denied His word, because Satan has hardened the hearts of men who didn't want to see His people receive the true living God. With God's prayer of solidarity to unified, and strengthen our hearts together with one faith of Jesus Christ to receive His blessing. He would un leash His divine mighty power upon all stronghold, break down all barriers between black white and everys other race on the face of this earth to come together as one in the eyes of the true living God Almighty. And to stop all these demonetizing force destroying His babies with no respect for life, in Africa where AIDS destroying His people. They will come from every walk of life and bring all their problem and concerns **There will be five crosses located upon the lawn of the Capital. In front of each cross a large dumpster will be placed to contain all prayer's concerns and problems.** God has shown me that when my people bow down and look up to heaven and direct their prayers to the one true living Almighty God. He will send down fire from heaven to consume all their prayers and concerns. At that time He would tear down and destroy all evil all over this world. He would rain down like fire from heaven and every saints assemble here would be touch by God anointing and awesome power that His word will be burned into their minds, hearts, and souls. God is speaking to us saint in **Acts 4:30-32** says, "By stretching forth thine hand to heal; and that signs and wonders may be done by the name of thy Holy Child Jesus. And when they had prayed, the place was shaken where they were assembled together; and they were all filled with the Holy Ghost, and they spake the word of God with boldness. And the multitude of them that believed was of one heart and of one soul: neither said any of them that aught of the things, which he possessed, was his own; but they had all things common. And your prayer once again I will take upon My hand and wipe away all your sins away and set you free. I will command you, thou shall love the Lord your God with all your heart, and with all your soul, and with all your mind. Thou you shall love your neighbour as yourself. I command you to keep away from those things I destroy. I command, you to obey My true living word." **Deuteronomy13: 4** says, "God said "ye shall walk after the LORD your God, and fear him, and keep His commandments, and obey His voice, and ye shall serve Him and cleave unto Him." In **Chap 28:1-2** says, "And it shall come to pass, if thou shalt hearken diligently unto the voice of the LORD thy God to observe and to do all this commandments which I command you this day, that the LORD your God will set you on high. All nations blessings shall come if thou shalt hearken unto the voice of the Lord your God."

If any man or nation disobey My voice, My command, and turn his own ways, when the Son of man coming in the clouds of heaven with power and great glory, only those who have been faithful and keep my commandments will appear in the heaven; all who disobey will be left behind. "These are the true words of the true living God. His Bible is the living testorment of the true living word of God." and of this day I will come to you in your midst and commend all these things unto you. I will unleash My power of the Holy Spirit upon every soul assembled in My presence like you you're never felt before, and the blessings will fall from heaven. Once you depart from anoung your brother and sisters you will never be the same again. What I give you, you will take back and teach to all people of their nations, because I 'm your God and you will be my people.

These are God's requirements and commandments, I am His messenger. I pray to the Divine power of God that you will let Him open up their hearts, and overcome our blindness, that we may see and understand the true living God is getting ready to bless the world. Lord, I pray, let the power of your Holy Spirit touch every reader of this book of God, to take heed to these words and prepare themselves for that day the coming of the presence of the Lord. **Act 10:33** says, "Immediately therefore I sent to thee; and thou hast well done that thou art come. Now therefore God, to hear all things that are commanded thee of God."

God Showed Me the River of Jordan and the Wildness

IN APRIL 7, 2002, God led me to a church outside of Greensboro. North Carolina. As I arrived I was greeted with love from the congregation. As they sing praise and worship songs unto the Lord, I felt the power of His presence in that church, and the power of His spirit was moving through the entire congregation. All my years, I, had never heard praise and worship the way I heard these young people sing. They were truly filled with the Holy Spirit of their savior. This is what God is looking for in His house. I pray to the Almighty God that churches will do what the Psalms say; sing to the Lord with Praise and worships. "Praise ye the Lord. Praise God in His sanctuary: praise Him in the firmament of His power. Praise Him for His mighty acts: praise Him according to His excellent greatness. Praise Him with the sound of psaltery and harp. Praise Him with the tumbrel and dance: praise Him with stringed instruments and organs. Praise Him upon the loud cymbals: praise Him upon the high sounding cymbals. Let every thing that hath breath praise ye the Lord." We are to thank Him for all His goodness, grace, and mercy, for what He has done for us. He wants to bless our hearts with His glorious peace and love. Why don't we praise and thank Him the way He is speaking according to **Psalms 150?**

As I was praising and thanking the Almighty Powerful divine Hand of the true living God, with my arms stretched toward heaven God opened up heaven and I saw a vision from God: the river of Jordan and the green grass. It was the most beautiful and peaceful scene I had ever seen. It were so awesome, the tears of joy were running down my face. I was praising and thanking the only true living God's. I saw saints of God churches all over the wilderness, wandering around and around as if they were lost; then He showed me churches moving close to the river of Jordan; God has saying to His saints We must go into the Jordan River to be sanctified, wash in the water, and through blood of the living lamb to be enter into the holiness of God Almighty and the sanctification of our minds, hearts and souls.

Psalm 107 4 says, "They wandered in the wilderness I a solitary way; they found no city to dwell in. hungry and thirsty their soul fainted in them."

In **Mark 1:9** says, "And it came to pass in those days, that Jesus came from Nazareth of Galilee, and was baptized of John in Jordan." But those churches were going round and round. I asked God "Why are they going around in the wilderness?" He said They hath put Me out and brought the world's system unto My church. Many of them are still in their old traditions ways; with hardening of their hearts, fearful of change. Many of their eyes are blinded to the true living word of God. Some are praising and worshipping with hip hop and rap music called man's gospel. Some have taken the true gospel of praise and worship and turned into man's words in contemporary gospel music, many churches have turn to rapping and hip hop music to drew young people into God house to be saved. Their worldly music, they are all worshipping Satan, not God. My church has failed to worship Me in spirit and of truth righteousness.

When they fall on their knees and call on the true living God. Ask forgiveness of the sin you have committed against Him. Christ will clean their hearts through His blood and led them to the river of Jordan.

Revelation Chap 2 and 3 says, "Ephesus has left thy first love, but thou art rich, and I know the blasphemy of them. Behold the devil shall cast some of you into prison. Pergamos and Thyatira but I have a few things against thee, because thou hast there them that hold the doctrine of Balaam, who taught Balac to cast a stumbling block before the children of my church, to eat things worldly idols, and to commit fornication. Satan has interred my church; commit adultery with her into great tribulation. Sardis I know thy works, that thou hast a name that thou livest, and art dead. Be watchful, and strengthen the things, which remain, that are ready to die: for I have not found thy work perfect before God. Laodiceans I neither know thy works that thou art neither cold nor hot, they are blind and naked. I counsel thee to buy for me So then because thou art lukewarm, and neither cold nor hot, I will spue thee out of my mouth. Repent I will come unto thee quickly. He that hath an ear, let him hear what the Spirit saith unto the churches; he that overcome shall not be hurt of the second death. Behold, I stand at the door, and knock: if any man hear my voice, and open the door, I will come in to him, and will sup (eat) with him, and he with me.: I couldn't stop praising and thanking the Almighty God with all my heart. Then my heart went out to those churches that don't love the Lord according to His will. In **Number 32:13** say, "And the Lord's anger was kindled against Israel (church), and He made them wander in the wilderness forty years, until all the generation, that had done evil in the sight of the Lord, was consumed." And there they shall die. What an awesome, amazing, and incredible and true living God I service. My heart was hurt because I didn't want to see our church lost in the wilderness. Oh Lord, I pray, please don't let them die. These are your children, Lord, give them another chance and let them take you back into your churches to be the head.

That Monday night at class, the instructor had just returned from Israel. He showed us picture he had taken around the Jordan River with green grass, exactly the same vision God has shown me. These things are hard to explain; only God knows what is going on in my life. What an awesome, amazing and incredible God. **Psalm 138** says, "I will praise thee with my whole heart: before the gods will I sing praise unto thee. I will worship toward thy holy temple, and praise thy name for thy loving kindness and for thy truth: for thou hast magnified thy word above all thy name"

God Showed Me the Gleam of Heaven

Mid May, 2002, I went out to a park to read God's word. I was sitting in my vehicle listening to a CD I want to Go to Heaven. I was looking up in the sky and all of a sudden I felt the presence of God in the vehicle. The Holy Spirit was strong and tears of joy start running down my face. Then God opened up heaven and I saw a vision. Oh what a sight I saw It was beautiful and peaceful scene. I saw those people up in heaven they were singing and praising God. Then they all starting looking at me smiling as if to say We are glad you are coming up here. Most of the faces I new. It was an amazing, incredible, and awesome scene. I started praising God, Lord, I want to go home to this place called heaven. Lord, this old world is not my home; and I am just passing through. Lord I want to go to a place not made by man's, but a place made by the glorious hand of Christ Jesus.

What an awesome and incredible scene. Lord, this old world is full of sins and heat. All around me is darkness; everywhere I go they are trying to stamp out God's word and every thing you and I stand for. This old world doesn't wants to hear about the true living God. They have their own gods. Oh Lord, how long will you let your people live in sins and bondage before you come to see about us? Lord, I am tired of this world, it is closing up around my soul. Lord, someday I will stand before you and say have I did all you ask of my soul? Oh Lord, I pray you will raise up somebody to go and turn this old world around and bring it out of the darkness into your glorious light that shine allover this world. Please Lord. God rise up someone like Moses. to lead your people out of bondage into a land where there be peace and joy forever and ever more.

The Healing Power of the Holy God

IN MID **June, 2002,** Thursday morning, an amazing event of God's presence happened at John Wesley College. That morning I arrived at school early and set in my vehicle thanking and praising God. In class the instructor asked who has prayer requests. When the students asked for prayer, they put their confidence, trust, and faith in God. One student said there was division in the church and the pastor was about to leave. Another student said her son have shoulders problem that kept him from playing summer baseball. Another student said her daughter had a breathing problem, and after seeing many doctors her result were the same and they have found a special doctor who would examiner her. Another student, new a young girl who had became pregnant before summer camp, and she has just been saved by the Lord, but she was afraid to tell her grandmother.

I had a strong compassion for these concerns. A student prayed and I felt the power of God's Holy Spirit shower down upon my soul so that I could not hold back the tears; God Spirit spoke to me and said the little girl is healed. I spoke to her and said Your daughter is healed by the power of God. The Holy Spirit kept coming upon me; I had to leave the classroom twice because God's Spirit was upon my soul so strong I could not sit down. And I didn't understand why all this was happen to me this way. Oh what a powerful and glorious hand of the mighty God. I pray God will release His Holy Spirit upon your soul. **Matthew** says, **12:15** says, "Jesus withdrew himself from thence: and great multitudes followed him, and he healed them all." It is God Almighty who has the power to heal; there is nothing in man. His healing is to glorify Him in heaven.

That Thursday evening the student whose daughter had the breathing problem prayed for my wife and Friday I said I would buy my wife flowers. She said have them sent; I did. My daughter came down from Maryland. Every since our problem started, when our daughter came down, there was always a conflict between her and her mother. This week I prayed to God, "Let there be peace in this house." Well this weekend brought peace for the first time in two years. What an amazing hand of the Almighty God who can overcome all problems. Just pray and let Him into your heart.

That Monday morning in class was one day of hallelujah, thanksgiving, rejoicing and praising to the one true living Almighty God: the student church division had a complete transformation Leaders and congregation came together to ask for forgiveness. And God restored the church back in order and everyone's heart was united under the one true living God. The student Son with shoulder problems, his shoulder was healing well enough to resume playing baseball. The student whose daughter had the breathing problem was completely healed. Two days later the student who spoke of the pregnant girl went to two doctors, and there was no trace of pregnancy. Hallelujah who says the God we serve is not a living and all powerful God? I pray your faith will be strength by this awesome, amazing, and incredible powerful hand of the true living God. When His true saints are assembled together among the divine trinity the Father, the Son, and The Holy Spirit are at work, something is going to happen, and it did. Whoever reads this book, I pray you will know and understand the awesome powerful God, and know how He showers mercy upon His people to bring them out from bondage and release them into the glorious blessing peace of God.

Who can say this God is dead? They don't understand the powerful God of all creation, who has all power, so that we may believe, and have faith and have confidence in the true living Jesus Christ.

Schools Belong under the Control of God and the Church

THE LAST week of June, 2002, My heart had been burden down about the way the government are running the school today, cutting programs, effecting students, type of material been taught is losing this country foundation and the pass history; the overt burden teacher. They're no God involving in their teaching as a fundamental life style. One day I was outside the classroom, looking up to heaven asking God want you do something about the school problem with our young people today. I don't hate the government I hate what is happening to our youth in school, not being feed the true living word of God. Lord, somebody has got to do something to stop this evil force that has been unleashed upon our schools and families, stop destroying the foundation of God and bring back the biblical life style.

At class Tuesday night the powerful hand of God Spirit were upon my heart, spoke and said I am going to releast the control of school from the government and releast them back into the hand of My churches.

The instructor said she was scheduled to attend a conference; the Spirit of God spoke and toll her to speak these words at the conforance to inform God's people to assemblem themselves and pray with this concern on their hearts. That God will break down the burden between the schools and government. God will bring the schools back where they stated. **Isaiah 22:21** says "And I will cloth him with thy robe, and strengthen him with thy girdle, and I will commit thy government into his hand: and he shall be a father to the inhabitants of Jerusalem." **Isaiah 9:6** says, "For unto us a child is born, unto us a son is given: and the government shall be upon his shoulder: and His name shall be called Wonderful, Counsellor, The mighty God, The everlasting Father, the Prince of peace."

That Friday morning I arrived at college early and I went into the chapter kneeled at the altar, and prayed to God, asking Is this your true word spoken unto me, Oh Lord, Give me a clear understanding this is your word, not Satan's. "I felt the power of God down upon my soul. That same morning the instructor asked who has prayer requests. I said God wanted me to ask for prayer. As I got ready to speak, an there was amazing feeling came over me like never before. I started shaking all over and I was shaking so badly I could not speak. As I was shaking the word came out of my mouth. This is what He said; I will break down barrier the between schools and the government, giving the school system back into hand of the church." I felt as if God were standing over me answer my pray I had just asked Him. Lord. I don't understand all of this. All I can say in you are God and there is no other like you. How can someone not believe in the true Almighty Hand of God? The instructor said, I would like to see your vision come true because the school system belongs into the hand of God's Church. His power was so strong upon me, I had to leave the classroom and go into the bathroom until I could calm down. Oh what a powerful presence of God I had upon my body; soul, and mind shaking me like a leaf on a tree.

I really can't explain it any better than this; you must be in the presence of God to know His Holy power and His glorious presence of His blessing. All I can Say power this God is so real and great I can't explain. I pray churches will feel the same presence of the true living God the way I feel His presence. God is calling on all churches in North Carolina. to start praying this vision God show me. He will bring it to pass. God wants His churches to assemble together and unite their hearts with this concern with a burden down in their soul and pray to the true living God, He will overcome the evil hand that had fallen upon our children so the school system will be put back into the hand of God and the church.

A Vision from My Heavenly Father

THE SECOND week in June, 2003, God led me to a church There the saints of God were singing, praising and worshiping the one true living God. I stretched out my arms upward to heaven. Looking up, with my eyes closed, I felt the power of God's Spirit come over my soul. The church was singing high and lifted up. Then God opened up heaven and I saw the clouds. They were so incredible, awesome, and full of amazing beauty, There was a row of cloud in front; then in the back I saw a long row of clouds high and lifted up. All across the back row of clouds, there were crosses lined all the way across just as far as I could see. I said, Oh Lord, what is this? Oh Lord God, I don't understand what all these crosses mean. Lord God this was an awesome and incredible vision. What a glorious scene, that I saw in heaven. **Revelation 5:12-13** says, "Worthy is the lamb that was slain to receive power, and riches. I saying, Blessing and honour, and glory, and power, be unto Him that sitteth upon the throne, and unto the lamb forever and ever." Lord sometimes I ask myself who am I for you to show me all these visions?

Then God brought the answer to my mind; these cross represent death. Everyone who died to Christ, their cross is represented in heaven and receive his cross for My sake has received his and her cross of eternal life in heaven. The only way Christ could return to the Father was to die upon the cross. **Matthew 16:24** say, "Then said Jesus unto his disciples, If any man will come after me, let him deny himself, and take up his cross, and follow me." Every person must die unto sin, be reborn to receive the cross of the kingdom of God.

That day Saints of God, I saw your cross and my cross, all God's children have a cross. He said carry your cross everywhere you go and you will abide in Me. But if you denial your cross on earth, He will deny your cross in heaven.

These cross represents the blood of the lamb that cleans all our sin away. It represents the Holy Spirit that makes us not ashamed of the Gospel. It represents resurrection power of the righteousness of God, to understand our lives according to the written word. It represents prayer, so pray and keep clean hands and purify your heart.

An Incredible Vision from God

August 13, 2003, I was in the park reading and study God's word and during my college homework, I stopped to take a break thanking and praising God, looking up to heaven. Saints of God, I saw something that frightened my soul. I could not believe what I saw until God spoke in my mind and said Jerusalem. **Revelation 21** says, "And I John saw the holy city, New Jerusalem, coming down from God out of heaven, prepared as a bridge aborned for her husband." Saints, I saw Jerusalem coming down from heaven; it covered about a third of the sky in the East. It was the most beautiful, amazing, incredible, and wonderful thing I have ever seen in my life. It was leaning to one side. Things my eyes saw I could not make them out they look like high tower or building, it lasted about thirty seconds. I had been afraid to tell anyone, because people would think I was losing my mind. I kept it shut up in my heart until **November 21, 2003,** At college, the professor was talking about Jerusalem rebuilding the temple, I asked a question about New Jerusalem, than the holy spirit came upon my soul and reveled it to me again and said Tell it and write it; don't worry I am with you. In **Habakkuk 2:2-3** says, "And the Lord answered me, and said, write the vision, and make it plain upon table, that he may run that readeth it. For the vision is yet for an appointed time, but at the end it shall speak, and not lie through it tarry, wait it because it will surely come, it will not tarry." I could not stay in the class room. The spirit was so strong, I had to leave and go out into the hall to calm down. I returned and then I started seeing it with tears still running down with joy. Saints of God, many of these things I don't completely understand, but I do know these are the same He spoke to His prophecy in the Old and New Testament of what is to come. When these things will happen, only God knows. No man knows the future of God's complete plan. God only gives us according to the lever of wisdom, knowledge, and understanding to act responsibly in caring out His will. **Zechariah 8:3-4** says, "Thus saith the Lord; I am returned unto Zion, and will dwell in the midst of Jerusalem: and Jerusalem shall be called a city of truth; and the mountain of the Lord of hosts the holy mountain. Thus saith the Lord of hosts; there shall yet old men and old women dwell in the streets of Jerusalem, and every man with his staff in his hand for very age."

John Wesley College professor

THE FIRST of November, 2003, the living God spoke to me about John Wesley College professors, and how they taught me. The Spirit of the Lord was upon my soul with an amazing feeling, with tears of joy running down my face. I felt so happy from all that I have learned from God. And it was all done through the Spirit of God involving these professors I can say without a doubt these are the greatest godliest men I have even met with the teaching tool through the gift from God. They are men/woman who have a wealth of rich knowledge with a true foundation of Biblical teaching strictly upon the solid rock of God's holy word. They taught me the Biblical knowledge from God's Holy Bible and about all His prophets and disciple; I had asked God to teach me the truth of His holy word. He answered my prayer. I received was just that. I pray to the living God for that other students have received the same level of training and knowledge that I have received and more. I thank God for these professors. There were two professors who became true friends in Christ to me. Dr Lindsey, when I was in trouble with Spanish, he opened up his office and taught me. Although this was the hardest subject I had even endure, I didn't learn very much. What I did learn he was there in my time of need. Also God, led me to go with him to Mexico City, the summer of 2003 my life was enriched and blessed being among him and his brother. I really enjoyed being there with them. Next, professor Matthew What a spiritually enriched person, with such living beautiful gift of God's grace with abundant of love in her heart, and soul to help other. When God sent me to college. I knew I could not make it own my own. God led me to someone who could help. My spelling it was horrible and she gave me the help I needed to survive. Lord, how can I thank them I don't have enough love in my heart to thank them Lord for all their support for three years. Lord I thank you for her life, she had been a real bless from heaven to help me through. I thank you Lord, for sending me to this college. You knew just what I needed. All the staff were a true blessing to my heart. I pray to God Almighty He keep them under His wings and cover them in the blood of the living lamb that their soul, will be kept until He call, them home.

Unknown Mystery of an UFO

ON FEBRUARY 28, 2004 an incredible thing happened to my vehicle, a good friend Jonnie a true man of God in Christ Jesus filled with the Holy Spirit. He and I had visited a church that night. After church I went with him home, we set discussing God's word. I departed about 11:15. p.m. As I was driving home I was praising and thanking God Almighty for all His goodness and mercy.

At about 11:30 p.m. I came to a crossing of a large street. The light turned green just before reached the street. I was driving about 15 m.p.h. As I started across I saw my truck hood buckle up from the front. Then I saw something brown looking come into my vehicle hood. Then it dispersed. On my left, I saw a white vehicle waiting to cross. Immediately, I went into a train. I didn't feel any impact or noise. I didn't stop. The street was well lit up. About a quarter mile away from home I came out the train. I heard a rattle from my truck. I start thinking why did I not stop? I drove home pulled into my garage and I looked in front of my truck. I could not believe my eyes.

I said Oh Lord, what did I hit; it was a V shape object. I saw it hit the dead center of the vehicle. The air bag didn't go off. That Saturday night I couldn't sleep. The next morning I was watching the TV. A man was preaching. The holy Spirit came upon my soul. God showed me a vision. I was preaching telling this story. The people on the right were praising God. The people on the left were saying I was crazy. Through Sunday God's spoke to me several time saying people are going to say you are crazy. I called the police but they didn't find any thing or another vehicle in this area involved in an accident.

The body shop could understand how it happened. The damage came close to five thousand dollars. After four years, I needed to take a physical. I told the doctor about the accident. After he completed all test the doctor reported I was in good health and there were no problem. I showed him the accident report and explained to him that God had sent a UFO (mystery) down upon my vehicle then he said something I didn't understand. He wanted to submit me to a mental ward for treatment because he though I had lost my mind. He said I needed to called my family to have me put away. I left the doctor's office without worrying. As I was driving home God spoke and said that doctor didn't understand. My son, he said, you are alright. I arrived home he had already called my wife; she was somewhat upset because the doctor said I was losing my mind and I must take more test to see the result of my problem. I refused to adhere to what the doctor said, so she called my whole family to make me go back and submitted to the doctor. I said no. I know what God said to me. I would not bow down to pressure for any one. I will stand firm upon the true word of God.

My wife and family got really up set with me. This was the first time my wife had talked to my family since God set us apart July 3, 2000. Then God was showing me this was done to get her back talking with the family again, and to show her concern toward me. **1 Corinthians 13:2b** says, I have the gift of prophecy, and understand all mystery, and knowledge; and through I have all faith.

Through this mystery UFO, God is beginning to open up my understanding to know the truth. Then God spoke to me about my sister Dorothy who was a blessing from heaven by calling and speaking to my wife with love from the family leading her back into the family? I thank Christ Jesus for using my sister to help my wife to see the light. And Lord I thank the God Almighty for my sister. She has always been the solid rock in bringing the family together. Oh Lord I pray your blessing from heaven will shower down among my sister's family. Also, let these same blessing fall upon the entire Odom family and unite us together as one body under the hand of the God Almighty Christ Jesus, the true Lamb of God.

God's Blueprint for My Life

GOD HAS a blueprint for everyone; it was developed for our lives before we were born. He already knows how our lives are going to turn out. He knows our lifetime encounters with Him and Satan. God knows who will be saved and who would not be saved; this is a mystery no man knows. **Jeremiah 1:5** says, "Before I formed thee in the belly, I knew thee; and before thou came forth out of the womb. He know just what kind of person we are going to be from the beginning to our death." **John 6:64** says, "But there are some of you that believe not. For Jesus knows from the beginning that they were that believed not, and who should betray him." Every man is born with an evil spirit and God has given him a gift of his own knowledge and understanding. At our second birth, every man receives God's Holy Spirit that lives in our heart, to directed and guided our lives by the hand of God. The life we are living from day to day is nothing we did of our own or what we do in the future, it is already laid out in everyone blueprint from God in heaven. What we do good or bad, it was program by God before we were born. **1Corinthians 2:10-12** says, "But God hath revealed them into us by his Spirit for the Spirit searcheth all things, yea the deep things of God. For what man knoweth the things of a man, save the spirit of man, which is in him? Even so the things of God knoweth no man but the Spirit of God. Now we have received, not the spirit of the world, but the spirit which is of God that we might know the things that are freely given to us of God." We are a living being connect to the Spirit of God to live our life in the order of Jesus Christ our Lord and savior.

God wants me to tell the world about this incredible, amazing blueprint He has for your and for my life. If you know God like I know Him you know that the God I serve is an incredible; God. He is glorious, merciful and peaceful. God, with all power and compassion of love, has placed these things down in my heart, mind, and soul. I had no idea this blueprint of my life would bring me to North Carolina and take me through such an incredible and amazing journey.

He used me while in service, to spread the gospel of Jesus Christ among other soldiers. This helped lead them to receive Christ as their personal Savior. As my life begin to develop into one of God's servant, His blueprint for my life through Christ brought about the incredible stories written in this book.

God can choose anyone He desires to choose to be His chosen one. It is all about love, faith, patience, and a pure heart. **James 2:17-18** says, "Even so faith, if it hath not works, is dead being alone. Yet, a man may say, Thou have faith, and I have works: shew me thy faith without thy works, and I will shew thee my faith by my work." God is saying I will judge every man according to his work.

God had taken me through some incredible things while I was in the service. It was only by the grace of God that safely brought me through those events. He promised, I will not leave you nor will I forsake you and I will stay right by you side, until the end of time. God's holy hand covered me every step of the way. He was continually blessing me while I was serving in the army.

While in the service, God led me to take every opportunity to further my education, by attending every school possible. I was sent to the Defense Equal Opportunity Management School. This course taught me how to speak to people with great respect and love for everyone, and how to become friends to anyone with the understanding of peace and love. Everyone must be treated with equal respect. There is no one no better than another. God. created us all to be Christ-like, we are all sinners and have come short of His glory.

His plan is for Christians to show love, compassion, and fellowship with other saints of God. Ask Him to change our hearts and break down barriers of hate and anger between us, and let the love of God overcome our problems. **Ephesians 2:14** say, "For He is our peace; who hath made both one, and hath broken down the middle wall of partition between us." Now we can be partakers of His promise to receive the gift of the grace of God given unto us to attain the working power of His Holy Spirit. I am not afraid or ashamed of the gospel of Jesus Christ, for it is the power of His salvation that has set me free. And taught me to learned how to work and talk to people in a loving way. God is guiding my life each and every day by teaching me to be more Christ-like. People say they feel as if we are brothers and sisters with common goals as I meet and talk with them. They say it is the love of Christ Jesus in your heart that care about us, trust us and have God's love for all. They become relaxed and it is easy to talk with them. Saints, with God on your side, you can confront and work through problems with a compassion of love for others. God desires peace and happiness for all people because of His loves for us. I thank God for placing His happiness, joy, peace, and love down in my heart according to your blueprint for my soul. I have been commissioned to do the work involving the will of the Lord. I thank Him for giving me the ability to speak to His people with compassion and a loving heart.

Oh God, you are the highest God. You are a God of love and care, with compassion that cover my soul with such peace, grace, and mercy, which overflow my heart, mind, and body. Lord God, at times you make me feel that I am in heaven. Father, I thank you. I will praise your Holy Name every day and night. Oh God, your blueprint for my life has given me such great knowledge and understanding how to love you the rest of my life. You have guided, molded and shaped my life to be your servant and to spread Your Good News. You hold the master plan for my life in the palm of Your hand. Oh God, You are my developer, engineer, chief cornerstone, builder, foundation, and master-crafter, and You guide my life day by day.

God's blueprint brought me to Christ at an early age of twelve From nineteen to thirty one years old I was lost in darkness; there was very little light in my life. For some reason the blood of God was still upon my soul and kept me soul from been completely lost.

In God there is no darkness of sin. There is only continuous light. For some reason He keep His light upon my soul. Satan was drifting me back into darkness but God never gave up on me. That is how much He loves you and me. He knows every hearts. He knew Satan would journey me outside the righteousness of God of my blueprint and into darkness. God knew how far Satan would drift me away, and when God willed return my soul back to Him.

You know the story of Job; in **Job 2** we find, "And Satan answered the Lord and said, Skin for skin, yea, and all that a man hath will he give for his life. But put forth thine hand now, and touch his bone and his flesh, and he will curse thee to thy face. And the Lord said unto Satan, Behold he is in thine hand; but save his life." God knows and He has authority over the mind of Satan, who is the father of sin and darkness. Satan would lead me to do something sinful but something would cause me to reject sin. I always wanted to be like my friends, and do what they did. Again, something would cause me to reject them and their ways. I had no clue what was happening to my life. It was God's blueprint of my life already programmed to send me into the world of sin to give me an understanding how the world system worked. I would see the dark side opposed to the light side. **Genesis 3:22** says, "And the Lord God said, Behold, the man is become as one of us, to know good and evil; and now, lest he put forth his hand, and take also of the tree of life, eat and live for ever." In **Jeremiah 11** says, "God controls evil." God was holding my hand and walking with me. He would not let me get so deep in sin that I would not want to return back to Him. God's blueprint insured that I would fall, but I would not stay down. He was preparing me according to the blueprint of my life for something only He knew the outcome of. I prayed to God and asked Him to forgive me of my sin, clean and set me, free.

Once again I had no idea my life would be turned around and set upon a solid Rock. **Romans 9:17** says, "For the scripture saith unto us, even for this same purpose have I raised you up, that I might shew my power in thee, and that my name might be declared throughout all the earth". I can truly say He has been with me every step of the way.

As I look back over my life I thank and praise Him how He watched over me during my dark days, I thank Him for bringing me through the storm, and leading me by His everlasting arm.

Lord, my soul is not worthy of rescuing; yet you showed mercy upon my soul and brought me back into the hand of my Heavenly Father. He loves me more than I can ever repay. How can I ever thank and praise Him enough for all of the grace and mercy He has shown my soul? **Ephesians 1:6-8** says, "To the praise of the glory of his grace, wherein he hath made me accepted in the beloved. In whom I have redemption through his blood, the forgiveness of sin, according to the riches of his grace. Wherein he hath abounded toward me in all wisdom and prudence."

God knows the blueprint of my life. He was working on my life, shaping it according to my blueprint. One day I was sitting outside of my house when a pastor and one of his deacons stopped by to talk with me about Jesus. That was the first time in twelve years someone had spoken to me about Jesus. The Holy Spirit led me back to the House of God. I joined Kent Baptist Church in Landover, Maryland. As time passed I became a member of the choir; later on I became a trustee. Later in my life with Christ I was ordained as a deacon. Through all of this, I still felt like I was cheating God. I never felt that these things were my calling; I felt I was not doing enough to please Him. My heart was somewhat empty, as if something were missing. I felt I could do more but I didn't know how. I was searching, looking for answers, I couldn't find anything to fill my empty heart. I really didn't know Jesus Christ, and I had a shallow heart. He knew my limitations and what I was capable of doing. Nevertheless, Oh God, I thank you for your Grace and mercy. You have brought me back into Your church that I may learn and understand. As long as I am able to speak, I will tell every soul I encounter about the love of Christ. What happened to my soul during those twelve years? By not hearing the word of God, I had lost all connections with Him and the gospel was hidden from my heart. I will never let this happen to people that I meet along my way. I will tell the Good News of Jesus Christ to everyone who is committed to hear. It is sad there are many so called Christians who can't stand to hear God's true word very long. If you talk about God as Paul speaks **Philippians 1:27a** only let your conversation be as it becometh the gospel of Christ." We weak Christian have been brainwashed by the world; the only time we should talk about Christ is in church on Sunday. If we live our life according to the Bible, then everything we do will come naturally during our everyday lives with God's guidance and direction. I am a living witness of God Almighty in that everything I do and say is to glorify God in Heaven. God has chosen me and changed my life to be an example of Him.

The problem is that people in the world are not hearing God's Word. **Mark 16:15** says, "Go ye into all the world, and preach the gospel to every creature." **Deuteronomy 18:18** says, "I will raise them up a prophet from among their brethren, like unto thee, and will put my words in his mouth; and he shall speak unto them all that I shall command him." Those who have turned away from God are lost in the world. God still loves them and he wants them to turn back to Him and repent of their sin. In **Ephesians 2:4-7** says, "But God, who is rich in mercy, for His love care wherewith He love us. Even when we were dead in sins, He hath quickened us together with Christ, by grace ye are saved. And had raised us up together, and made us sit together in heavenly places in Christ Jesus. That in the ages to come, He might show the exceeding riches of His grace in His kindness toward us through Christ Jesus."

God Knows Just What You Need

WHILE I was at Kent Baptist Church, Jesus took me through lot of training as His blueprint was guiding my life. Pastor Carr, who is a great man of God, was an inspiration to my life because of his profound knowledge and understanding of God's Word. It was evident that God used the pastor as a shepherd to help shape and mold my life. I would never have known the value of his training if God had not brought it to my attention in the year 2000. God holds the key to my future and He knows when everything will come to my understanding of God. Now I know what all his training meant for my life. God was teaching me to do His will and preach His gospel. I can truly say that Pastor Carr is a unique pastor who works closely with his deacons through development of spiritual training and helping them to develop skills for improving interpersonal relationships. The competence of our training was strengthened through my personal witnessing to others. God developed me into a more caring person while at the same time He was developing my skills for building church fellowship. I thank God for allowing me to cross his path. My life was truly blessed by him. Pastor Carter is also a great man of God who has the ability to work with young people by leading them to Christ. I know God has a great ministry for his life. I pray the Almighty God will continue to lead him in the pathway of righteousness, enlarge his territory, and lead him to greater heights. Sister Diggs is the greatest music teacher I ever known, although I had a difficult time learning to sing. I thank God they let me make a joyful noise with them. The whole choir really blessed my heart the years I served Christ with them. I thank you and I love you all with my whole heart. I pray the holy hand of God will really bless you all with His peace, mercies, kindness, and humbleness through the mind of Christ.

The training I received consisted of many books and training classes. Some of the materials used were Experiencing God and Knowing and Doing the Will of God by Henry T. Blackaby & Claude V. King; Systematically Through the New Testament by Thomas D. Lea & Tom Hudson; Basics of the Christian Experience; Christian Theology Training and personal and group Bible study. God was preparing me with His Word for what only God knows.

Deacon Davis, Deacon Hayes, and Deacon Gaffney are three mighty men of God. They greatly influenced my life when our paths crossed. These brethren have great knowledge and understanding of the Word of God. Their leadership roles were significant to the ministry in the body of Kent Baptist Church. The pastor, deacons, and congregation were one body of Christ, united in love, to do the will of God. Don't let me forget my good friend Deacon Barbour, another mighty man of God who walks with God. I can truly say every one of you has touched my life and I pray our Heavenly Father will lay His loving and merciful hand upon each one of you personally. I love you all with my whole heart, with all my love and care.

There is another great man of God who had great influence on my Christian life. Pastor Nix, my brother in-law. Each time we met he was willing to share the word of God. He explained it in a way that I could understand. He is a follower of Christ who is always committed to help someone in need. I pray the hand of the Almighty God will continue to build him up in ministry of the true living Christ Jesus. He is a man of God who doesn't compromise with God's true living word. I love him with my whole heart.

In October of, 2002, God's Holy Spirit spoke these words about my brother in-law's wife, my sister Julia. I was on my way back from the hospital speaking the love of Jesus Christ to His people. The Spirit was upon my soul, and tear of joy were running from my eyes. Your sister has prepared a place in heaven. She has such great love for my people; she had offered up herself as a living sacrifice of offering and blessing unto My Holy Kingdom. Julia, God had granted you according to the riches of His glory, to strengthen your Spiritual soul with His mighty power and holy blessing. God had given you a special gift of giving. God brought this to my mind, as you make cake and pies, giving them freely to people in needs, and those who are blessed. I could not understand how you could do this with such joy. Will God change my heart to see this is not your doing, but its the spirit and love of the true living God, that works through and upon your heart and soul to service Him in such a special way? God gave up his Son for us all; you are only following His example. I pray that God Almighty will place down in my heart a gift of love and joy the way He has given you, my sister. As I write these word with the he tears of joy running from my eyes, I know God hears my prayer. The greatest gift of Jesus Christ is a heart of love to give up ourselves to serving other.

In **Act 20:35** say, "I have showed you all things, how that so labouring ye ought to support the weak, and to remember the works of the Lord Jesus how he said, it is more blessed to give than to receive."

My Mother and Father Gave Me a Solid Foundation

AS I WRITE these words, God's blueprint would not let me forget my mother and father, who brought me into this world by the hand of God. These two people strengthened me by teaching me about God's authority, discipline, obedience, and instruction for my home life. They took us to church and Sunday school. This is the reason I am here today, by the love of God and our parents. God and our parents built a solid foundation that I was able to stand on. Oh Lord God, I thank you for my parents. I know I was not always good to them or You, yet they love me anyway. My mother was a special mother to all my brother, and sisters; the love she gave us no one else could give to us. She was a mother who cared for her children. Oh God, she has been a blessing to her children. My father deceased early during our life. He was a God-fearing man, and he provided for us the best he knew. Later he went to be with the Lord, leaving my mother with eight children to care for by his second marriage. I thank God they were able to lead us all to Christ at an early age. When my mother and father were alive, I remember many times they would fall on their knees and call on God to take care of their children. They would pray and seek God's faith in the midst of storms. My family was not rich; we were poor, but rich with love. My father had his own farm but with such a large family of twenty children, there was very little to go around at times. I would see the hurt on my parent's faces. They had to struggle to support their family. They would go lacking so we could eat and have clothes to go to school and have clothes to attend church. We had to work on the farm, go to school, come home, work feeding the livestock, cut firewood, and do our homework. Year after year this was the life we grow up with. As I was growing up there were times I would disobey my father, but he would always cause me to change my mind by using the leather belt. **Proverbs 23:13-14** says, "Withholds not correction from the child: for if thou beatest him with the rod, he shall not die. Thou shalt beat him with the rod, and shalt deliver his soul from hell." In **Ephesians 6:1-3** admonishes, "Children, obey your parents in the Lord: for this is right. Honour thy father and mother, (which is the first commandment with promise.) That it may be well with thee, and thou mayest live long on the earth." Now my mother is going on to be with the Lord. I am the oldest. As I look back over my life, I am blessed to be alive; I am blessed to know God is my heavenly Father. I am blessed to have such wonderful and loving parents who guided my life in the right direction. Oh I thank the Almighty God for my sister and brothers. We are all blessed by the direction given by our parents and the blessed hand of God that has guided us and is still guiding our family.

God brought to my mind in **May of, 2002,** when I was young, and all my brothers, sisters our aunts and uncles and friends would always ask my father who is the one that will lead your people. I never really understood what they meant until later on in life when they explained it to me. My father had sons named from the Bible: Elisa, Simon, Paul, Moses, Abraham, James, and Joseph. God was supposed to rise up one to lead his people. But my name was Henry and I had a speech problem, I stuttered when I talked, and they would make fun and say, "Not you." I never did let this bother me. I knew I would become a "Nobody," So how could God choose me; who am I Lord? I feel I am still not the one. God has chosen me but I don't fully understand all this means. I know one day my Lord will reveal it in time, if I just wait and put my trust in Him.

My half sister Mattue has been a blessing from God to help shape and mold my life. I love her with my whole heart; she is a God-fearing sister. She also been a blessing in the community, helping to raise other families' children and bringing them up with love, respect, and the grace of God. She was a great support to our family after our father passed on. She was a blessing to our mother in her time of need. I pray the holy God will continue to cover her with his hand. July of 1999 I visited her and she let me borrow a book called The Layman's Bible Encyclopedia. How did she know this book would be a major force in my life? O God I thank You because You are an all knowing God; You know just what I needed. What a blessing that my heavenly Father has provided all my needs. In **Philippians 4:19** say, "But my God shall supply all your need according to his riches in glory by Christ Jesus."

Lord, let me acknowledge You, Christ Jesus my Savior, because you are the truth and living God. You are full of love and compassion. You are my shepherd, who leads me into your paths of righteousness. God, lead me into the blessed hope of my salvation and the promise of eternal life. Lord, I pray whoever reads these words will be touched by the hand of God. May Your grace by unto them and peace from God our Father. The peace of Jesus Christ continues to bless you in all spiritual blessings in heavenly places.

During my early years growing up I always wanted to learn how to play a guitar. I was able to save up enough money to purchase one. I wanted to play like Chuck Berry, the rock and roll singer. I tried and I tried. I could not learn how to play. A man came to our house and he said, "Son, first you must sell your soul to Satan;" then you will learn how to play. "You must go out and sit on a graveyard and ask Satan to teach you to play." I took his advice. I was young and I didn't know much about God. But first I had to get up enough nerve to go near a graveyard. Time passed but I finally went. When I arrived I could not sit on the grave. It seemed as if something was preventing me from sitting on the grave. I became afraid and ran away and never went back. All these years I have not though about it since, until the last week of **April, 2002.** God brought this back to my mind and showed me that He had prevented me from selling my soul to Satan. I started praising and thanking God for not letting me sit on that grave. Tears of joy were running down my face. Oh, what a mighty God I service! All through my life God has been there for me, according to my blueprint that only God knows. Only God knows which direction our lives will go. He also knows what our futures will be like. **Isaiah 26:3-4** says, "Thou wilt keep him in perfect peace, whose mind is stayed on thee: because he trusteth in thee. Trust ye in the Lord for ever: for in the Lord JEHOVAH is everlasting strength."

Strengthen Your Heart with Confidence

GOD'S BLUEPRINT was designed to split my wife and me up. God had to work upon my life and prepare me to do His will. This was the second part of my task from God. His plan took me through the fire; these were the hottest days of my life; I thought God had forgotten all about my soul. At times I felt I was burning in hell. That's how bad it was I thought Satan was winning the battle by pulling me down into the pit, and God was going to allow it to happen just to see if I could hold on to His unchanged hand or if I would give up on Him. God's grace and mercy would not let Satan have his way in my life. He was in control the whole time I was going through the fire with my wife. He knew just how much I could bear and how much purging was needed to purify my heart, body, and soul. God set my life plan in motion to see how I would react under the pressure, the fire that was burning all around my soul. This was a time of testing, of strong faith and will power from the Almighty God. **Galatians 2:20** says, "I am crucified with Christ: nevertheless I live: yet not I, but Christ liveth in me: and the life which I now live in the flesh I live by the faith of the Son of God who loved me, and gave himself for me." There are going to be times in our lives when we must go through the burning furnace of fire when God wants to purify our lives. Until He get you ready hold on-have faith. **Psalms 130:5** say, "I wait for the Lord, my soul doth wait, and in his word do I hope."

At first, I did not agree with what God was doing in my life. Things were happening so fast and I was caught completely by surprise. I would fall on my knees and cry out to the Almighty God, How long; how much can I bear? Lord I don't hear you; where are you? When will you let my soul come free from this furnace of burning fire? He never answered my prayer. I would always read in **Psalm 27:6** says, "And now shall mine head be lifted up above mine enemies round about me: therefore will I offer in his tabernacle sacrifices of joy I will sing, yea I will sing praises unto the Lord." I was hurting and felt like giving up. He was right there all the time. I didn't understand why this was happening; there was no sign. This was a decision I had to make, but I did not know if this was God or Satan. Through it all I didn't give up. I kept my faith and trust in the One who had brought me this far. God says we must suffer as He suffered. Those of you who have held to His unchanged hand know that God is preparing you for something only he knows the outcome of. These thing were already set according to my blueprint.

From July 3, 2000, to October 3, 2000, I prayed to God morning, night, and through the day. No answer! During these days and night, I saw all I had lived for slipping away from me. There was nothing I could do to stop it.

That great day of October 3, 2000, God finally spoke. "Go tell your story, study My word, and your marriage will be saved." I felt the awesome power of God come over my soul with love and peace. I felt relief from something that was holding me down. I start praising, glorifying, and thanking the Almighty God in heaven. Oh, what a true living God we serve.

Little did I realize God wanted me for Himself! He wanted me just as I am. He wanted to break me, shape me, mold, me and make me over again. He had to break the mold of my life, purify me, and re-form me in His image. All of this was to prepare my soul for God's blueprint for my future to come.

My wife and I were taken apart by God. She asked me to sign separation papers. She kept "turning up the heat in the furnace. There were troubles happening all around me, and God knew it. Then things began to happen that were amazing! I would experience fear and worry and God would calm my worry and replace it with love, peace, and joy. All of these are the gifts of the Holy Spirit of God. The Spirit comforted me in the time of trouble. Situations will come your way but remember that God will bring you out of the fire without being burned. As you read in **Daniel 3,** notice the power of God's hand at work in the three Hebrew boys who did not bow down to idles because they were servants of the most high God. He says trust Him and put your confidence in Him. He loves us. He is calling us to be His disciples to go and work for Him.

I pray you will read these words and be strengthened in your heart to ask God to overcome your problems. Depend, on lean and put your trust in Him. **Psalms 118:8** says, "It is better to trust in the Lord than to put confidence in man. It is better to trust the Lord than to put confidence in princes."

God Provided Angels to Comfort My Soul

GOD HAS placed his angels around my head according my blueprint. In 1998 I started smelling a sweet smell. I would always try to find out what it was and where it was coming from. I would ask people of God and they would not know. When God split up my wife and me I would smell the scent often, every day. I spoke with a pastor and discovered it was an angel of God. He has given me the knowledge and understanding of his word. **Psalms 34:7** says, "The angel of the Lord encamped round about them that fear him, and delivered them." **Psalms 91:11** says, "For he shall give his angels charge over thee, to keep thee, in all thy ways." **Exodus 23:20** says, "Behold, I send an angel before, and to bring thee into the place which I have prepared." God has given me the ability to communicate with the angel. I would smell the angel's scent and ask a question. If the answer were true the scent would go away. If the scent lingered, the answer was no. That amazing scent is with me all the time. It an awesome feeling to have angels around you all the time providing you with such a sweet smelling scent from Heaven. There is nothing on earth that can compare. This is more than incredible and amazing. Are you in tune with your relationship with God? You can receive this same blessing. He is not a respecter of persons. His blessing is for all Saints. I praise and thank the Almighty God all through the days and through the night. There is no other god in heaven or on earth who can do what God has done in my life. If you know the Lord the way I know him, then you know an amazing God. He has a blueprint for your life. Won't you let Him take you on a spiritual journey?

I will bless and glorify the name of my Lord for His abundance of love, peace, and grace. I pray that I may be kept in the understanding of the truth of His word. Lord, lead me into a quiet and peaceable life, in godliness and honesty that I may be acceptable in the sight of my God and savior.

Don't Worry; God Is Your Protector

IN ACCORDANCE with God's blueprint for my life, God carried me through some miraculous things. One summer, during school vacation, I went to Norfolk, Virginia, to live with my brother. I was to visit my cousin who lived on the other side of the city. I only saw her once. I told her mother I would come to visit them one day. About two months later, I decided to go over. I was coming from out in the country where everyone was family and friends. There were no gangs. I had never heard of or seen a gang until I visited Norfolk. I didn't think anything about it. As I got near my cousin's house three boys came up to me. They wanted to know what I was doing in their neighborhood and where I had come from. I started to explain and looked up to see about twenty boys had surrounded me. I never saw them coming. I didn't know where they had come from so quickly. I figured this had to be the gang I had heard about. One of them got in front, while the other was in back of me. They were ready to jump me. The one in front drew his hand back to strike me. Out of nowhere my cousin jumped in and stopped his hand, pushed him back, and said to leave him alone.

God brought this back to my remembrance to remind me that He was right there to protect me from any harm. He said I will never leave you and I am always standing by you. **II Samuel 22:3** say, "God of my rock; in him will I trust: He is my shield, and the horn of my salvation, my high tower, and my refuge, my saviour; thou savest me from violence."

Oh God, I thank you for saving my soul from the hand of Satan. I was in trouble and you delivered me out of my distress. What a mighty God I serve.

Psalm 136:1,4,12 says, "Give thanks unto the Lord; for he is good; for his mercy endures forever, to him who alone doeth great wonders; for his mercy endures forever. With a strong hand, and with a stretched out arm; for his mercy endures forever."

Trust and Have Faith in God

GOD'S BLUEPRINT took me through another period of my life. Prior to going on full-time active duty with the National Guard, I was already assigned to the National Guard and was working with General Motors at the same time. I had just taken the post office exam.

There was a sergeant major, who was full time active duty. He asked me to take a full time position. I said no; I'm not interested. A month later, he called me again. I told him I had been accepted to work for the post office. A week later, the sergeant major called me and offered me a full time position as assistant operational sergeant. He told me we must fill the position or we will lose it back to the National Guard Bureau. I said I would come by to see him. That same week, I visited the sergeant major, and he sent me to see the Captain. He said, "We have interviewed eighteen soldiers and no one was qualified." I was amazed and asked. "Why do you all think I am qualified? He replied We have seen what you are capable of doing." I said, "I don't think I am any more qualified than the other applicants are." He said "We want you for this position." I said, "I need to talk with my wife, since I have already been accepted at the post office."

I went home and explained to my wife. I felt God leading me to accept the full time army position. On Friday I called to accept the position. Six month later, a warrant officer came and said I have some bad news. I said, "What are you talking about?" He replied, "Your position has been abolished. There are no other positions open." I told myself I should have accepted the post office position; now I needed to look for employment. I asked God, "What is going on? Help me Lord; I need you." The next day the warrant office came and said "You are the luckiest person I have ever seen. The National Guard Bureau reinstated the position."

It was strange, but I was not worried. I believed God would make a away. I don't understand why people fail to trust and believe in Jesus Christ. Some people believe in luck, but I trust in the true living God. Satan tried to hurt me by showing me that God can't be trusted. God is all knowing and He is the Powerful Almighty God. He says who believes in Him shall have life and will be blessed. **Psalms 4:5** says, "Offer the sacrifices of righteousness, and put your trust in the Lord." in **Psalms 112:7** says, "He shall not be afraid of evil tidings his heart is fixed, trusting in the Lord."

God's mighty hand continued to move in my life while in the service. Six years into this position there was a time for other opportunities. There was another position that came open involving controlling the budget and preparing orders to send soldiers to school. I applied for that position. I wanted a change and I really wanted to work in that position. I was not accepted. As time passed I continued as the assistant operation sergeant. Later I became the operation sergeant as a sergeant first class. My job was to prepare training schedules, review training schedules, prepare operation orders, request training areas, review ammunition requests, and develop yearly training-plans. I also commanded and controlled the battalion headquarters and five other companies.

One day my commander wanted to know if I was interested in the position as a First Sergeant of a company. I thought about it and said this would be too much of a load. He said I would continue my same duties and be the First Sergeant I had to refuse for three simple reasons. One, I never would see the execution and result of all the planning and coordinating I did two, I would never know what went right or wrong during the execution and evaluation phase of the result. And three, I was not qualified to become a First Sergeant.

God trains, shapes, and molds us for His purpose, to carry out His will. He equips us with love, faith, knowledge, and understanding of His word. We should be eager to see how well we can please Him by doing his will He has already given us. Sometimes we are eager to accept something while on our journey that we know God has not placed in our benefits package. These thing can be attractive, and a temptation to us. This is a problem in church. Leaders are not supposed to place people into positions without knowing their spiritual gifts that God has given them, yet they are placed into positions not in accordance with their gifts. This causes confusion and problems in the church.

I Corinthians 12:7-10 says, "But the manifestation of the Spirit is given to every man to profit withal. For to one is given by the Spirit the word of wisdom to another the word of knowledge by the same Spirit. To another faith by the same Spirit; to another the gift of healing by the same Spirit, to another the working of miracles; to another prophecy; to another discerning of Spirit; to another divers kinds of tongues; to another the interpretation of tongues." After I said no to the position, he told me I would never make Master Sergeant, as I didn't say anything. My faith was in God and whatever he had for me in His blueprint for my life. There was nothing I had to worry about. There is no man on this earth that can change what God has already promised.

I knew all the time God wanted me to tell people to put their trust and faith in Him. It doesn't matter when people try to pressure you into what they think is right. Don't give in. Trust God. Only God holds the key to our direction and future. If you know who your Heavenly Father is, no one can discard your dreams or block your blessings. God is a never failing God. I am amazed as I type these words, God's Spirit is upon my soul, and God took me from Sergeant First Class through the rank of Command Sergeant Major. This is the highest rank in the Army as enlisted soldier Oh God, I thank you. I was able to stand firm in the hand of God and believe every good and perfect thing came from God above. While I was standing firm with God, He was using me to spread his Good News to His people and bring His people to salvation and the true knowledge of Jesus Christ.

Lord God, I will never leave you or forsake you. Lord, you are the God I love and I trust with my whole heart because you have been everything to me. Lord, I know you love me more than I will ever know. I can never thank you for all you have done for me. I pray and hope all Christians will put their trust in you and let you be the head of their lives. If they will do this, they will never leave you again, because they will be amazed at what a powerful hand You have.

Power Is in the Faith of God.

WHAT AN incredible powerful, God we serve. He knows all things. The position I applied for and didn't receive at the time I requested. God gave to me in His own time. I completely forgot all about it. The Holy Spirit came upon me the week of **February 22, 2001**, and brought all this before my mind. My eyes filled with tears of joy and God said write these words in your book. This will teach My people how to be patient and stand on faith. It is amazing and incredible what God has don in my life! He reminded me that He gave me all these things because I was faithful to Him and He wanted me to tell the saints what it means to be faithful to God. After ten years had passed, God moved me into that position. If it was not for the blood of the cross, this could not have been possible.

Galatians 5:5 says, "For we through the Spirit wait for the hope of righteousness by faith." **Psalm 52:9** says, "I will praise thee forever, because thou hast done it: and I will wait on the name; for it is good before thy saints." He looked down on me and saw my need. He gave me everything I need in life according to His blueprint. Oh what an incredible God I serve. He is amazing; I don't deserve any of this! There are others who are worthy than I, am. I have felt God's presence upon my soul and it is an incredible feeling. If heaven is like this, Lord, I am ready to go. But I know He has more work for me. I must stay focused and do whatever He has waiting for me, according to my blueprint. I will live every day of my remaining life to please His will, It is not about me; it is all about my Lord God Almighty. I know one day He will call me home and I want to be able to say, "Yes Lord I did my best."

I will continue to pray for all Christians that they may seek the will of God and receive His power to serve other with love. **Act 6:5a** says, "And the saying pleased the whole multitude: and they chose Stephen, a man full of faith and of the Holy Ghost."

The Power of God's Holy Spirit

WHAT I am about to say is so incredible I don't know how to explain it. Every day since **July, 2001,** God had cover me with his blood, water, and Holy Spirit; it is an amazing feeling to be in the presence of the Holy, true; living God. What I am saying is you need to know the power of His presence. It is something you must feel for yourselves to know and understand that God is real and personal. I know He is with my soul every day. I know the awesome feelings that come upon my soul of God's eternal glory from heaven. My mind, my heart, and soul are so at peace with God. His love covers me with such a great compassion and tender mercy. It is His redeeming love of His holiness and precious peace of sanctification. I ask God sometimes why this is happening to me this way. Then His Holy Spirit will bring it to my mind. "You been faithful to my every word. You are going through pain and suffering for my namesake; you have been patient and obedient. You carry your cross everywhere you go. You stumble, but you don't fall. You are doing as I command you. You always pray for my people. You go to hospitals to visit the sick, and pray for them. You visit nursing homes and pray, read scripture, preach, and teach Sunday school. You speak my words to everyone you meet by blessing them with my Love and care." God had told me He will touch everyone I come in contact with. He will cover them with His blessings. He is my shepherd and I will continue to carry out His will. Every day my handkerchief is wet with tears of joy because I can't hold the tears back when I think about my heavenly Father who loves me.

He wants to love all His Saints and to have them receive the same blessed feelings from the Holy Spirit of God, to know His power, and strength, and the knowledge of God to open up the mysteries of God, His wisdom, and understand of His word. All we have to do is know Him wholeheartedly, and to love Him with all our hearts, minds and souls. Seek to gain knowledge of His word and live by faith and help other in need of pleasing God.

He knows my heart is not holy like His; therefore I must call upon Him each day. He takes my sins upon His shoulders, and carries them to the foot of His cross. He washes me in the true living blood and water of Christ Jesus. He has redeemed my soul by His blood. He has created in me a new heart with love and grace, and mercy of His righteousness. He has given me a Comforter, which is the Holy Ghost. The Holy Spirit lives in the temple of my heart, which is the church and the church, goes wherever He lead us to go and do God's will.

Joel 2:29,32a says, "And also upon the servants and upon the handmaids in those days will I pour out my sprits. And it shall come to pass, that whosoever shall call on the name of the Lord shall be delivered." Therefore will Lord wait, that he may be gracious unto you, and therefore will he be exalted, that he may have mercy upon you: for the Lord is a God of judgment: blessed are all thy that wait for Him.

The Great Commandment of God's Love

THE MOST effective way to spread the Good News is by the love of Christ. God's people are to tell others about the love of Jesus Christ and the love that God has for them. Love will change people's hearts. Love will cause people to open up and talk to you. They will in turn show love to you. Love is missing in the lives of people today. Family love is missing. Church love is missing. Love has been replaced by the world's system of materialism. The world's system has become a controlling factor in people's lives. It is the things of the world that have taken us from the love of Christ. People of today, must understand the things of the world won't last. Every time man invents another item, we have to buy it. We have become a people who worship idols and images of false gods. The material thing such as the Internet cell phones, automobile, evil TV shows, expensive clothes, expensive tennis shoes, these things and more have replaced God in our lives. For many Christians we place God so far back we only give Him two hours on Sunday. I pray to the Almighty God that people will give up on the world system and put their trust and love in the Almighty and everlasting God. He is a God who will never fail; He is a God of love. He wants to place love in our hearts. Love is the most effective way to bring people back to their first and only true love. He said we must have the mind of Christ to spread the love of Christ to the people of Christ. His love will bring us out of darkness. All through Christ's life on earth, He showed love and compassion to all of his people. He said, "Love one another." When we disobey Christ by not showing love to His people, we are not doing the will of God. People are still in darkness and hurting, looking for something to fill their empty void.

Oh God, we need more of your children to come out from the world, and ask to be clothed in your righteousness of your true salvation. Then they can go out and spread the Good News of Jesus Christ. People are really hurting and they need to know where they can find relief. God is the answer. He is a healer and a loving God.

In the great commandment found in **Matthew 22:37-39** says, Jesus said unto him, "Thou shalt love the Lord thy God with all thy heart, and with all thy soul, and with thy entire mind. This is the first and great commandment. And the second is like unto it. Thou shalt love thy neighbor as thyself."

Family, church, friends and neighbors do we really understand what this verse means for our everyday living? It means just what it says: love the Lord with all our hearts, souls and minds. What does these word mean? Does it still mean we have time for the world? No we must involve Christ Jesus, love in everything we do to glorify God in heaven. All through the Bible when God's people sacrifice their soul, unto Him, they are able to live peacefully and receive all His blessing promise of Jesus Christ. Families must pray together and ask the Lord to lead them, guide them, ask Him to allow them to help someone today, and let Christ love precede out of our mouths to bring peace to someone else soul, heart and Christians, you will be surprised if you show God's loving words to someone in your walk, or friends, at work, wherever God's lead you to help someone, and you will be blessed to see their faces. What is happening to us saints? We have let the world full our hearts. We don't know how to live our daily life with Christ Almighty.

Our biggest downfall is very little love for our neighbor; the world has made ourselves secret not to get involved or not doing anything to help someone in need. God said love your neighbor; how can you love someone you don't know anything about them? Loving your neighbor does mean you know someone that you can help or someone in trouble and they need your help, but you fail to get involved because the world says every man is for himself, God's commandment doesn't mean anything to our hearts, souls, and mind anymore..

A neighbor is a friend, neighbor next door, community, or anyone who is in trouble and in need of help. You know the Good Samaritan in **Luke 10:29-33** read this and understand, "A certain man fell among thieves they wounded him leaving him half dead, a pries saw him, he passed by. A Levite didn't wonted to get involve. But a certain Samaritan had compassion and help him." What God has given us with His love in our hearts we should be glade to help our neighbor. This is what God call love and faith is in action in **James 2:15-16,17** say, "If a brother or sister be naked, and destitute of daily food, and one of you say unto them, Depart in peace, be ye warmed and filled; notwithstanding ye give them not those things which are needful to the body; what doth profit. Even so Faith, if it hath not work, is dead, being alone." We say we love the Lord and our neighbor and yet we fail to do His will by not show love and helping our neighbor, God said O vain man that faith is dead.

Every morning I pray and ask the Lord to lead, direct and guide my footsteps and lead me to help someone along my way. Saints, it is unbelievable how God uses me with His love to help my neighbors who are in real need. Every neighbor God allows me to help is done by His Holy Spirit speaking to my soul and saying give freely with no return. When you pray and ask God to lead you to help someone He will do just as you ask, this you will not have to worry, God will not let anyone trick you out of something you think they don't need. God always know the heart of a person; no man can fool God. Christians, many times God will put us through situations to test our faith, you have money that you need for something very important, but God will put His spirit upon your soul to give this money to someone in need. You don't know how bad this person needs this money, but God say give it, because He knows that person's need is more important than your need. Will you obey or disobey God's calling? Giving is from the heart of love. If we Christians have not been taught how to have a loving and compassionate heart to help our neighbor, than our heart is not right with God, we have a closed heart for those in need; only Christ Jesus can change our hearts to service God calling. This is why many Christians of today don't have a strong faith; their lives are not producing spiritual fruit for the Lord; our works are dead. Christians, our problem is that we think we know everything; we are too quick to listen to our pastor, and are not asking God how to read and study His Bible for ourselves, listen and heard what God is saying to us and asked God to give you a clear understanding of His holy word, that you may have a loving heart to help your neighbor in need. God say if you let me teach you the truth, your life will be richly bless by the Holy Spirit of the true living God Almighty.

Galatians 5:14-15,18 say, "For all the law is fulfilled in one word, even in this thou shalt love thy neighbour as thyself. But if ye bite and devour one another, take heed that ye be not consumed one of another. But if ye be led of the Spirit ye are not under the law." **Ephesians 4:25** says, "Wherefore putting away lying, speak every man truth with his neighbour: for we are members one of another

The backslider, who has gone back in the world, God loves you. He wants you back in His house. God promises if you come back to Him, He will bless you more than you were blessed at first.

It is God's will for His church Christians to spread the Good News about the love of Jesus Christ and telling lost soul how they can be saved and God will manifest His love in their hearts. The love of God can do incredible things in your if you are committed to let Him take charge of your life.

God wants Christians to go and tell the lost sinner that Jesus has already paid the price.

God's love can make you a new person by transforming your life into Christ likeness.

God's love can make you walk and talk differently, more like Christ.

God's love can cause you to live a happy, peaceful, and joyful life, with the love of Christ.

God's love can make you Christ-centered, by walking in the footsteps of Christ.

God's love can make you Christ-like, by carrying your cross of Christ daily.

God's love can change your hatred to love for all others. This is the will of Him.

God's love can stop your worries and give you peace of mind and comfort. He wants every one to live peacefully.
God's love can heal your sickness and make you well. God says pray for one another to be healed.
God's love can overcome your problems, and give you joy. Put your trust in Him.
God's love can bring you back to Christ because Jesus Christ is standing, waiting.
God's love can bring sinners to Christ. God is standing at your door knocking.
God's love can overcome your enemies and give you confidence to stand firm in God's hand.
God's love can change our negative attitude to a Christ-like attitude. Look to God, put your faith and trust in him, and get understanding of God's word.

God wants us to be Christ-centered, with an open heart of love. When our heart is open, we can receive the thirteen blessings of God's love that He has for us. He wants to give us peace and joy down in our hearts. He wants to give us His knowledge, purity, glory, kindness, meekness, and faithfulness. Christ wants to show love, but first we must come into a true understanding, loving relationship with Him. Each day we must strive to be more Christ-like with our talk, and with our walk. He wants us to love Him more than the world. He wants us to walk in His footsteps. God said, My greatest commandment is to love me with all your heart, mind ,and soul; the second love your brother as you love yourself. **Colossians 3:14** says, "And above all these things put on charity, which is the bond of perfect ness. I am a true, living witness."

He has placed these thirteen blessing in my heart, mind, and soul. God has given me the knowledge and boldness to spread His Good News wherever I go, in my talk and in my walk with the Lord. He wants His children to have compassion for the poor, hurting, and lost people by showing love. He didn't save us to sit down and look down on the poor unsaved people. (Don't look down on your brother or a sinner.) Ever since the beginning of time, God has been using people to spread the Good News. God did not bring us this far to stop the plan and purpose He has for our life. Our blueprint is God's master plan that he has for our life. This plan is for us to love Him and our brother.

We are going through a critical time in history. Children are dying more today than ever; the rich are getting richer, and the poor are getting poorer. Satan and his mighty army are on the march. There are more churches today than ever, yet we are losing the battle. Where are God's people? And what are they doing? God needs His people to spread the Good News more than ever. Satan is taking over God's churches, the family, and marriages. These are the three most important elements of the church. Satan knows this. He is working hard to destroy these three elements. Satan's job is to kill, steal, and destroy. Christians, I pray to Almighty God that you will spread the Good News of love among the poor who are hurting. Please have compassion on these people and tell them about the love of Jesus Christ. Your encouragement will give them hope, comfort, and confidence. Tell them your testimony and how God saved you from your life of sin. Be real and show a Christ-like attitude. Don't be ashamed of God. A real child of God has the love of God in his/her heart and soul. By doing this you are bringing glory and honor to Him. As you do this, your heart will be richly blessed by His mighty power from Heaven.

We Must Suffer But Give Thanks to God Almighty

I PRAISE and thank God, the Father of our Lord Jesus Christ! The Father is an all-merciful God, who always gives us comfort. He comforts us when we are in trouble, so that we can share that same comfort with others in trouble. **Psalm 23** we read, "Yea, though I walk through the valley of the shadow of death, I will fear no evil: for thou art with me; thy rod and thy staff they comfort me." We will share in the terrible sufferings of Christ, but also in the wonderful comfort he gives us. We suffer in the hope that you will be comforted and glorify the name of the Lord. Let your suffering strengthen your heart that you may become more like Christ. We saints must understand we are to suffer for the gospel of Christ Jesus. Don't let its deter us; it will only make us grow stronger in the Lord. It will test our faith in the Lord. As we suffer, let us praise and give thanks to the Lord. We are people of strong faith, courage, and determination to spread the Good News of Christ Jesus. Let not your hearts run weary or be troubled; instead rejoice and give thanks to the Almighty God. Lord, help us carry on your good work, reaping the harvest of lost souls. Let us comforter them in love, helping them make a decision to receive Christ. We are to comfort those in need, those who are hurting. Be a friend to them. Show them you have a compassionate heart of love toward them.

When you work for Him be patient. Endure your suffering like Christ. Don't become disappointed. When thing don't seem to go your way, remember who is in charge. The biggest disappointment you can make is getting ahead or put yourself in place of God. If you do this, you will suffer more than you can bear. Remember, you are not in charge. Always remember your Heavenly Father is in control of your Christian life.

Saints and fellow friends of God, I want you to know what a hard time I had in my days. My sufferings were so horrible and so unbearable at times I felt like giving up. It seemed certain I was losing the battle; my wife was winning and God was nowhere around. I was preparing to give in to her. Instead the grace and mercy of God came knocking at my door. God said, "My son, I'm with you always." He reached down with His holy hand and picked me up. "You are going to be my disciple; I will prepare you to go through suffering for My name' sake. Stop; put your trust and faith in Me. I will test your heart to stand fast in your suffering. I will always be there to deliver you from so great of trial of affection." Suffering is God's purpose to test our faith, strengthen our hearts, and build up our knowledge and understanding to stay strong because these things will come: temptation, trial, oppression, sickness, diseases, and other problems will come, so remember this is done to glorify your Heavenly Father during your suffering. **Roman 8:17** says, "And if children, then heirs; of God, and joint heirs which Christ; if so be that we suffer with him, that we may be also glorified together." Fellow saints, we must start trusting God, who raises His Son from the dead to life. God saved us from the dead in sin. **II Corinthians 1:4-5** says, "

Who comforted us in all our tribulation, that we may be able to comfort them which are in any trouble, by the comfort wherewith we ourselves are comforted of God. For as the suffering of Christ abound in us, so our consolation also abounded by Christ" My prayer to God is that these words will give comfort to our hearts in time of suffering. Also I pray you will glorify and give thank to the Almighty God for sending us through trials of suffering, because when you come through, there will be a transformed by the renewing of your mind. You will never be the same against. Saints look up and believe in the saving grace of the divine power of our Heavenly Father, the one who we love so dearly. We give all praise and honor to His holy Name. The Almighty God will hear us and answer our prayers during all our troubles.

God's Power in Prayer

DO YOU believe in the power of prayer? I am a true believer and I pray and hope you have that same belief. The power can raise the dead, the power can heal the sick, the power can overcome darkness, the power can overcome your financial problems, the power can overcome your marriage problems, and the power can overcome your family problems. There is no end to what the power of God's prayer can do. Put your trust and faith in Him and believe in what you are asking. I have heard about your faith in the Lord Jesus and your love for all of God's people. For I never stop being grateful for you, as I mention you in my prayers. I ask the glorious Father and God of our Lord Jesus Christ to give you his spiritual knowledge of the power of prayer. The Spirit will make you wise and let you understand what prayer truly means. My prayer is that the light will flood your hearts and that you will understand the hope that was given to you when God chose you for His purpose. And my prayer will help you discover the glorious blessings of fellowship together with all of God's people.

There are times in our lives when we get caught up in the darkness of the world. I was victimized by sin away from God, and the power of His prayer had departed my soul. I was left with a shadow heart that caused Satan to take my soul back into darkness. When I tried to pray, asking for my needs, my word didn't have any feeling or no real meaning. God didn't hear my prayers. There were sins in my heart; God would not answer. **John 9:31** says, "Now we know that God heareth not sinner: but if any man be a worshipper of God, and doesth his will, him he heareth." I would pray and ask the Lord forgiveness for my sins. **Romans 6:14** says, "For sin shall not have dominion over you: for ye are not under the law, but under grace". Lord, I have turned my back and I have sinned against you. Oh Lord cleanse my unrighteousness; release me from the bondage of sin. Take my sin to the foot of your cross, and wash me in the blood of the lamb. And the power of His prayer set my soul free. Now you shall stand in His holy place with clean hands and pure heart free from sin. I prayed and received my blessing form God, and righteousness from the Lord of His salvation. He will hear and answers your prayer if you are committed of confessing your sin to God. **Matthew 26:41** says, "Watch and pray, that ye enter not into temptation." You must be totally committed to study His word. Attend church. Let His light shine through your heart with love, and be filled with the Holy Spirit of Christ Jesus.

Jesus is standing by, waiting to hear from you, ask Him for your needs, by prayer and fasting. I truly believe prayer and fasting work. Let us turn our hearts to God and seek His guidance for prayer and fasting. We all have sinned and come short of glory in God. Don't let your sin keep you away from God's glory. Saints God has given us the Holy Spirit that comes with the power of prayer; don't hold on to it; release it unto God. He wants to hear from you each and every day. When we pray, we are in communication with God. You are glorifying His name in heaven.

This is the most powerful weapon we have to fight off Satan. Don't let it become dull. There are many saints who don't know they have such an awesome and powerful weapon. There are some who don't know how to use it. This is why so many are not able to fight off Satan. Prayer will draw us closer to God. The more we pray to Him, the stronger our relationship with Him will become. Prayer will give you peace of mind. Talk to God; don't be afraid of Him. He loves you. He wants to walk with you. He wants to talk with you along your journey.

He is there to guide your every footstep. How can we refuse a God who wants to love us with His tender mercy and care? All He wants to do is build a home in heaven just for you. I pray you will not let Him down. He is standing by waiting on you. Oh Lord, I pray right now that you will open up the hearts of those saints and provide them with the knowledge to know how to use the most powerful weapon at their disposal. Let God bring you joy, with all glorious love, and have an everlasting abundance of peace. Whenever trouble comes your way, fall on your knees and look up to heaven and call on the Lord. And say, "Oh Lord my God, come and see about me. The enemies have come upon my soul. I need you to fight my battle." He will hear your cry. He will come and rescue your soul. Saint asks God to purify your hearts, and comfort you during tour trials. Prayer is not only behind close doors. Prayer is just talking with Him. You can pray anywhere, anytime, in your vehicle, walking, singing praises to Him. He wants to have an open communication with you, so tell all your troubles. At times He wants us to be quiet and along with Him. Turn off the radio, TV and music and spend real personal and quiet time with Him, read His word, meditate on His word, and pray to Him.

One of the greatest gifts God has given me to pray for people. Each night He wakes me up around 3: a.m. depending on what time I go to bed. He has given me forty-three nations/countries, Presidents, world leaders, soldiers around the world, churches/leaders, families, poor people, schools/colleges, young people, hospitals, nursing homes, and my entire family and friends. I pray for each one individually from two to four hours each night and read His word, that thy will come to Christ and let Him be their savior and bring peace into their hearts, feed the poor and heal the sick, and draw saints closer to Christ Jesus. At times when I pray I feel the power of God speaking through my mouth. The church, families and the world are in real trouble and they need someone to pray for them. These people God's has laid upon my heart. I pray He will hear and answer my prayer. Will you ask God to help you pray? Do you have any love for God's people, saved or lost?

All through the Bible there are examples of prayers God has for us:

Matthew 9:38: Pray ye therefore the Lord of the harvest send forth laborers to harvest.

Luke 21:36: Watch ye therefore, and pray always, that ye may be accounted worthy.
Ephesians 6:18: Praying always with all prayer and supplication in the spirit.
Psalm 6:9: The Lord hath heard my supplication; he will receive my prayer
Matthew 21:22: And all things, whatever ye shall ask in prayer, believing, ye shall receive.

Prayer and Fasting Are More Than Just Talk

On November 23, 2002, there was a real burden upon my heart for several reason. My heart was heavy because of my love for all God's people all over the world, especially for Christians. Also, I was having difficulty with one of my subject at college. I could not gain the knowledge I needed to please my professor or God, and I felt like giving up. I would pray, "God, you sent me to college and this is one of my requirements (Spanish), but my mind will not open up that I may learn. "Lord, I need help, Lord. I can't make it on My own." Lord heard these words, and I sat down and wept, and mourned many days, and night on fasted, and prayed before the God in heaven. Oh Lord, God of heaven, the great and terrible God, have mercy upon my soul, hear my prayer of thy servant, which I pray before thee, Oh Lord, help my soul to gain the accepting knowledge I need to learn Spanish, and help your people to seek you and Lord give them salvation and grace.

Well, these things were weighing heavy upon my shoulders. I talked to God about going on a fast and pray until He made these things right. I would just drink water. The day of Thanksgiving I ate breakfast, after that I would not eat food for the next forty days. Thanksgiving of 2002, my wife cooked a big dinner. It was the first time since July of 2000. That food looked and smelled so good; it was tempting my mind, but my heart knew that was not right. I told her I was going away for the weekend to study and pray to God in a quiet place.

For the first five days I was ready to give up the fasting, I was hungry and my stomach was hurting. Cramps, aches, and pains would come over my body. I could not sleep. I was feeling so bad, I said, "Lord, forgive my sin. I can't do what I said I would for my love for your people." Lord, I don't understand why this is happening to my soul. A year earlier He had me to go on a fourteen-day fast and pray. I didn't feel this way, Lord I can't go on now. "what was I to do?" Satan is trying to make me give in. **Genesis 32:24-28** read, "and Jacob was left alone; and there wrestled a man with him until the breaking of the day. And when he saw that he prevailed not against him, he touched the hollow of his thigh; and the hollow of Jacob's thigh was out of joint as he wrestled with him. And he said, Let me go, for the day breaketh. And he said, I will not let thee go, except thou bless me. And he said unto him, What is thy name? And he said Jacob. And he said, Thy name shall be called no more Jacob, but Israel: for as a prince has thou power with God and with men, and hast prevailed."

That Sunday I returned home still feeling the same way ready to give up. That night God spoke to me and said, "Forty, forty, forty. I said, "Lord, is this you speaking or is this Satan? Satan get away from me; I rebuke you in the name of Christ, flee from my soul." The word started again, "Forty, forty, forty," I said, "Lord what are you saying? Do you want me to go on a fourth day fast and pray?" Immediately I felt fine. All pain left my body, and I knew He was calling me to go on another journey and He would carry me all the way. Then God took me to **Deuteronomy 9:18** says, "And I Moses fell down before the Lord, as at the first, forty days and forty nights: I did neither eat bread, not drink water, because of all your sins which ye sinned, in doing wickedly in the sight of the Lord, to provoke him to anger. I prayer therefore unto the Lord don't destroy the people be patience have mercy upon them redeemed them through your blood and set them free from sin, Oh Lord please hear my payer."

I am here to tell saints of God be careful what you pray and commit yourself to do for the Lord. If you think the storm and the fire is too strong, don't give up. He is only testing your heart and faith, but He will carry you through.

God created our blueprint according to His plan and purpose for every soul to carry out His will. He knew I would face persecution and suffering from Satan for His namesake. In **Psalm 109:21** says, "But do thou for me, O God the Lord, for thy name's sake: because thy mercy is good, deliver thou me." God uses evil to come against us, to test our faith and strengthen our hearts, souls, and minds, to carry out His will.

At Christmas my wife cooked another big dinner and I was tempted but my heart kept me on God's course. God led me to Maryland to visit my family; I had been fasting and praying for twenty- three days. Food was all around tempting my flesh but God would not let my soul bow down to Satan. Then He led me to some drink orange juice, then He led me on to Richmond, Virginia, to visit my sister. My sister was upset because I had lost so much weight. She was afraid I would get sick or something else could happen to me. I told her I was feeling fine. God was carrying me. While there, God allowed me to eat a piece of bread and an orange.

Then He led me to visit my family in Emporia Virginia. That Sunday my niece and sister were preparing for church. I asked them May I could go with them? They said, "Oh yes, we would love to see you go." We visited a church my father would take us to during the summer months. I hadn't visited that church in over forty years. God led me to tell a testimony and the power of God's Holy Spirit came upon that congregation; it was amazing how God moved in people's lives. The Holy Spirit was upon me so strong I knew then He was working through me. It was nothing about me, only the power and Spirit of my heavenly Father.

I returned home on day twenty-seven of fasting and prayer. On day thirty-three I was teaching a Sunday class at the nursing home and halfway through I felt dizzy and weak. I tried to go on, but I had to sit down. The nurse came and told me I needed attention. They all rushed in to see about me. They checked me and found no problem. I told them what God had led me to do and that I had not eaten any food. I had stopped drinking juice and had no water in seven days. The nurse said, "You need to drink something" I said, "No I promised God I would go all the way with His help." I still felt dizzy so I drank a cup of cold tea. Amazing things happened to me and I do not understand why. The nurse said my face turn white as snow. No other part of my body changed, only my face. I don't know why. I asked God but He gave me no answer.

For the remaining days I was very weak but my mind was very clear. I lost so much weight I had to cut two more holes in my belt to hold my clothes up. I could walk fine but I couldn't stand very long, **On January 8, 2003**, after forty days, God led me to eat food for the first time, and I thanked Him with my whole heart. Saints, with God there is no limit. What God can do through you if you have faith, with clean hands and a pure heart!

I indicated I was praying to God to help me to understand and speak Spanish. While on the fast, one night about 3:00, 0 clock in the morning, I was speaking Spanish perfectly and clearly, but I didn't know what I was saying. I start praying and thanking Jesus Christ. I new then my prayer had been answered; now all I had to do was keep studying, and wait. In His time I will speak just as He showed me. He will send me to feed His people who are hungry for His true living word. I have a strong compassion to see them come to Christ and receive their salvation.

Three Is An Important Number of God

THE MIDDLE of February, 2003, God brought to my mind three threes: the year 3/3/03, the first time in history this date ever appeared in AD. Then He took me into **I Corinthians 13:13** says, "And now abideth faith, hope, charity, these three; but the greatest of these is charity." **II Corinthians 13:1** says, "He said this is the third time I am coming to you. In the mouth of two or three witnesses shall every word be established?" Christ began His minister at 30, He was crucified at 33, His resurrection was on the third day, in Revelation 20 their three kind of people stand before God; dead, small and great. The Father Son, and the Holy Spirit are three in one. There are many three in the Bible they are important to the coming of the Lord. What is God telling me?

Well all through His Bible He has shown me many visions about what will come in the near future.

One Sunday I was teaching a Sunday School class at one of the nursing homes. After I had completed the lesson, God led me to go to another nursing home. I was there talking and sharing the word and love of Christ to the patients. Then He led me to a lady in another room. I started talking to her and she started telling me all her troubles. She said the nursing home had taken all the money for her huband and she only had thirty dollars to pay a five hundred-dollar bill. And it had to be paid on the third of March 2003. She kept talking about it would be due on the third of March and she was very worried. She didn't know what she was going to do. She kept saying the third and I can't pay my bill. She was eight-five years old and she had been a pastor. She said "Would you pray for me." I said "Yes," and then the Holy Spirit came upon my soul. God spoke to me and said "Ask her does she know what the third day, third month, and third year of two thousand is?" She said "No" so I began to tell her. Tears started running down my face and I felt the presence of God all around my soul and tears started coming from her eyes too. I told her Your bills are paid by God, the devil can't stop the mighty hand of God. Put all your problems in the hands of God; your worry and problems are over. He is going to poure out a blessing like you never seen before. "She said, "Oh thanks you Lord!" She said, "In all my years no one ever encouraged me the way you did." I told her it was nothing about me; I was sent to her by God I prayed for her that, God would keep her in perfect peace and perfect health then I departed. Two weeks later I saw her; God had answered her prayer on that day. Glory to the Holy Name of the prayer answer God.

As I was driving home the Holy Spirit spoke and said, "Those things I showed you 2003, God has begun to pour out His blessing among every nation."

On the third day of March I finished my test. The college had just come out with the summer schedule. I had been praying they would have English, which was one of my requirements for graduation, but they didn't have it I said, "Lord why? I thought you wanted me to finish this summer." I only needed twelve more credits. I felt bad; I had go back in the fall. A student spoke to me and told me God had something for me during the fall. I left and went out to sit in my vehicle to talk to God. As I was driving home something happened, and I felt a calm come over my soul. I felt at peace. I felt happy. I knew God was in control of my situation and there was nothing to worry about. That night I was praising, thanking, and worshiping Him with my whole heart. Lord God, you are the God of the whole creation; You know all thing, and You know my whole blueprint, Oh thank you, Lord.

The next day was the fourth of March. I witnessed God's blessings right in front of my eyes. That same day, saints told me some amazing blessings they had receive. Churches and saints, gird up your loins and get ready to see the power of God begin to fall in your world. That evening, God spoke and said Russian, Germany, France, Poland, Vietnam, Pakistan, Greek, England, Japan, India, the Middle East, South America, Central America, North America, and many other nations are becoming hungrier and thirstier for the word of God. Their needs are serious and they need a savior. I am their Lord God who can fill their empty hearts. I am rising up generations of people to go and feed them. Tell my church to called upon My holy name and ask for forgiveness of sin, and purify their hearts to become righteous in the eyes of God Almighty. I will come in to prepare my churches to receive her blessing. Prepare her hearts to go and feed the lost, hungry, and the poor and teach them the love of Christ Jesus. They are looking for the true word of God to ensure they have eternal life after death. Because God has shown mercy on whom I will have mercy, and I will have compassion on whom I will have compassion, you are not my people; but with mercy you shall be called the children of the living God. The nations, who follow not after the righteousness of God, now are calling and seeking the righteousness of God. **Isaiah 61:10a-11** says, "I will greatly rejoice in the Lord, my soul shall be joyful in my God. For he hath clothed me with the garments of salvation, he hath covered me with the robe of righteousness. For as the earth bringeth foth her bud, and as the garden causeth the things that are sown in it to spring forth; so the Lord God will cause righteousness and praise to spring forth before all the nation."

Save My Little Babies

FOR MANY years I have seen families torn apart, babies destroyed, and my heart weighs heavy every day and night. **The night of March 16, 2003,** I could not sleep because these things were on my mind and heart and kept me tossing and turning all night. About 3:30 in morning God spoke to me and "said save my little children three times." I got up and wrote the information down.

Oh my heavenly Father, you are the most high God, my heart is heavy, but let me first praise and glorify your holy name in heaven and on earth. You are a God of grace and mercy; how I love to praise the Lord and the King of Kings. God showed me these words in **Psalms 21:11** says, "Their fruit shalt thou destroy from the earth, and their seed from among the children of men. For thy intended evil against thee: they imagined a mischievous device, which they are not able to perform" **Psalm 27:10** says, "When my father and my mother forsake me, then the Lord will take me up." Man have committed abomination unto God by shedding His blood through their city, and women they are in the midst of it, they have defile themselves." **Ezekiel 22:12** says, "In thee have they taken gifts to shed blood; thou hast taken usury and increase, and thou hast greedily gained of the cities by extortion, and hast forgotten me, saith the Lord God."

Lord, from the depths of my soul to the rock of my salvation, my heart is increasingly troubled. Oh Lord, I cried out unto You with my voice. Oh Lord hear my prayer; come and save your babies from the wrath of Satan, and let them live. The world has gone mad. Your babies' lives are being taken right before your eyes. Men and women don't see any value in the life of Your creation anymore. Lord, you are the creator of everything upon this earth. You told man to watch over and keep it; now man has taken upon himself to destroy what you have created. How long, how long will you let man destroy your kingdom Oh Lord? **Romans 10:3** says, "For they being ignorant of God's righteousness, and going about to establish their own righteousness, have not submitted themselves unto the righteousness of God." Oh Lord, man needs to be put back in his rightful place. Every life is precious in the eyes of the Lord. We see how far love has departed from man and woman. Something as precious as a little baby is a soul, mind, heart, and a body to be loved by you. Their hearts are like a sold rock, wax cold, hateful and angry. How can people created by God be so evil toward little babies who can't help themselves? Lord, from where you have created us we have gone our own way, and have no regard for human life. Women, what happened to your moral sense of responsibility and duties to your child? When you destroy your baby, you are destroying Christ Jesus; do you think you will not see him or her again? You are wrong, remember man cannot destroy the soul and spirit of a baby or man. Don't you know your baby is calling you right now? Yes, they are calling all mothers. Babies are saying, "Mommy I love you, I miss you, why did you not save me? Why don't you want me? You don't love me Mommy?" **Psalm 22:1-2** says, "My God, my God, why hast thou forsaken me? Why art thou so far from helping me, and from the words of my roaring? O my God, I cry in the daytime, but thou hearest not; and in the night season, and am not silent." I found someone who loves me very much, and His name is Jesus, and He gives me everything I need in a mother and a father. Will you come and see me? I want to see you. Mommy, I am waiting to see you; I love you. Yes, mother and father, you will see them at the end of time and it will not be a time for rejoicing without God.

Save your babies; they belong to God, not you. God give them to you to keep, to teach them with love, to teach them right from wrong, to let them know about Jesus Christ, so let your life be a good, moral, and righteous example of Christ toward them. Remember, God didn't take your life; why would you take your baby's life? Remember these are not my words; as I write what my Father tells me, because the Holy Spirit is upon my soul as I write these words, I am only a messenger from God.

Lord, I pray women will read these words of the true living God and understand their sense of responsibility toward, babies. Wait upon the Lord and ask Him to give you strength to go through these dark days. Refrain from sex until marriage. Having babies is nothing to play with. Just because you feel no one loves you, why would you go make love, to get a baby to love? All your planing is built on nothing but sinking sand. Soon the wind will blow and your love will come crumbling down. Then you will think, "Why did I do this?" Many young ladies and men will have sex because they think it is fun or it feels like love. For a little while it is all right, then reality sets in. "Now what do I do? I have a problem, how should I handle it?" Satan is your father, and he will tell you to destroy it; you don't have time for a baby. There is more fun I have in the world for you. We are seeking higher gratification in the job market; highest standard of living, and a convening way to live happy, free from babies, to have more glorious time for ourselves and to have a good time pleasing our hearts.

Ezekiel chap 23:37,39,45 says, "That they have committed adultery, and blood is on their hands, and with their idols have, they committed adultery, and have also cause their son/daughter whom they bare unto me, to pass them through the fire, to devour them. For when they had slain their children to their idols, then they came the same day into my sanctuary to profane it; and, lo, thus have they done in the midst of mine house. And the righteous men they shall judge them after the manner of adulteresses, and after the manner of women that shed blood; because they are adulteresses and blood is in their hands."

Do you see how the enemy works in our lives? Those of us who don't know the Lord, Satan will do whatever is necessary to keep your mind and heart from the true living Christ. Ladies, do you know everything God does? He starts with a beginning and every baby is the beginning of life. Satan knows this is God plan. When you give Satan the authority to destroy God's babies, you haven validated the sacred plan of God. Because Satan knows this is the beginning of life of God's plan.

Lord, I pray you will save your people from the hand of Satan and release them into the hand of the true living God. I pray for their repentance and remission of sins and it shall be preached unto every man, women, boy and girl, and among all nations, beginning here in the United States. And let this be a reminder to all to turn ourselves to our Heavenly Father. **John 15:7** says, "If ye abide in me, and my word abide in you, ye shall ask what ye will, and it shall be done unto you." Ask the Lord to overcome the darkness of your heart and set you free. Lord, prepare me for your sanctuary to have clean hands and a pure heart that I may praise and worship your Holy name. And Lord, give me your comfort and salvation that I may abide with you the rest of my days.

These words the Holy Spirit brought to my heart to write unto the church. The church has abandon its rightful responsibility in supporting the most serious problem facing families today: involving young women/men in destroying life. (1) the church is to be an outreach among problem families. (2) Take time out of its busy schedule and teach families and young people why it so important not to have sex un-marriage? Teach them the conquest, heart ache and problem they are going to face. (3) Teach them the love of God doesn't want them to destroy their babies after making a mistake. First of all, put your trust, faith, and confidence in the true living God. Church, help them, comfort them, and give them encouragement to hold to God's un changing hand. Explain to them God's grace, mercy, and love are there for them. Teach them to refrain from the same mistake. (4) When there is a baby, this is where they need the love of Christ Jesus from the family and churches the most. They need help from the church with positive speaking attitude. Saints, do not destroy them or the family with your negative conversation (5) In God's eyes there is no one perfect; we are all sinners making mistake. Who gives us the right to bring judgment and evil upon someone because they made a mistake? Lord, help us to speak positively regarding your every word by teaching someone why it so important to save a baby.

This is the third time God led me up on top of the mountain and opened my heart and eyes wider to see the true mysteries of God's word. He said this nation is cursed because individual who had aborted their babies and have not called upon God asking for forgiveness of sin. And the country has not refrained from destroying God and His babies. He knows we all are going to make many mistakes in our lifetime, "but we never stop, we never learn, we never seek God for our sin of forgiveness." God will bring curses upon us because we are too proud to ask God for forgiveness. We are willfully disobeying Jesus Christ. God said in Jeremiah, I will pour their wickedness upon them, I will bring evil upon the men/women of the nations. God is speaking for this is the will of God to turn us over to the will of Satan. We must refrain from fornication: that every one of you should know how to possess his vessel in sanctification and honorable unto Christ Jesus, to be redeemed through the blood of salvation unto eternal heaven. So let us trust the Lord by calling upon His holy name, and ask Him to forgive us from our sins, and redeem us through the blood of the lamb, and clean us from all unrighteousness and make us white as snow, that we may receive His promises.

Father, Where Are You?

MY HEAVENLY Father spoke to me in early **April of, 2003,** with a strong convition of compassion about fathers who have abandoned their children and are not living up to their responsibilities. Who do we think we are that we can play with God's life? How dare we decide that we will not live up to our duties and responsibilities of the life we helped create? Has Satan taken us so far into darkness that it does not bother us anymore? God is not pleased or satisfied with our actions. Do we really not understand how many burdens we place upon the mother? God is looking down with tears in his eyes and wondering why He created man.

What God showed me may shock you. One day on my way from college I stopped at a red light. Sitting there God showed me a man walking across the street and said, "Man is like a dog running after every female he can find." I thought about what He said. Then I wondered, why would He tell me this? For the next three months I tried to get it out of my mind, but I could not. **On June 3, 2003,** at about 1:30 a.m. in the morning God led me to read **Isaiah 56:10-12** says, "His watchmen are blind: they are all ignorant, they are all dumb dogs, they cannot bark; sleeping lying down, loving to slumber. {Meaning they love to run around to find ladies who are willing to lay with them.} Yes they are greedy dogs, which can never have enough, and they are shepherds that cannot understand; they all look to their own way, every one for his gain from his quarter. Come ye, say they, I will fetch wine, and we will fill ourselves with strong drink; and to-morrow shall be as this day, and much more abundant." Man has abandoned all righteousness of God and he is under the control of his father the devil.

Man kind there, is hope to bring you out of all your problems and unbelief, your Heavenly Father still loves you and He wants to give you a better life, whereby you will be able take responsibility for your child, with the knowledge and understanding of God's love to help you live a peaceful life with Christ Jesus supporting your family.

Young men, one thing you are doing is so wrong, you will help bring a baby into this world, but when the time to face up to your responsibility you go and get yourself in trouble with the law.

You go to jail or go to prison; there you are free from your responsibility. You receive three meals a day, you sleep in your bed, and you join all your friends. You all get together and talk about the negative things you have done. As God says you are ignorant, not to know you are under the control of Satan. As long as you stay under his control your life will remain this way. Only God can release you from the wrath of Satan by confession and forgiveness of your sin through the blood of the living lamb of God.

He has show me a vision that young men will come for their children and will take care of them because it their responsibility. Your children are calling for their fathers. They are asking their mothers, "Where is my father?" What will she tell them? It is hard for them to sleep at night, because they miss their fathers. It is hard for them to study at school knowing their father is in jail or in prison. Fathers, how would you feel if you were in their shoes? What has happened in your life? Please do not bring this upon them. Have a heart of love so that your child will grow up and be proud to call you father. Men, I pray to God Almighty that you find it in your heart to help the one you left with the burdened down heart. Trying to be a mother and a father is not easy.

I pray you will be a true working father to support the mother and child. Marriage or no marriage, I pray God will intervene in the situation to make it right in the eyes of the Lord. Lord God, I pray for those young ladies who have stood up and waited on the blueprint You have for their lives. And I thank You that You saw her and have mercy upon her soul, by You change her life to follow the plan You have set before her life. And that she will be rewarded for her strong faith in the Christ Jesus taking care of the child.

Ladies and men, I pray to God that ye might be filled with the knowledge of His will in all wisdom and spiritual understanding, that you might walk worthy of the Lord unto all pleasing, being fruitful in every good work, and increasing in the knowledge of God. I pray He will strengthen you with all might, according to His glorious power, unto all patience and longsuffering with joyfulness. Give thanks unto the Father, which hath made us meet to be partakers of the inheritance of the saint in the light of God. Who has delivered us from the power of darkness, and has translated us into the kingdom of His dear Son. These are the words of the living God for those young men who have departed their responsibility.

The True Bible Is Missing from God's People

THERE ARE many churches that don't believe in the Old Testament, and this has been troubling my heart. Why would God write the Bible from Genesis to Revelation if He only intended for us to use only the New Testament? This is shorting the completed knowledge God intended for His saints to know. "No this is not God will's," this is man/Satan's will to keep us in darkness of God's word. God created the OT as an example for us not to make the same mistake as the holy people of God. **John Chap 1** in the beginning was the word, and the word was with God and the word was God. Every word is for our understanding of who God is and how we must follow His example by learning His prophecy and follow their example for the righteousness of God's will. His Spirit will guide us to follow Him the same way. **II Timothy 3:16-17** says, "All scripture is given by inspiration of God, and is profitable for doctrine, for reproof, for correction, for instruction in righteousness. That the man of God may be perfect, thoroughly furnished unto all good work." Without the knowledge and complete understanding of the Old Testament our life foundation can't fully understand the New Testament. In the NT there are many reference to the OT that was reference by Jesus and His disciples. Christians, we are being mislead by not understanding the complete Bible. Saints want you call on God and ask Him to show us the truth, and stop listening to man false teaching. Oh Lord, I pray our soul will not die before we become completed knowledge of Your word. **Deuteronomy 4:2a** say, "God is speaking, ye shall not add unto the word, which I command you, neither shall, ye diminish from it." **Proverbs 30:5-6** says, "Every word of God is pure: he is a shield unto them that put their trust in him add thou not unto His words, lest he reprove thee, and thou be found a liar." **Revelation 22:18-19** says, "For I testify unto every man that heareth the word of the prophecy of this book, if any man shall add unto these things, God shall add unto him the plagues. And if any man shall take away from the words of the book of this prophecy, God shall take away his part out of the book of life, and out of the holy city."

In late March of, 2002, God spoke unto me and said before the end of time, man will remove His Holy Name from His Bible. God, I don't understand The church is confusing its members about what being preached today from many Bibles, because in the congregation there are at lease five difference types of Bible and all have differing translations, so how can they keep up with what is being preached or taught? As I attend churches I have a King James Version and even I get lost and confused because their Bible doesn't always say what my Bible reads. Lord, your time is drawing near day by day. Saints, when are we going to wake up to the truth of God's holy word? Man is taking God's Bible and turning it into his own words to comfort your soul and make money, saints this is not pleasing to God Almighty. The word written in His Holy Bible is of God Himself; every word is alive. Because every word is the living spirit of Father Son and Holy Spirit. As you read His word God's will speak to your hearts with His holy spirit. If you are a true living child of God and you have man written Bible and you read it and if God doesn't speak to your heart, than you don't have a Holy Bible who word is of God Himself. I pray you will wake up before its become to late and seek the Lord for the right answer in chose the right Bible.

Night and day I am praying exceedingly that we might know the truth of Your every word, that it will give us a complete understanding in the perfect will of God Almighty. Oh Lord give us stronger faith to carry out Your will. God our Father, and our Lord Jesus Christ, direct and guide us by Your Holy Spirit unto You Heavenly Kingdom.

God Is in Charge of Satan

IN THE last week November, 2003, these are God spoken words many Christians don't believe God will bring sickness, sin/evil upon His people, yet all through the Bible, God uses sickness sin/evil for His purpose. To bring about correction, righteousness, strengthen our faith, strengthen our hearts, and to punish evil wrongdoing. Also it will prepare our hearts with confidence to face Satan in the future. Remember, God is in charge of all evil and He uses it for His purpose in our lives. When we let Satan take us out of the will of God, Satan then leads us to commit sin, because this is his will to take us out of God's will, when we become weak and our fires have gone out, and we lose the focus on God. Satan can easily lead us back into sin. Sometimes God allows these things to happen in our lives to bring glory unto the Lord. This information is written in His Bible, involving God's holy people who disobey His commandment and covenant. We need to read God's true Bible, to learn how God allows sin to come upon His people. There are many ways God allows sin to come upon Christians: preparing us for His purpose through trial and tribulation, sickness and problems, and on and on. There is no limit. God is a mystery, and many saints don't understand. Oh Lord, I pray you will help us open our hearts to see Your truth and understand who You are. Oh Lord, speak to us and teach us Your righteousness of Your true word. Here are some examples of God controlling Satan to bring evil. God put an evil spirit upon Saul, against David, **Jeremiah 16:10b** says, "The Lord pronounced all this great evil against us?" **11:23** says, "I will bring evil upon the men." **Isaiah 45:7** says, "I form the light, and create darkness: I make peace, and create evil." **Nehemiah 13:18** says, "Did not our God bring all this evil upon us? The Lord I will bring evil upon this place." **John 13:26-27** says, "Jesus allow Satan to entered Judas Iscariot."

It is a sad day we are living in, We Christians will buy all kind of books and read them, but when it is time to read our Holy Bible, the world has taken all our time, yet we go to church one to two hours on Sunday and hear what the pastor is saying to us. Are we really there to gain God's knowledge and to understand His purpose for our life and take it out and service His needy people. Or are we there to pass time, to look beautiful?, Or to show off our new clothes? What if someone asks you to explain what was preached. Could you open your Bible and explain? Or has it become a rhythm because my parents went? I hear many Christians say, when we leave church, I don't want to talk church anymore. Outside the church building we have our free will and we make our own choices to do or say as we please. This is the work of Satan; there is no God in their hearts.

If we are true children of God the church will live inside our hearts. Where we go the church goes also. Lord God, help us Oh Lord. What happened to us today as so called Saints of God? Why are we not standing upon His solid word? Where is the progress in our spiritual growth in the Lord? Where is our fruit? Why have we put all our trust in man's preaching, and not studying God's true holy word to let Him speak to our hearts? Our life is supposed to be control by God's Spirit; yet we are under the control of an evil spirit of Satan. **Duet 28:59, 60** says, "God, bring all sickness and diseases upon thee."

On the first of October, 2003, God led me to a church. During prayer time, I went up front as the pastor prayed. My arms lifted up to heaven, the holy Spirit came upon my soul, and God showed me a vision and said darkness has come over His church and family. And Satan has taken control and is leading My people down the road of destruction. Tell them I am coming back for My church and I will take control.

John 1:5-7 says, "The light shineth in darkness; and the darkness comprehended it not. There was a man sent from God, whose name was John. The same came for a witness, to bear witness of the light, that a men through him might believe."

The Secrets of Our Hearts Bring Destruction

GOD LED me for the third time up on the mountain in the presence of the living God. He opened up my heart to His knowledge and understanding, to know the truth of His holy word. Then he put into my heart the fear of the Lord and said this is the beginning of wisdom: a good understanding, having all knowledge and righteousness of His true commandments the secrets of saints hearts has been weigh heavy upon my heart for some time. Many churches and saints believe we must hold on to the secret sin of our life and against others we have wronged. **The last week of October,**

2003, the "Lord spoke and said secret three time", and write these words to teach my people the truth about holding on to their secret hearts. These words I pray you will read and take heed to the true living word of God. He has taught me the truth of His living word by opening up my heart to recognize the truth when I see or hear something wrong. I have heard many false words being taught to God's people about our secret. Don't tell; God knows our hearts, just believe and He will set you free. Show by uplift hand if you don't want to open your mouth, yes God knows our secret hearts. These words are not from God, but mans false teaching leading us down the pathway of wrong, unrighteousness of destruction and straight into hell. The body of Christ is to have no secret. All through the Bible God is saying open your mouth and confess your problem. Don't hold these secret things in your heart.

As God led me into the hospital, nursing homes, many older and young people are victims of their secret heart with their past sins shut up in their hearts, denying any room for God. When I speak to them I see their past sins in their faces and heart and in their voices; they have become hardened, and don't want to hear the true word of God. If I speak the words "Jesus Christ" about confessing sin, they will draw up or turn their heads away from me. Lord, I don't understand why church leaders let so many of God's people fall so deeply into their sin, away from the true righteousness and love of Jesus Christ. The church must be an open place to release our sins unto God or teach us to call on God to break our secret sins. The elders and strong wise men of God are there to help us pray and ask God to break that evil spirit of shaker and curses from our past.

I know how it feels to have secret sin in our heart. I was a victim for twelve years, my heart was heartened, and I didn't want anyone to tell me anything about my hidden sin. I would venture my anger out toward anyone who tried to tell me I was wrong. I thought I was all right by hiding my secret sin; no one had the right to know my secret. Little did I know that Satan was controlling my life, preparing me for hell forever and ever.

One night after twelve years it all came to an end, and Satan was defective once again. God led me to fall on my knees and call on the Lord; Oh Lord, God, I am a sinner; have mercy on my soul. I have turned my back on you and taken on the evil spirit of Satan who has been controlling my life. Lord, please, I want to come back to you. Lord redeem me through your blood, and set my soul free from the hand of Satan. From that moment, my life has not been the same since there is no secret in my heart. Jesus speaking in **Jeremiah 23:24** says, "Can any hide himself in secret places that I shall not see him? Saith the Lord. Do not I fill heaven and earth? Saith the Lord " **Ecclesiastes. 12:14** says, "For God shall bring every work into judgment, with every secret thing, whether it be good, or whether it be evil."

The family secret sin has become a shaker of bondage in many family members involving sexual abuse, hate and anger between brother and sister. Parents bring hate and curses upon their children, running them away from home. There is no God, no forgiving. Children have no respect toward their parents, parents having no respect for children, mother and daughter, father and son saying things involving hate with damage affecting other. What comes out of their mouth is corrupted communication, sex involving husband and wife in committing adultery. As we grow older these things are hidden in our hearts. If these evil secret spirits are not broken with confessing our sin unto God, we will never be set free to see the righteousness and blessing of our Heavenly Father. **Matthew 6: 14-15** says, "For if ye forgive men their trespasses {sin}, your Heavenly Father will also forgive you; but if ye forgive not men their trespasses, neither will your Father forgive your trespasses." Church, saint, and family, it is very important to forgive others of our sin. Please don't hold this secret sin in your hearts any longer. May God have mercy upon your soul. No man can destroy Satan from our secret soul except the blood of the living lamb of the God Almighty. I pray you will call on Him, ask the Lord to forgive your secret sin against parent/sister/brother from the hate and evil we brought against our parents, and other. Lord makes our souls free through the blood of the lamb. **II Thessalonians 2:3** says, "Let no man deceive you by any means: for that day shall not come except there come a falling away and that man of sin be revealed, the son of perdition." God say I will open up your secret to the truth and you will flee from my righteousness. **Deuteronomy 29:29** says, "The secret things belong unto the Lord our God: but those things which are revealed belong unto us an to our children for ever." Saints I pray you will take heed of the word of God, because holding on to our secret sin has a tremendous impact on our health and physical condition, and our family lives.

1. Holding on to our secret sin keeps our hearts hardened with hated and anger towards others.
2. Holding on to our secret sin can be very deadly toward our family and friends.
3. Holding on to our secret sin is damaging toward the body of Christ.
4. Holding on to our secret sin will bring bitterness and negative conversation.
5. Holding on to our secret sin brings on depression, stress, anger, guilt, bitter resentment, hypertension, heart attacks, grief, and many other diseases.
6. Holding on to our secret sin can cause us to reject ourselves and destroy others.
7. Holding on to our secret sin will destroy marriages and family unity.
8. Holding on to our secret sin will cause us to lose peace of mind and cause us to reject God.

1 Corinthians 5:5 "God will deliver our secret into the hand of Satan for the destruction of our flesh." God wants to make us right with Him, He want us to be sincere in asking for forgiveness of sin. In **Ephesians 1** God wants to redeem us through His blood, the forgiveness of our secret sins and break the curse that hang over our heads. He wants to make us rich in His grace and mercy. He has predestine us unto the adoption of children by Jesus Christ, to the praise of the glory of his grace. He hath made us accepted in the beloved of His kingdom. We are the children of God, let us not hide anything, secret upon our heart, release it unto God Almighty so we may receive these promise of Jesus Christ.

Saints, these things build up in our hearts and from time to time Satan will bring us to a point in our lives where evil becomes so great, we will explode with hate and anger that become very damaging and destroy people who are in our path. Saints, this is why so many of us are sick, weak with all kinds of diseases and afflictions that affect us. The doctor is sitting back, waiting for us to bring our secret to him. God sent His Son down here to defeat Satan through His shed blood of the lamb. Churches and saints of God, why are we holding on to our secret toward ourselves for so long? God has more in store for us if we confess our secret hearts unto Him. Saints, stop listening to man and study Gods word and put our trust in Him only.

Saint, we have put ourselves in the sight of the doctor; do you know they are developing medicine to combat against our secret sin that will stop our worrying and give us a release from our problems? They will never cure our sinful problem. Only God can do this, because no doctor has the ability to detect an evil spirit, but they will tell you something to give you medications. Saints of God, where is our faith in the true living God? We claim we service Him, so why don't we bring our sin to the saving grace of God our Father? Saints, I pray to God that, we will not continue to hold these things in our secret hearts. I pray we will read the Bible, study, and see the truth for ourselves.

Ps 90:8 our secret sin is in the light. Ps 44:2 God know the secret of our heart

Ps 139:15 I was made in secret. Prov 25:9 discover not a secret to another

Is 45:19 I have not spoken in secret? Matt 6:4 God shall reward the openly man

Rom 2:16 God will judge the secret of men. Jer 23:24 can any hid in secret places

II Cor 4:2 renownced your hidden things, Eph 5:12 you will be ashme in secret.

Christians Judging Others Wrongdoing

As God continues to develop my life on a special journey as a messenger of God to witness and tell testimonies unto churches all around North Carolina. God is teaching me the righteousness of wisdom, knowledge, and understanding the strength of salvation for the fear of the Lord in His treasure, involving right and wrong. Many churches it is sad to say, lack knowledge of a true Christian to remain faithful unto God. I heard leaders say to me that in the past the church was full, but they can't say what is happening at the present. As I venture out into the community, I talk to many saints who have departed the church for many reasons. The biggest reasons I hear them say is about sin in the church and wrongdoing of member outside the church. Yet they don't see any reason why they should be back into the house of God. How can we judge someone what we are not doing right? O Lord, hear our prayer Lord, come and see us; we are in need of a true living savior to teach us the right knowledge of our love toward our sisters and brothers in Christ. Lead us back into Your house and help us to love you, Jesus Christ, with all our minds, hearts, and souls. Oh Lord, please teach us how to praise and worship your holy name and remain in your kingdom.

Lord, we sit home bringing judgment upon other Christians about their wrongdoing. Yet we have departed from the church, thinking we have the right knowledge, and understanding of the truth to judge others sins. Yet we don't know our Heavenly Father is not pleased with us so-called Christian.

We true Christians who are led by the Spirit of our Heavenly Father to a church with problems, Christ led us there for His purpose of correction. God puts us there to help the church to call on God for correction of the true knowledge and the love of Christ Jesus. Stay strong and be faithful to His calling and wait on His timing. Many times we fail to wait and depart from Gods righteousness. Do we think we have the right to judge others wrongdoing, this is not of God. We take our children out of the church; we still don't see any wrongdoing, keeping them home, filling their hearts up with the world's way. Lord, do we really understand our actions and purposes, about the truth of God? The children see and do as we teach them to judge and talk about God's people. This is a real problem that in God's house. Families are not taking their children to church or involving them in the actives and programs that will help strength their growth, teaching them about the love of Jesus Christ. We are setting a bad example and Satan is taking them under his wing and preparing them for hell. This is not pleasing unto God. **I Corinthians 4:5a** says, "Therefore judge nothing before the time, until the Lord come." Lord, do we Christians know our actions are wrong by blaming our brother or sister? We are to help them see the brightness of God's light of glory in us, and not let us show disrespect unto our brother and sister. **I Corinthians 8:12** says, "But when ye sin against the brethren, and wound their weak conscience, ye sin against Christ." Oh Lord, I pray you will help us find our way back into the house of the Lord and open our hearts up to the truth of our purpose in life. May the richness of God's blessing and grace strengthen our hearts until we reach our designated eternal life in heaven.

God's Power Brought Me Through

WHAT A mighty hand of God that brought my soul through two wars and out of so many storms. Satan tried every way to destroy my soul, but the divine power hand of the Almighty God is what kept me safe from all hurt and danger. Satan had all of his chances but he was not able to destroy my soul. I was covered by the blood of the lamb of Jesus Christ. He never fails me because of His incredible love and the mercy He has for my soul. I count it a joy and a blessing from my Heavenly Father that He has redeemed my soul from the hand of Satan to allow me to tell God's incredible story of my life. These stories may go out to the whole world, so that everyone who reads them will know the powerful holy hand of the incredible Almighty God. He has the last say about whose soul will be redeemed. He has put me through an amazing and awesome test to face the wrath of Satan's hand. It was a test of my faith I never care to go through again. But to please my Heavenly Father I will do whatever He asks, because I know He is right by my side, and I love Him the way He loves me. **1 Peter 1:7** says, "That the trial of your faith being much more precious of gold that perisheth, through it be tried with fire; might be found unto praise and honour and glory at the appearing of Jesus Christ." In this world our lives will face many trials and tribulation. This will make our faith grow stronger in the Lord, if we don't give up. When God saves His people from the grasp of Satan, He always has something in store for them.

I am a true, living witness of all that God has taken me through. He wants me to tell you that whatever you are going through, He will bring you out; He will set you apart to glorify His name. He will put you through trials to test your faith. After going through my trials, I praised God for delivering my soul with His righteousness, strength, and mighty power. Lord, you have brought me from a mighty long way. You brought me through the storms, fire, rain, suffering, and pain, I thank you, Lord. **Psalm 91:15** says, "He shall call upon me, and I will answer him: I will be with him in trouble; I will deliver him, and honour Him." Lord, hide me in the shadow of your wing. I give thanks to God, the Father of my Lord Jesus Christ. You have been my rock, my fortress, my salvation, and my savior. I will never stop praising your holy name.

For there is hope laid up in glory for me in heaven, whereof I heard before in your word of truth in the gospel. **Colossians 1: 10-13** says, "That I might walk worthy of the Lord unto all pleasing, being fruitful in every good work, and increase my knowledge of God. Strengthened with all might, according to his glorious power, unto all patience, and long suffering with joyfulness. I give thanks unto the Father, which hath made me meet partakers of the inheritance of the saints in light." Who hath delivered my soul from the power of darkness, and hath translated me into the kingdom of his dear Son Lord Jesus, I praise you with my whole heart and I love you with all my soul and mind.

II Timothy 1: 6-10 says "Wherefore I put thee in remembrance that thou stir up the gift of God, which is in thee by the putting on of my hands. For God hath not given us the spirit of fear; but of power, and of love, and of a sound mind. Be not thou therefore ashamed of the testimony neither of our Lord, nor of me his prisoner: but be thou partaker of the afflictions of the gospel according to the power of God. Who hath saved us, and called us with a holy calling, not according to our works, but according to God's own purpose and grace, which was given us in Christ Jesus before the world began. But it is now made manifest by the appearing of our Savior Jesus Christ, who hath abolished death, and hath brought life and immortality to light through the gospel." For every word you read is from God; these are not my words. Every day God would tell me what to write. It is amazing how God would come to me in the spirit of my heart and mind, telling me what to write, and I would take out my pad, and pen, and start writing God's word.

I Have a Strong, Loving Compassion for All God's People

BEFORE WRITING God's book, He had given me such a strong loving compassion for all of His people, especially for the church, families and those sinners who don't know Christ. It is the love of my Heavenly Father who places this down in my heart to lead me to help all I can through His strength and power. These are the people who make up the body of Christ. **Colossians 2:2** says, "That their hearts might be comforted, being knit together in love, and unto all riches of the full assurance of understanding, to the acknowledgement of the mystery of God, and of the Father, and of Christ." Love is the greatest mystery in the Bible, because it is the living spirit of God for Christians to love all His people as He did. **Galatians 5:14** says, "For all the law is fulfilled in one word, even in this; thou shalt love thy neighbour as thyself." God has inspired me to write these stories from His spoken word about the inspiring love and compassion I have for His people. It breaks my heart when I see God's people take his word lightly and not obey Him. Many Christians of today say they love the Lord but are not committed to do the work of the Lord's will. I pray for your soul, that your desire might be filled with the knowledge of His will in all wisdom and spiritual understanding, that ye might walk worthy of the Lord unto all pleasing, being fruitful in every good work, and increasing in the knowledge of God.

We have brought the world's system into God's house, and it has taken control. We have run Him away from His house. I will pray to the Almighty God that the churches will listen to God speaking to them. God spoke to me in December, 2000, and said, "Go tell My churches, I am coming back, and the churches are to remove the world's system out of My house." It will be spotless with no wrinkles, blameless and without sin. Some Christians today feel they can live on both sides of the fence, serving the world and still saying they love Jesus Christ. I pray to God that His people will know they can't love two masters. **Matthew 6:24** says, "No man can serve two masters: for either he will hate the one, and love the other; or else he will hold to the one, and despise the other." We cannot serve God and man.

Sinners: I have a strong compassion in my heart for them, but I hate what they are doing to themselves. With rap and hip-hop music they are taking their frustration out on their parents and neighbors, because they didn't show them love in growing up, no discipline, no morals/ethics, and no standard. Many parents are living in sinful condition, not believing in God, and the church has abandoned them. So young people grow up with all this hate and anger in their hearts. The evil music they record is a reflection of their lifestyle, living in corrupt neighbors. Young people in school are driving the bus drivers crazy with no control nor respect; in the classroom they drive the teacher insane by disrupting the class with their evil behaviors. Parents, why don't you love your children? God gave them to us as a gift from heaven; do you not know they are precious in the eyes of the Lord? How long will we stand by and see them fall by the waste side of Satan? Parents; when are we going to wake up? God is the only answer. Asks Him to remove the blinder from your eyes. I pray to the Almighty God they will turn from their wicked, and sinful ways. Go down on your knees and call on the Lord. Let Him give you the love of Christ Jesus; come in from out of the storm. **1John 3,** God is saying these children of the devil whosoever doeth not righteousness is not of God; he that committeth sin is of the devil. They don't know they are selling their soul to Satan. All the other rock stars gone before them, soul are burning in hell, and every person who buys and listens to their music is cursed following down the same road selling their souls to Satan, by worshiping the dead. It is so sad that there are so many Christians who have become slaves to Satan. The worldly music system is turning our young people to the dark side of Satan, and away from the love of Christ Jesus. Where are the churches that are supposed to be alight for Jesus Christ to help our young people reframe from this sinful music and evil ways? Not only young people; our older generation is just as involved as young people are. Many saints of God are also involved, and we are supposed to represent our Heavenly Father. But yet they are letting it creep into the House of God. Lord, what is going on with your people? Lord, you have given us the greatest commandment of Your love, yet it is missing from Your peoples hearts, minds, and souls. **Psalm 55:1-3** says, "O Lord give ear to my prayer, O God, and hide not thyself from our supplication. Attend unto us, and hear us we mourn in our complaint, and make a noise. Because of the voice of the enemy, because of the oppression of the wicked: for they cast iniquity upon us, and in wrath they hate me." **Psalm 51:1-2** says, "Have mercy upon us, O Lord, according to thy loving kindness: according unto the multitude of thy tender mercies blot out our transgressions. Wash us thoroughly your blood from our iniquity, and cleanse us from our sin." Oh Lord, I pray you will release your people from the hand of Satan, and deliver them into the kingdom of heaven.

Family: God has given me a strong compassion for today's families. I was brought up in a family who taught me knowledge, and understanding to fear God. I love my father, and mother. By having these kinds of parents, all my sisters, and brothers are Christians; they love the Lord. So I know what a God-fearing family should be like. When I see families torn apart with no love of God in their hearts, my heart is heavy and goes out to them. I love them the way I love Christ. There are so many families today who don't know Jesus, and they have forgotten the commandment of God. **Deuteronomy 8:11** says, "Beware that thou forget not the Lord thy God, in not keeping his commandments, and his judgments thee this day." I pray to the Almighty God that families today will come to know the love of Jesus Christ. Families are a major part of the body of Christ, which is the church. Churches are hurting today because families have been torn apart by the ways of this sinful world. **Ephesians 4:12-13** says, "For the perfecting of the saint, for the work of the ministry, for the edifying of the body of Christ till we all come in the unity of the faith, and of the knowledge of the Son of God, unto a perfect man, unto the measure of the stature of the fullness of Christ." The Bible is quite explicit on these things involving, love, morals, discipline, obedience, veneration, responsibility, and respect for one's father and mother, toward their children, setting forth the need of love, care, and guidance in the family, and a spiritual religious relationship with Christ. These things are the keys to holding the family together. God said, "I will build my church upon a solid rock." This means the family house must be built upon a solid rock. If it is not, the church will crumble. I pray the family will build their families on a solid rock for the Lord. The family must save God's church by cleaning it out, by removing the world's system, and by restating God's churches back upon the solid rock on which it stands. He said "Go tell my church I am coming back and my church must be clean, spotless, blameless without sin." **Revelations 3:7** says, "And to the angel of the church in Philadelphia write; these things saith he that is holy, he that is truth, he that hath the key of David, he that openeth, and no shutteth; and shutteth, and no man openeth. Thy has kept my word, and hast not denied my name." Families, I pray you all will unite your loving hearts together and look unto the Lord for your guidance and direction for your lives to live day-by-day, through your faith, and believe God is your savior the Lord Jesus Christ.

God's Shallow Hearted People

In December, 2000, God showed me all those so-called Christians with shallow hearts. They were all returning back into the world of darkness, with very little light shining. Shallow hearts bear no fruit. They are looking for easy answers, and they cannot deal with hard work for the Lord. They are not able to get involved with church activities, or study His word, or attend Bible study, their lives are too busy. These things take away our precious time. As newborn Christians, we will rejoice in responding to the glory of the Lord, and praising His Almighty Name. As time pass is we lost the little love we had for Christ, because this lifestyle not in the church. We remember the good times in our minds, and Satan is ready to return us to our old natural man of sin. Because when we heard the word it falls on hard ground; it will not produce any fruit. Sin is in our hearts closing off God's Spirit. Our spiritual life will die because God's word will not grow in our hearts. We will attend church services, yet the word of God will not penetrate our hearts. The word enters our minds, not our hearts. Why do you call, me Lord? As soon as the word goes out, the devil goes and takes it away. Pray and ask God to cultivate our hearts each day, asking forgiveness of our sin, so His word will fall on good soil in our hearts to produce good fruit for the Lord. **Luke, chap, 8** the soil of their hearts is so hardened that a word from God cannot penetrate it. What is the condition of your heart? You are allowing the evil world to constantly enter your hearts through television with sinful movies, sexual and sin. Cursing has become so common that it doesn't face us so- called Christians. They sit and watch those demonic wicked shows. God said as you sit and watch, your souls are cursed with a curse along with those who are cursing. The sinful music you listen to, the sinful books you read, and the sinful thoughts you have in your mind and heart. When we allow our hearts to become hardened, and desensitized by these things of the world, God 's word will not penetrate our hearts or bring any changes to our spiritual lives. These things of the world mean more to us than Christ. We are disobeying His true word, and allowing Satan to take the advantage of us with a curse from God; He is not pleased when He is disobeyed. He is speaking **Luke 8:7** says, "And some fell among thorns; and the thorns spring up with it, and choked it. And that which fell among thorns are they, which, when they have heard, go forth, are choked with cares and riches and pleasures of this life, and bring no fruit to perfection." This is one reason we must study and meditate on God's word day and night. God never leave us locked into sin. He always provides a way for us to escape the wilderness, and sinful world. **1 John** says, "God said if we confess our sins, He is faithful and just to forgive us our sins, and to cleanse us from all unrighteousness."

Psalm 25:4-5 says, "Shew me thy ways O Lord; teach me thy paths. Lead me in the truth, and teach me: for thou art the God of my salvation; on thee do I wait all the day."

These are God's words that will help draw us to a close relationship with Jesus Christ.

a. God's word will heal us, and deliver us from destruction; God's word will spring forth out of my mouth: it shall not return unto me void, but it shall accomplish that which pleases God.

b. Things are going to happen against us, and we will go through trials and tribulations, and face hard times in life, but praise and worship Him. Joy will come in the morning, peace and love will be in your hearts.

c. I will stop dwelling on all bad and negative things in my life. Instead, I will dwell on all positive things to bring glory to Christ Jesus.

d. God can make bad things change into positive things for your life. Ask God for forgiveness, stay true to His Holy word; be obedient to God's word and His commandments.

e. I will praise God every day, and night, for what He has done for my soul.
f. God commanded His light to shine out of darkness, into our hearts of light.
g. God, give us your spirit of wisdom to understanding your holy word.
h. Love will cover a multitude of sins. As stated in Proverbs 10:14 "Wise men lay up knowledge; but the mouth of the foolish is ever destroyed."
I. The fear of the Lord prolongeth days; but the year of the wicked shall be shortened.
j. The fruit of the righteous is a tree of life; and he that winneth souls is wise.
k. You can experience God with a relationship that will pass all understanding.
L. Fellowship with the body of Christ is an important part of fellowship with God.
M. God's will fight your battle, if you give it to Him and stop trying fight it yourselves.

Don't Let Your Problems Lead You Away from God

I WAS controlled by Satan for more then twelve years, then God led me back to church. After being there for some time, God led me up front and I asked to be reinstated back into the house of God. I told them I was saved, and a Christian, so they accepted me. No one ever asked me to ask God to overcome my past sins. I continued to attend church, not concerned about my sin. I was there, but I could not get anything out of the preaching, I could not understand what was preached. I kept feeling something missing in my life; I could never find out what was wrong, my heart was still filled with sins. **Psalm 95:8** says, "Harden not your heart, as in the provocation, and as in the day of temptation in the wilderness." It was going on two years back into the house of the

Lord. One night at home God led me down on my knees to pray. I was praying to God and asking Him to forgive me of the sins I had committed against Him and others. All at once something came upon my whole body is if it had taken a hundred pound off my shoulders. It was the Holy Spirit of God taking my sins to the cross and washing my soul in the blood of the lamb; I had been set free from the hand of Satan. I felt so relieved, so at peace, and the joy of the Lord. This feeling I will never forget. I praised and thanked the mighty hand of the Almighty God who set my soul free from the hand of Satan. From that night I never felt lost or away from God. That next Sunday my eyes and heart were open and I could understand God word. **Colossians 1:12-13** God has accepted me back into His kingdom; "Giving thanks unto the Father, which hath made us meet to be partakers of the inheritance of the saints in light. Who hath delivered us from the power of darkness, and hath translated us into the Kingdom of his dear Son." God wants me to tell pastors, and church leaders they need to start asking lost Christians, about their past sins before they become a member of the body of Christ. If this doesn't happen, God will not forgive us just because He leads us back to church. Our past sins will remain in our hearts. There are so many so-called Christians in the church today who have returned and never ask God for forgiveness of their sins. It is up to the pastors and deacons to tell God's people what they need to do to be set free before they are accepted back into the body of Christ. First they must ask God to clean their hearts from unrighteousness. They must humble themselves. They must not try to justify themselves. They must not hold on to secret pride but give it all to the Lord, and receive His blessing.

Psalm 32:5 says, "I acknowledged my sin unto thee, and I said, I will confess my transgressions unto the Lord; and thou forgavest the iniquity of my sin. Selah."

If this doesn't happen it will cause sin in the body of Christ, and Christ doesn't live in sin. This is why God is calling on churches to turn back to prayer, because the body of Christ is hurting from the heartiness of our hearts from our past sins. He said this people attend church every Sunday but yet they do not ask forgiveness of their sinful hearts. We must call on the Lord with a sincere heart of prayer. Prayer has taken a back seat in most churches. God is calling on churches to turn back to old time prayer. All through the Bible prayer was the greatest weapon they had to call on God in time of trouble; also, it was a daily commitment unto God to keep them in line with His will. Somehow we feel we have found power in the world and ourselves to keep us in line with God. We have been mislead by Satan; he is leading us down the broad road of destruction. God is calling on churches to commit a major portion of Bible study into prayer. Once a month, devote your services time to teach everyone the knowledge and understanding of prayer and how important it is to their daily walk with the Lord, How can prayer set us free from our sin? Like of praying would stop our spiritual growth in Christ Jesus.

Many saints don't understand the power of prayer. Instead, we are struggling with all kinds of problems, like going to the doctor and spending all of our hard-earn money trying to get well. "The doctor is glad, Satan is happy, and we are sad." God is standing by with tears in His eyes, saying why don't my people believe and trust in the power of healing prayer of Christ Jesus. His plan is for us to be in perfect peace, and in perfect health. I am a true living witness that if we learn to pray to our Heavenly Father, praising and thanking Him for our salvation, and say "Lord my old body is racked with aches, and pain," He will hear us. I pray, Lord, You will take control, and deliver these things that are trying to destroy my body and soul. Oh Lord set me free, by cleaning all my past sin. Lord, forgive me; I am not worthy to stand in your presence. Oh Lord, help me to feel the power and glorious of Your precious hand to guide my life by Your Holy Spirit, and lead me into a peaceful day with grace and mercy, and give me Your understanding of Your love you have for my soul. Then, Lord, lead me to help someone in need, and I will show them the love You place upon my heart and soul. I pray You will save their souls. Pray, and believe He will answer your prayer. Be patient and wait.

God Is Speaking; Are We Listening?

December 13,2001, I heard God's spoken word**:** God is our Father; He is our creator. He is our sustainer, for those who have been reborn through the blood of Christ Jesus, and who love Him. He is a mother a father, and He speak to us as His dear children, because He is our Heavenly Father. Christ speaks to us in so many different ways. He speaks in His own time and in His own ways. We have no control over when or why Christ speaks to us. God doesn't speak to everyone the same way. He speaks to reveal His ways, His purpose, and His will. God speaks by the Holy Spirit, through the Bible, through prayer, through our daily trials and temptation, and through the church. These are some ways God speaks to us. During my walk with Christ, He spoke to me in the nature voice, through my ear, in my heart and mind, through vision, through dreams, by the Holy Spirit, through other Christians, through television, through preaching, through fellowship, the Bible, prayer, and fasting. God spoke during His creation of the world; today He is still speaking to man. God is speaking to Christians, but we still don't recognize Him as our Heavenly Father. **1 Corinthians 2:10** says, "But God hath revealed them unto us by his Spirit: for the Spirit searcheth all things, yet the deep thing of God." He wants to have a close and loving relationship with you and I. He wants to speak to us as His Holy people. He created us, and freely accepted us as His children, and made us ready to meet Him in heaven for eternal life.

We are to study His word, attend Bible study, attend church regularly, read our Bible daily, and walk in His ways by standing fast in all God's ways. We need to recognize God when He speak lesion be quite. He will reveal His purpose to us by giving us an understanding of His will. The greatest things we can do to hear Him speak are visit the sick, feed the hungry, visit those in prison, go out and harvest the lost soul, and help feed the new baby in Christ. This is the life of Christ. Then we will hear from our Master; we can speak to Him and He will speak to us with a regular conversation. At times He wants us to be in a quite place where He can speak to us alone. Let our hearts be in tune with the true word of Christ. Our minds must be focused on Him with a pure heart and clear hands. When Christ speaks we should recognize, and be committed to accept His calling. The Bible is the most complete and updated Book ever written, and every word is God Himself. God spoken from Genesis to Revelation; He is still speaking to you and me. "This Book is alive; it is God Himself." Pick it up read it for yourselves; pray and ask Him to speak to your heart; ask Him to reveal His purpose for your Christian life.

One of the saddest things of today is that we don't fear God nor seem to understand God creation from heaven to earth regarding national destruction and weather: God is warning, and speaking to us through floods, earthquakes, tornados, hurricanes, violent thunderstorms, lightening and fire. God, said I, will bring my wrath upon nations because of their disobedience. **Job 37** says "At this also my heart trembleth, and is moved out of his place. Hear attentively the noise of his voice out of his mouth. He directed it under the whole heaven unto the earth. Out of the south cometh the whirlwind and warm weather: cold and fair-weather cometh out the north. After it a voice roareth; he thundered with the voice of his Excellency; and he will not stay them when his voice is heard. His thundered marvelously with his voice; great things doeth he, which we cannot comprehend. For he said to the snow, be thou on the earth; likewise to the small rain and to the great rain of his strength. He sealeth up the hand of every man; that all man may know his work. He causeth it to come, whether for correction, or for his land, or for mercy. **Jeremiah 47:2** says, "Thus said the Lord; Behold, waters rise up out of the north, and shall be an overflowing flood, and shall overflow the land, and all that is therein; the city, and them that dwell therein: then the men shall cry, and all the inhabitants of the land shall howl." Hear what the pastor is saying about His word. God's word is alive, the word is God. When we read it, He will reveal Himself to us. **John 1-2** says, "In the beginning was the Word and the Word was with God, and the Word was God." The same was in the beginning with God. This is a mystery of God; He will open up our hearts, and give us a clear understanding of His knowledge of who He is, if we obey Him. **Isaiah 40:5-6** says, "And the glory of the Lord shall be revealed, and all flesh shall see it together: for the mouth of the Lord hath spoken it. The voice said, Cry. And he said What shall I cry? All flesh is grass, and all the goodliness thereof is as the flower of the field." Saints, our blessing is right at our fingertips All we have to do recognize when God is speaking, humble ourselves, pray, seek God's face, and submit our whole hearts to the mighty hand of God our Heavenly Father. Stay focused according to His will, and then He will bless your hearts. **Isaiah 28:2** says, "Behold, the Lord hath a mighty and strong one, with as a tempest of hail and a destroying storm, as a flood of mighty waters overflowing, shall cast down to the earth with the hand." We must understand who we serve, a mighty God, a powerful God, a God we should fear, and a Father who wants to hold up His bloods tined bandier before us. We need to be committed to sacrifice our time for the Lord, We Christians must be rooted, and grounded in the word of Christ, and not let Satan find ourselves drifting back into the world where there are all kind of voices. **1 Corinthians 14:10-11** Paul is speaking; "There are, it may be, so many kinds of voices in the world, and none of them is without signification." Therefore if you don't know the meaning of the voices, check your Bible to ensure it is God speaking. In the Bible God spoke to Adam and said to maintain His garden. He spoke to Able and said leave your home and go to Canaan and I will bless you. He spoke to Jacob on his journeys. He spoke to Moses many times, and He spoke to Mary Magdalene at the empty tomb. God never stops speaking, He is speaking all the time, revealing himself and His purpose to all Christians. **II Corinthians 4:13** says, "We having the same spirit of faith, according as it is written, I believed, and therefore have I spoken; we also believe, and therefore speak." As you read these words, He is speaking to you. will you open up your heart, let Him come in, and speak to you? We must pray, and ask God to open our eyes, mind, hearts, and souls to hear and receive what He is saying to us. There is nothing hard about God's He knows just how much we can bear. When God calls us for His purpose, we must humble ourselves, be obedient, and follow His plan. You will hear many voices speaking to you. If you know this is not God speaking, rebut it right away. Don't let it confuse you.

This is why it is so important to study God's word and understand the knowledge of God by having a true relationship with Him. Because Satan is all around us waiting to destroy God's plan and the purpose He has for our life, because Satan can speak to us as gods.

There are many Christians who don't have a clear understanding of God speaking. When we hear or feel we have been called by God, immediately our leaders will say we have been called to preach. Before we know it we are preaching. When He calls us this is just the first stage. By the time God gets through molding, shaping, sending us through the fire, and teaching us, to do this it could take anywhere from two years to ten or fifteen years, or longer, all according to His plan. When you hear God calling, wait, be patient until He reveal His purpose and plan He has for our lives. Don't let someone talk you out of what God has given you. This is one of the biggest problems facing churches today. Many leaders called by God are not committed to wait on the Lord to receive their fullness of God's purpose in preparing their spiritual lives. When hard times come they are ready to leave the church and this is happening all over. "They have missed His calling." "God didn't call everyone to preach." there are many other purposes of God's Good News. He said we must go through suffering, trial and tribulation, and be tempted. God has to prepare us for His final planning that we may stand upon a soiled rock and be not removed for the purpose of God. **II Corinthians 3:5-6** says, "Not that we are sufficient of ourselves to think anything as of ourselves; but our sufficiency it of God who also hath made us able ministers of the new testament; not of the letter, but of the spirit for the letter killeth, but the spirit giveth life." He wants to speak to us but we have closed the door on Him. He wants to love us; He has a plan for us. Open the door and let Him back into your lives. He wants to speak to us to prepare our hearts to carry out His will by spreading His Good News and helping feed the poor and lost.

He has called me on many missions! He spoke, go into My churches and tell the story of my wife and all what I have sent you through. Oh I thank God for strengthen my spiritual soul to know who God is so I can recognize His mystery and His calling for my purpose in life. I am here to tell you when God calls you to work for Him, there is nothing like it. The peace of God, passes all understanding. Joy and meekness are manifest unto the exceedingly great precious blood of the Lamb. The understanding of His knowledge and the glory of His outstretched arm that covers my soul with His blessed feeling is one nothing on this earth can describe. When God speaks listen and hear what He is revealing to you, humble yourself, be obedient to His calling. God has the same blessing for your life. My prayer is that the

Lord holy word will go out to the world, to all people understanding, so that every soul will become trained to know the knowledge of God when He speaks.

God's Open Hearted People

IN NOVEMBER, 2000, God's spoken word: An open heart's, Christian seeds will fall on good ground, spring up, and bare fruit one hundred fold. The good grounds are listed in **Matthew 13** says, "With an honest and good-hearted saints, having the word of God deep rooted in their soul to bring forth fruit with patience." Having a desire in life with Christ always produces openhearted saints with love of His word to multiply much fruit. That is why we must regularly pray and ask Him to take inventory and cultivate the soil in our lives daily. I often ask, have any obstacles or sin entered my heart with ought knowing? My flesh is weak, and I need God every minute of the day to keep me in His will. I will work hard for God, I will not let the world temptation enter my heart; I will remain sensitive to His word. I pray every day to walk with Him that I will not be concerned with the cares of this world's. In His Spirit I am quick to take action, to stay away from the cares, and concern of this world. I will always pray, stay focused and put my trust in the true living God who has brought me this far. Then I remember what He did to save my soul, and there is no way I can repay my salvation. I must go down on my knees day and night praying, calling upon the Almighty God, Oh Lord, I thank you, I praise your Holy Name from the bottom of my whole heart. You are the amazing and all powerful God whom I service.

Open hearted Christians, disciples, and saints, we must humble ourselves under the mighty hands of God. We are His servants, we are the ones who carry our cross. We are not ashamed of His gospel. God is our shepherd, He abides in us, we abide in Him, and Christ is the vine; we are the branches. Christians, glorify God in the highest, by lifting up the Son of man, and have a strong belief in Jesus Christ. Receive the full inheritance of the righteousness of the living word of God, and be justified by His faith. Saints of God also have been ordinances by the power of the blood of Jesus Christ as they give up their minds, hearts, souls and bodies as living sacrificial lambs upon the altar to be entered into the Holy, Holy of Holy of the mercy seat of God. We will become the light of the world. Christians will teach and tell the world about the love that God has for sinners. Saints have a loving relationship with Christ and His blessing. Be filled with the combination and doctrinal of God's word; have a spiritually filled heart with an excellent and delightful attitude toward all of God's people. His open hearted Christians are the ones who go into the world the way Jesus Christ did. They go unto the poor to help them, and speak the word of God that will give them confidence and hope. We go into the darkness, and spread the word of Christ to feed those left behind, always praying that God will save their souls.

Matthew 25:35-40 says, "For I was an hungered, and ye gave me meat; I was thirsty, and ye gave me drink: I was a stranger, and ye took me in: naked, and ye clothed me: I was sick, and ye visited me: I was in prison, and ye came unto me. Then shall the righteous answer him, saying, Lord, when saw we thee a hungered, and fed thee? Or thirsty, and gave thee drink. When saw we thee a stranger, and took thee in or naked, and you clothed thee. When saw we the sick, or in prison, and came unto thee? And the King shall answer, and say unto them, Verily I say unto you, Inasmuch as ye have done it unto one of the least of these my brethren, ye have done it unto me." These are the Christians who bring glory and honor unto Jesus Christ. We are to go out and bring back the lost sheep who have gone astray, and those who have fallen asleep. We are to bring them back into the house of God. He said we are to be Spiritual Light unto all of His people; we are the ones who give hope and a light to the blind and sinner through the world. God doesn't want us to look down on our brethren and sisters by telling them about their problems, but to help them with the support of our love, giving them confidence, and courage. Tell them there is a bright side to life. Tell them your testimonies, how Christ led you out of your sinful situation.

True saints will build their homes upon a solid rock. Christ is the chief cornerstone, and the building will be fit together as the

Holy Temple of the Lord. True saints will produce fruit. True saints will dwell in their hearts with faith; being rooted and grounded in the true love of Christ. True saints will stand strong when storms arrive, when trials come, and stand when evil comes against them. God said in **1Peter** in order to be a true saint, we must suffer for even hereunto were we called: because Christ also suffered for us, leaving us an example, that we should follow his step. True Saints of God will know the hope of their calling and will be faithful to walk worthy of the Lord into all pleasing, being fruitful in every good work by faith. And being strengthen with His glorious power unto all patience with the increasing in the knowledge of God. True saints know the love of Christ, which the presence knowledge, that we are filled with all the fullness of God's glory. True saint have been adopted into the inheritance of the predestination of God's Heavenly Kingdom.

a. Let God control every area of your life.
b. Be committed doing God's will and Purpose in your lives.
c. Be mindful how you dress, eat, what you look at on TV, and resist Internet temptation, so God will be pleased with you every day.
d. Lord guide me, lead me, plow me, cultivate my life daily, bring forth good soil that your seed may fall on good ground and bring forth good fruit.
e. I need to grow stronger daily in the Lord's word to become more Christ-like.
f. The sum total is what all I do for the Lord.
g. I must face the Lord, through the redeeming power, and mercy of Jesus Christ, and stay free from sin.
h. I wanted the resurrection power of Jesus to set me free, and give to me power over sickness and cast out sin.

II Thessalonians 2:13-14 says, "But we are bound to give thanks always to God for our brethren beloved of the Lord because God hath from the beginning chosen us to salvation through sanctification of the Spirit, and belief of the truth; Whereunto he called us by our gospel, to the obtaining of the glory of our Lord Jesus Christ."

These openhearted saints of God are led by the spirit of God to follow His example to live day by day serving Him in every way possible, by taking care of our family in God's ways to glorify Christ: helping the poor, the hungry, the weak, and those who are lost in their sin. This is the example of Christ and His disciples for us to follow. Also show your self to be an example as Christ; on your jobs and around your friends, everywhere you go, remember everything a saint does is to glorify Christ Jesus. These things will continue to grow and strengthen our faith with the knowledge in Christ Jesus. **Proverbs 8:31-33** says, "Rejoicing in the habitable part of his earth; and my delights were with the sons of man. Now therefore hearken unto me, O ye children: for blessed are they that keep my ways. Hear instruction, and be wise, and refuse it not."

Saints of God, when you speak the truth and follow His example, there will be times the weak evil so called Christians will come at you with their evil-speaking tongues of fire, trying to stop you from speaking the truth in the glory of Christ Jesus. Many will sit in church with their mouths closed and don't want you to say "Amen "or praise and worship God, yet this is what God is calling on churches to do to follow the example of His Bible.

II Corinthians 4:3-4 says, "But it our gospel be hid, it is hid to them that are lost: in whom the god of this world hath blinded the minds of them sit in churches which believe not, lest the light of the glorious gospel of Christ, who is the image of God, should shine unto them for God, who commanded the light to shine out of darkness, hath shined in our hearts, to give the light of the knowledge of the glory of God in the face of Jesus Christ" To open their hearts to exalted Him with praise, worship, glorifying His name in heaven and saying Amen to the pastor. Saint our hearts must be right with God, involving praising and worshiping the true living God. Saint let us show the Lord God Almighty we are His dear children, giving Him the highest praise. In Hebrews, God says, having therefore, brethren, boldness to enter into the holiest by the blood of Jesus. By a new and living way, which he hath consecrated for us, through the veil, that is to say, his flesh? And having a high priest over the house of God. Let us draw near with a true heart in full assurance of faith, having our hearts sprinkled from an evil conscience, and our bodies washed with pure living water. Let us hold fast the profession of our faith without wavering (for he is faithful and merciful). And let us consider one another to provoke unto love, and to good work: Not forsaking the assembling of ourselves together, as the manner of some is; but exhorting one another: and so much the more, as ye see the day approaching.

Oh church of God, you have set a great example unto other churches; they must look unto us, and how God's saints must conduct themselves. We must let God be in charge. Christ is the Head of the Church. And hath put all things under his feet, and giving him to be the head over all things to the church, which is the body, the fullness of Him that filleth all in all. This church is the representative of Christ Jesus. **Ephesians Chap 4:4-6** says, "There is one body, and one Spirit, even as we are called in one hope of your calling One Lord, one faith, one baptism. One God, and Father of all, who is above all, and through all, and in you all." From whom the whole body fitly joined together unto the body of Christ. For the work of the ministry, for the edifying of the body of Christ, tell we all come in the unity of the faith, and of the knowledge of the Son of God, unto a perfect man. **Revelation 22:16-17** says, God is preparing His church bride in order for His return at the marriage supper. "I Jesus has sent mine angel to testify unto you these things in the churches. I am the root and the offspring of David, and the bright and morning star. And the Spirit, and the bride say. Come. And let him that heareth say, Come. And whosoever will, let him take the water of life freely."

God Is Coming Back for His Church

On December 23, 2000, God's spoken word Oh God, your Christians are suffering, hurting with pain, sickness, and sin in their hearts from the lack of true gospel given by Jesus Christ. Church leaders, I have heard so many false teaching words toward God's people during praying time, come to the altar, don't tell your troubles, problems, or what is hurting you; the Lord knows your heart; I will pray for you. Or show by up lifted hands that needs pray. Yes it is true the Lord do know our heart. "This is false teaching". God says open our mouths to confess our sin and the things affecting us unto the altar of God Almighty or what ever our problems. Lord, forgive me of my sin and help me with my problem affecting my soul and body. I pray to the

Almighty God that you will help leaders overcome their false teachings and teach the congregations the truth written in the Bible Open their mouths unto God Almighty, confessing their sin unto Him asking Him to forgive whatever their problem are.

Psalm 103:3 say "Who forgiveth all thine iniquites; who healeth all thy diseases. Who redeemed thy life from destruction; who crowneth thee with loving kindness and tender mercies."

I have seen saints come to the thrones of grace for prayer the pastor will talk about problems, but no one will pray or they will pray not knowing what their problem is. I see the look on their faces when they return to their seat with disbelieved. "As to say why did I go up there?" People have stopped me after church and asked me to pray for them. There are real problem in churches today. Our young people are drifting away from God's house. Because of the lack of love, many saints are hurting with all kinds of problems sitting right in the church. Leaders are too busy or they are failing to commit themselves to help them. Church leaders today need to be more sensitive toward these saints of God, and family problems. Leaders, please help them to overcome their problems, and then prepare their hearts to get them involved with outreach minister to reach the lost hurting souls.

Saints, do we really know why we attend church? Each Sunday we come to hear the word, and depart the same way. There is no spiritual growth in our life; no increase to strengthen our faith. The church memberships roll are declining. Remember, the churches belong to Christ. He is calling on churches to call on God to clean their hearts. There is much work in the world for the churches to be involved in. In Acts, the disciple waited on the promise of God. He opened up the window of Heaven and poured out His Holy Ghost upon them, and it empowered them to go forward. And the first churches was started. Church this is God speaking to us in **Act 4:2-4** say, "Being grieved that they taught the people; and preached through Jesus the resurrection from the dead. And they laid hands on them, and put them in hold unto the next day: many of them, which heard the word, believed; and the number of the men was about five thousand. And they continue witness to the world about testimonies of Jesus Christ Life." The church belongs to God; He wants His church to be a testimony to the blood, the cross, the resurrection, and the Holy Spirit, teaching the community, and the world. He is standing by, waiting to pour out His blessing upon His people to empower them to be a witness to Jesus, resurrecting of power to bring the church commandment in line with God's plan.

a. First God says bring prayer back into His house, turn a major portion of Bible study into prayer time, bring your burden to the altar, and ask Him to cleanse your heart and create a new true rightful spirit.

b. Ephesians 4:12 for the perfecting of the saints, for the work of the minister, for the edifying of the body of Christ

c. Ephesians 4:13 Tell we all come in the unity of the faith, and knowledge of the Son of God.

d. Prayer Lord, you will teach churches to become witnesses, disciples and evangelists to take your word to the lost and hungry.

e. Prayer Lord, help leaders to start outreach program to support their communities, to bring un-churches into the house of the Lord.

f. Pray Lord, help churches start new classes, and teach us according to God's knowledge and gifts from the Lord.

g. Prayer Lord, we can do all thing through You who strengthen us in Your resurrecting power.

h. Oh Lord, help us to turn Your church back over to You. Teach us to see and understand Your word as the true living bread, is the river of true living water of life. Oh Lord, give us your vision in the direction that You want us to follow your plan.

i. Oh Lord help us to manage your church not according to our understanding, but to Your will. Help us to receive clean hands, and a pure heart to carry out your will.

Lord, why are many churches leaving their problems neighbor, moving out into a safe community free from sinful area build large churches? Do they feel they can service You better away from problem and sinful areas? They believe if they build large buildings, people will come. Yes this is true; easy/weak Christians will depart from small churches, and come into a large church. Here Christians, they can hide, they feel less threat, they meet their other weak friends, they have the same mindset. It is easy to set in a large crowd, there is no pressure, no involvement, here no one will confront us directly to get involved. Our sins will not be exposed, we feel safe, we feel comfortable and we will not feel guilty of our sin.

Many large and some small churches are dead during praising and worshiping because their so-called praise and worshipping is not the true living word of God. Many song I hear have too many man's words and very few of God's word. Praise and worship teams are like of true knowledge from God. To praise God, we must praise and worship Him in spirit and truth with His holy word from the true living Bible that has the life of God's Spirit. With God's right instrument and singing, His word will empower His Spirit to take over the church and penetrate our hearts. Lord God, help us where we are weak, build us up and make us strong in your righteousness involving praise and worshiping you, Lord. Also, many churches empower their music over their singer with drums drowning out the words.

Many so-called Christians sitting in church don't have any knowledge involving praising and thanking God. They go out in the world, open their mouths and make all kinds of noises praising and worshiping man. They come into God's house with their mouth shut, not praising or thanking God for all His grace and mercy and not saying Amen to the preacher. "God said we have become like dead wood sitting in the church; their lives needed to be resurrected back to life through the blood of the Lamb. Psalm, Let the people praise thee, I will praise his word, and I will deliver thee of trouble thou shalt glorify My name.

Easy/weak Christians sitting in large churches, God sees us running from Him, and running to hide. "No matter where we go, we can't hide from God. He is taking down our name in the book of the Lamb according to our works. Leaders of today know how to market people to fill their large churches. They are more concerned about the number than the quantity of saints. Many are not being taught or trained how to go out and spread the gospel of Jesus Christ. God is saying we have run away from the problem areas. Who will help bring my people out of their sinful problems? When we run from the problem, people become more sinful, because there is no one to tell them about the true right from wrong, and no one showing love of Christ Jesus. God says my churches are my eyes and ears to see, and help correct the problem. How can we do His will? If we are nowhere around the problem, how will they be saved? Christ went into the sinful problem areas to save the lost.

Churches are to be representative of the community; they are to service the community of it spiritual needs, and supported the families needs. We are to support and help hold the community together. When the community is hurting, the church should feel their pain, and help heal their wound, by showing their love of Christ Jesus. The churches are supposed to establish programs to get un-church people involved with activities, that require skillful planning of God's will, to get their minds interested and focused on the Lord. They need to see how church members treat them with love and care. We are God's people, set apart for His kingdom. Because we are different than the world. They will look to see how we are different than them. The love of His compassion should overflow in our hearts that it will fall upon those in need.

Today the world is having more problems in community and neighbor than ever before; it is out of control. Churches are to be there to help combat the problems, with the help of the Lord. Families are being torn apart; young people are running wild. They are doing their own thing. There is no supervision, no directing, and no one guiding them in the right direction. And they feel they are right on all issues. God house has abandoned them; their lives have no discipline, no morality and no standard of God's love. Those brave churches that remain behind; I pray to the Almighty God they will open their doors, and let the un-churched into God's House. Go out in the community and share the Good News of Jesus Christ and the love of God with a strong compassion for the lost. **Luke 14:23** says, "And the lord said unto the servant, Go out into the highways and hedges, and compel them to come in, that my house may be filled. This is why we are calling Christians to be witnesses of Christ. Pastors and leaders, teach your congregation they are to minister the word of God everywhere they go because they are the church. **Hebrews 1:14** say, "Are they not all ministering spirits, sent forth to minister for them who shall be hears of salvation?" So saints, let get busy doing His will. Go out sharing the Good News of Christ to the lost and pray He will lead them into the house of God.

Christ is looking for churches who are committed to get involved with His people and teach them right from wrong and love them all, regulars of their sin Tell them come in out of the rain.

a. Christ wants programs to support kids after school.

b. Christ wants program that will take young people on organized trip into new areas, to teach them the foundation of His word.

c. Get them involved with Christian organized sports.

d. Christ wants programs to take kids to summer camp to learn about Jesus Christ, by teaching them the principle of Biblical fundamental skill, knowledge, and understanding God's will for their lives.

e. Christ wants us to establish programs and activities to keep the young people off the street.

f. Christ say those churches who get the community and neighbor involved will grow spiritual in the Lord, and as they continue to grow they will start new churches in another community where it needed. "God is calling on leaders to establish churches in problem areas to reach problem children, not to build large churches out of the problem-free area just to say, I have a large church with a large membership on my roll."

Many churches today are focused on just preaching the word of God, and establishing programs for the already saved Christians. They are not concerned about the churches families problems or about the lost un-churched. Church leaders are supposed to know their families and their problems. Get with the family of God and identify these problems and teach and help families to overcome their problems with prayer and support. Paul saw problems in the church; he called on the leaders to do something correct them. Today we are the same leaders to help the sheep that are hurting with problems. Young Christians come to church looking for comfort, peace, love, joy, happiness, and understanding of God's word. But the church doesn't see the real need of young Christians, because they don't have time to get them involved. The churches are feeding them meat and they can't digest it. They become displeased, so they stop coming because their spirituals need are not met.

Do you remember what happened in September 11 after the wrath of God. People filled the house of God They were looking for answers from Christians and God. We saints of God failed them, because the churches continued their regular order of service by feeding everyone strong meat. They should have changed their order of service to be more accepted to their needs, by opening up our hearts with compassion of love, embracing them with open arms, reaching out and comforting them, telling them. We love you as God love us. We should have let them see Christ-likeness through us.

Hebrews 5 12-14a says, "For when for the time ye ought to be teachers, ye have need that one teach you again which be the first principles of the oracles of God; and are became such as have need of milk, and not of strong meat. For every one that useth milk is unskillful in the word of righteousness: for he is a babe. But strong meat belonged to them that are of full age." Oh God I pray pastors, deacons, and leaders will become more involved with church members and serve them the way God intended for them to be served. "God said; I made you the shepherds over my people and you are to feed them and take care of them; by supporting their needs by showing love, and compassion for His people." Don't lose them back out into the street.

Young Christians must be involved with church activities, and program; giving them responsibility. Once a month, let them take full control of the entire service. Let them chose their own pastor, approved by church leaders. By doing this they will tell their friends to come and see. If you want to see your young Christians grow spiritually, give them responsibility, make sure they have a strong loving leader who will help direct and guide them in the right direction of the Lord. If the churches will not teach and use them, you will lose them back into the world. Church must always have leaders to take charge of young people and train them by their age group, making sure they are active in church activities.

Developing Young Christians

THE HOLY Spirit spoke to me about young Christians in 2002 and again in 2004. He made it plain by opening up my eyes to see the truth. About how young Christians life are to be trained and grow up in Christ Jesus, direction, guidance, and righteousness

This is what God showed me: leaders of the church as young babies in Christ coming in to the saving salvation of eternal life with Jesus Christ. This is like God planting a young fruit tree in the field to grow and produce fruit. But before it can produce fruit, the tree must be supported by the church families in helping it grow up in the right spiritual maturity, spiritual disciplines, spiritual love, spiritual morality and spiritual ethics. Also it must teach them the right happiness and growing strong in the fulfillment of their young Christians lives. That will teach them how to learn and receive the true knowledge of God. So they can have a brighter future in Christ Jesus to produce fruits.

The pastor must charge the entire body of its responsibility toward the growth and devolvement of these young Christians in the true knowledge of God. Having strong growth, involving true righteousness of Christ Jesus, helping build strong maturity with a solid foundation of the Biblical principle with the understanding of Jesus Christ. Saints, help those young Christians to grow strong in the right direction in reaching their full development in the fulfillment in the embodiment of God Almighty. It takes more than a family to grow young Christians in the right direction in a world full of evil and hate against God's righteousness. The family must be taught the body of Christ is there to help them in every way possible to help direct, guide, and lead those young Christians. If we fail God's plan and don't take advantage of training our children under Christ guidance, God are going whole us responsible if Satan take them back out into the world. I pray to the God Almighty the entire churches will fall in line with God's plan and do what is right toward these young Christians.

Church Get your heart right with God.

Deuteronomy 4:10b says, "Gather me the people together, and I will make them hear my words, that they may learn to fear God all the days that they shall live upon the earth, and that they may teach their children." **11:18a-19** says, "Therefore shall ye lay up these my word in your heart and in your soul, and ye shall teach them your children, speaking of them when thou sittest in thine house, and thou walkest, thou liest down and thou risest up **v22b** I command you, to do them, to love the Lord your God, to walk in all his ways, and to cleave unto Him."

God Is Coming Back with His Holy Spirit

On December 11, 2000, I was at work. What I am about to tell you is very important from God Almighty, so read this. **For forty five min the Holy Spirit of God showered down upon my whole heart, mind, body and soul**. I asked God: what are you saying to me? What do you want me to do, Lord? Why is this happening to me, Lord? Is there someone you want to heal? I don't understand what is going on, Lord? "Well, for the last six month, I have had a real concern about God's house involving pastors leaving, and deacons not following God's plan. They are still following their old traditional ways. They are afraid of changes. He is moving all the time. He said you can't stay where you are and go with Me; you must change from your old traditional ways, pick up your cross, and follow Me. The world's music has entered into God's house. His lost people are not being saved. Pastors are preaching His word; very few are being saving for Christ. It is the church's responsibility to help bring His people into a saving salvation. God said the world's instrument and music are not to be in My house. There were two students standing by, they was talking about instruments and church music, and the Holy Spirit came upon me so strong tears were coming from my eyes. The glory of the Lord was all over my soul **and He started speaking through my heart. I pulled out my writing pad and pen and God told me to write these words. As I started to write, I felt Him moving the pen in my hand and words were appearing upon the paper. It was incredible and amazing what was happen right in front of my eyes. I want you to tell My church people to get ready. And remove the worldly music, worldly instruments, and the world's system out of My House. Tell My people to get their hearts right with God's. "He kept saying." "Tell My people I am coming back for My church and My House is to be clean, spotless, blameless, and without a wrinkle. Tell my people to confess their sins, they are to study My word, and they are to attend church regularly. They must go out and tell my lost sinners about the**

love of Jesus Christ, and how they can be saved. Leaders in God's House are to be knowledgeable of My word, and My plans for My church. Church leaders must attend training seminars to gain the knowledge that I have for them."

He said, I will teach you more than you have ever known. "God said" I am coming back, and my leaders must know My word. "He said Whoever reads My word in this Book will be touched by the Holy Spirit, because these are the true words of God". As I type these words of God the Holy Spirit and His glory are upon my soul. "He said, I want My church to be alive, with the love of God, and the Holy Spirit down in their souls." "He said, I love My people. I want to have a closer and loving relationship with them that will pass all their understanding." "He said" "I created you in the likeness of My image, and you were made in the eyesight of God." "He said My people are going away from me like the lost sheep. I want My Christian people to go out and bring My people back to the House of God. Tell them I love them despite their sin, and I will love you more than you will ever know if you just confess your sin. Isaiah 53:6 says, "All we like sheep have gone astray; we have turned every one to his own way; and the Lord hath laid on him the iniquity of us all." I am their God and I want my people to sing praise and worship song. God said, Tell my people what I told you; don't explain anything, just tell them, they will read My Book, I will teach them the power of My holy word, and they will receive the Holy Spirit of Jesus Christ.

Prepare Your Children to Be Rooted and Grounded in the Love of Christ

On March 1, 2002, the Holy Spirit spoke to me while I was in my classroom at John Wesley College. This is what God said: Go and tell my church to abandon their old traditional ways, where God is not part of their service. God loves you and He wants to establish a loving and peaceful relationship with His church. He is calling you to come and join Him where He is already working. He wants to prepare our hearts to receive the truth word of God, and the knowledge He has for us.

"He said You are going to see a mobilization of the young generation of Christians beginning all across the world, and this generation with God's Spirit will open up the eyes of blindness in their old traditional ways and hearten hearts. These young Christians will come from the North, they will come from the South, they will come from the East, and they will come from the West. And they are coming into God's house all over the world, doing the work of the Lord. The darkness of My church will be overcome with the gloriousness of the bright light of the Holy Spirit of God; it will open up your stoned hearts."

Luke 13:29 "says, "And they shall come from the east, and from the west, and from the north, and from the south and shall sit down in the kingdom of God."

The powerful hand of God is going to unleash His mighty power by open heaven, and showering down His blessing of His Holy Spirit. He is going to bring the fulfilling of riches of His heavenly places into the house of God. **Isaiah 32:15** says, "Until the spirit be poured upon us from on high, and the wilderness be a fruitful, and the fruitful field be counted for forest. And the work of righteousness shall be peace; and the effect of righteousness quietness and assurance for ever."

He said, "My people must be rooted, and grounded in My word."

Then God show me Satan is also mobilizing his army to combat against God's work, and Christians who are not well rooted and well grounded in His word, will become part of Satan's army, as well as those who are committed to hold on to their old sinful ways. **Isaiah 14:12-15** says, "How art thou fallen from heaven, O Lucifer, son of the morning! How art thou cut down to the ground, which didst weaken the nations! For thou have said in thine heart, I will ascend into heaven, I will exalt my throne above the stars of God: I will sit also upon the mount of the congregation, in the sides of the north: I will ascend above the heights of the clouds; I will be like the most High. Yet thou shalt be brought down to hell, to the sides of the pit." Christians, beware of false gods. Satan is beginning to establish up on high to appear as Jesus Christ himself (the antichrist). Churches, I pray to the Almighty God that you will teach His people to understand the real truth of the living word of God, and what He means to their daily living, with Christ deep in their hearts. These are the true word of God; I am not trying to frighten anyone. I am a messenger of God reporting what He commands me to write. He wanted me to tell you about His mighty power. You are going to see the awesome power of God the Holy Spirit, which is about to be unleash to the entire world and into God's churches all over this land. His people need to know and understand the Holy Spirit of God. "He said In that day I will pour out my Spirit upon those who believe in me."

God is already pouring out his Holy Spirit upon those who are true believers by studying His word and attending church. Attend Bible study, and spread the Good News for Jesus Christ. He says, "Once you do these things, and gain My knowledge, then I will pour out My Holy Spirit upon your soul. I will give you a purpose in life." He said, "Many of My churches today are putting more emphasis on today's, music with man's word of the world,. instead of putting God word in song that speak to people with the Holy Spirit, with praise and worship." Also, churches are putting on all kind of performances, and programs just to make money and please the saints. His House has become a house of worldly materialism of entertainment. Oh God, I don't understand your churches of this day. Churches are using all kinds of worldly ways such as rap and hip-hop music to bring young people into God Church with no true foundation. Pastors and member are leaving churches more today than ever. **Revelation 3:15-16** says, "I know their works, that thou art neither cold nor hot, I would thou wert cold or hot. So then because thou art lukewarm, and neither cold not hot, I will spew thee out of my mouth."

we don't want to wait on His timing. We want to see the plan with our eyes; we want everything right away. Our faith is weak, and with no God involvement. Saints of God I pray you will get to know who God is, and to know the church belongs to Him, not man. Let God take His rightful place in His own house, and pastors take your rightful place as shepherd over the sheep. The greatest need in God's house today is the true word of God, by teaching the congregation their responsibilities and purposes as Christians, what are their gift? How does they help the body of Christ? What are their responsibilities as a child of God? What are they to do during the week? How are we to minister our faith in God to the lost? How are we to walk in the way of the Lord to carry out our purpose as Christian? How are we to live our daily lives in front of family, friends and co-workers?

These things are to be apply in our everyday lives serving the Lord; everything we do must be done to glorify God in heaven, not ourselves or man. The church has lost its direction in how individuals are to live their lives as a Christians: our lives are to be completely different from the world's way of living. This is one of the main reasons churches are failing God; because they want to be like the world. How will Christians live differently from the world if the minister is not teaching them? Jesus taught people about the things in the world that everyday people did; this is how He related His words to them. Today the things we do in the world are the same. So, ministers, why are we not teaching God's people about the things we are accusative with in this world where we are living in day by day. Help us to know and understand God's plan and purpose for our daily lives. Saints are to be a light to the world preaching the Good News. Saints, God said we are in the world, but not of the world. I **John 2:15-16** says, "Love not the world, neither the things that are in the world. If any man loves the world, the love of Father is not in him, the world is lust of the flesh and eyes and wicked. Saints remember every thing we do must be to glorify God."

The shepherd is to feed the sheep by providing these true answers to them. It is good to go to church, but if you don't know about these things for our lives, how can you serve God? The leadership of your church is responsible to help teach the saints by equipping them with their purpose of the true living knowledge of God Almighty, and drawing us closer to Him with a loving relationship. He longs for our souls to be fed with the right spiritual

Churches have forgotten to call upon God, by not learning how to follow His will and direction to bring people into His church. Churches are not using the most powerful weapon they have, which is Prayer. "Oh Lord, I will pray for Your churches, that will go down on their knees and pray to the Almighty God, asking You to forgive their sin. We have sinned against You, Lord. Help us to clean up Your house and bring it back in the name of Lord Jesus. Oh God, we need you, Lord, to make us the church You have called us to be. The church belongs to you, Lord, and you are the head and we are the body."

Last summer I visited a church in Virginia. As I walked into the church, I felt a spirit of electricity moving among the people I knew it was not God's Spirit. It just didn't feel right, and then I thought this is the same way I felt in my youngster days, dancing in clubs. That man was playing that electric guitar so strong you could almost hear it talking. I could not believe my eyes or believe what I was witnessing in those Christians. That electric spirit was moving through the church. I felt the electricity as if Satan spirit were telling me to move with the saints, but I could not, because I knew it was not God's Spirit talking to me. I felt really sad. I said "Oh God your saints have let Satan's instrument and music into your house just as you spoke, and you saints don't even know it."

Christ is the head of the church, and the head of the body; the congregation is the body. He is the first to rise from the dead. He is the everlasting God, He is the most High God, He is all fullness there of. **Revelation 4:11** says, "Thou are worthy, O Lord, to receive glory and honour and power: for thou has created all things, and for thy pleasure they are, and were created." Yet man is using it to please himself. **I Chronicles 16:29** says, "Give unto the Lord the glory due unto his name: bring an offering, and come before him: worship the Lord in the beauty of holiness." Churches, this is God speaking of who He is and churches, we are taking Him too lightly; we are disrespecting the power of the Almighty Hand of God. We don't fear God anymore. Churches, lets: get right, put our trust in Him, and let Him lead, direct and guide, our every step according to His will. Let us not try to get ahead of His will, or go off on our own, creating and developing our plan for His church. In the past we talked to God and He answered our request according to His timing. Somehow today nutriment. The body and soul are to grow in spiritual maturity to produce fruit for Christ. If the soul doesn't receive the right food the body will die; our body is a living organ of Christ's Spirit. Its need is the nutriment from the shepherd as he lead his sheep to greener pastures to receive God's blessing. This is the way God wants His Christians to be fed, off rich food from the true word of God, and to know our purpose and responsibilities. With true living bread and water, we will never hunger or thirst.

Churches are robbing themselves of wonderful opportunities for God to speak to them by not encouraging their people to share what God is during in their lives. There needs to be more understanding, with guidance and right directions as to what plan or purpose God has for their lives. Churches should encourage their people to stay on the right path that leads to heaven. Young and older people need to pray in small groups, this will break the fear to open up their hearts and speak the way their heart lead them. Young people need to testify what God is doing in their lives. Sunday school or Bible studies are a wonderful opportunity for people to testify to their life-transforming work of God They do not always know the proper Christians testimonies but the Holy Spirit will uses it to impact the church. In beginning of a new believer, their hearts are not yet strong so feed them milk, not meat. Help them grow stronger in the Lord. Feel free to share with others what God has done for them, but be careful not to let Satan trick us It is a terrible thing to give credit to Satan for something that didn't come from God.

God Is Standing at Your Door Knocking

THE LAST week of November, 2000, God spoke these words: "Sinners are ready to be harvested Christians, prepare your hearts to lead them to Christ. The sinner's fields are white and from the river they are jumping up. They are fed up with the world's system; they are hungry for the true word of God." I looked over and I saw fields all over the land and they were white and waiting for someone to come and harvest them and tell them about the love of Jesus Christ and how they must be saved from their sins. They have become tired of things in this world; their hearts are empty for real love. Their parents fail them, their friends fail them, the world has failed them and the church is failing them. The only place they can find love is in the true word of Christ Jesus, who has the true living bread and the true living water that will give them the saving grace of Jesus Christ. He is standing at your door knock; will you let him in. Sinners, God loves you just as you are Don't you hear Him knocking. Open up your hearts and let Him be in charge of your lives. Be more like-Christ by changing us through the blood of the lamb. Christ sees us as dirty filthy rags, poor and lacking in His knowledge. We are lost, and going astray, running everywhere, looking for love. Yet He still loves us. He will shower mercy upon us. He wants to pick us up, clean us off, and make us His dear children. Christians must show their love in Christ toward those in need. we must see them through the eyes of Jesus; because we are all sin and came short of the glory of God. Let us come to a true understanding of Christ Jesus by telling our story, and showing true love by helping feed the poor and leading them to Christ. They are standing by waiting; will you help them?

There are many brave saints who are real soldiers for God. They are on the battlefield every day spreading the Good News and winning soul for Christ, as He led them to the throne of grace.

Oh Lord, I pray to the Almighty God that the churches will come out from behind the four walls and be committed to mobilize themselves to do the will of God. Bring the lost into the house of God to receive their salvation, and other blessing He has for them. He wants to have a rightful relationship with them; He wants to fill the empty void in their hearts. He wants to give them the true living water so they will never thirst again. He wants to give them love, peace, joy, compassion, and comfort them with affection, grace, hope, knowledge, and fill them with the Holy Spirit and give them the understanding of the true word of God. In Genesis we find in chapters 1 and 2, that in the beginning God created the heaven and earth and everything by his outstretched arm. Everything he made was good. In chapter 3 man was the beginning of sin. Man has been in battle with sin ever since. God sent His Son Jesus Christ down to set us free from sin; He has made a way out of sin by His blood on the cross. **Isaiah 11:2-3** says, "Promise and righteousness is with us who love the Lord. And the spirit of the Lord shall rest upon him, the spirit of wisdom and understanding, the spirit of counsel and might, the spirit of knowledge and of the fear of the Lord. And shall make him of quick understanding in the fear of the Lord."

1 Sinner, do you believe there is a true and living God?
2. Do you believe God sent His Son to die on the cross to overcome sin so that you and I may be set free?
3. Do you believe there is a heaven and hell?
4. Do you know what heaven and hell are like?
5. Do you believe God sees your every move?
6. Are you contented with your life, living in sin?
7. Do you believe living apart from God that you are living in sin?
8. Do you think God approves of your lifestyle apart from Him?
9. Do you believe God loves you despite your sin?
10. Do you know where your soul will go after death?
11. Do you believe there is eternal life after death, such as heaven or hell?
12. Do you believe your good works alone, by helping the poor, hungry, helpless and those who are down and out, will get you into heaven?
13. Do you believe faith alone in all you do, will get you into heaven? James said faith, if it hath not works, is dead.
14. If you were to die tonight, and your soul stood before God, and He asked you why He should let you into heaven what would your soul say to Him?

Families Today

In January, 2001, God's spoken word: was as follows: I looked over and I saw all of those families, and there were so many broken homes with no love. Families are torn apart with no morals, no discipline, no standards, no honor for one's parent, no respect, and no responsibility. These problems and many more are facing families today, and they have a great impact on the church, family, school, and community. God first created families, then He started the church to represent the family to be the body of Christ. God's plan is to show love, honor, disciplines and respect to each other, and to train them in the true knowledge of Jesus Christ. His commandment provides for the preservation of the basic unit of society's structure of the family. Parents instruct your children in the nurture and admonitions of the Lord concerning their responsibility toward their children.

Our families have become in bondage with the material things of this world. There are more things made by the wealthy man today than ever. Many of them have become major distractions in family living. The more we buy, the farther we are moving away from God. It a sad day we are living in. He is not pleased, we have become magnetized by everything we see and can't live without. Many of these things have become idle worship in our family life today. We have become slaves to the world's system. We are trusting in the world for our way of lives; we saints have let Satan take prayer out of school; and the right to beat our children to keep them in line with God's standard We have become afraid of Satan; we are no longer depending on Him. The Bible is no long real to our life, and ever day living. For this, we wonder what went wrong with our children. The world has become their teacher, because we parents have failed God. We teach them how to shot guns, we teach them how to smoke drugs, we teach them how to kill, we teach them how to steal, we teach them how to use bad language of cursing, we teach them to drink alcohol, we don't show any love, any respect, and we don't teach them about the love of Jesus Christ. With all these things, why can't we see Satan is controlling our lives, leading us straight to hell? God is speaking in **Ephesians 3:14-16** says, "For this cause I bow my knees and I prayer unto the Father of our Lord Jesus Christ. Of whom the whole family in heaven and earth is named. That He would grant you, according to the riches of his glory, to be strengthened with might by His Spirit in the inner man." But yet we are spiritually blinded. The world system we so depend on is controlling our lives. Many families have committed themselves to Satan. Today there are so many families' children who are at the mercy of Satan, and Satan is causing our children to destroy themselves and other children. The most important part of a family's structural has been torn apart, and the only way we are going to turn this around, is to go back to the basic Bible and call upon the Lord to help us raise our family in the correct understanding and righteousness of Christ Jesus.

Proverbs 22:6 says, "Train up a child in the way he should go: and when he is old, he will not depart from it." The Bible is a simple direction and guide for our lives There is nothing hard about God, and we made Him hard. How did families make it through life before all the worldly things came about? Families, pray, put your trust in the living God. Believe in Him, and He will make a way for your soul. This is the same God. Why don't we believe and trust Him for our provision each and every day? He knows our hearts, He knows our lack of trust. His love for us has not changed, and His promise has not changed. He is a jealous God and He want us all to Himself. He wants to have a closer and a loving relationship with us. He wants to receive His rightful place at the head of our families. Pray and ask for forgiveness of your sin, and say "Lord, I am sorry, Please take my family back into your kingdom." **Romans 3:23** says, "For we all have sinned, and come short of the glory of God."

In **Job 40:14** say, "Then will I also confess unto thee that thine own right hand can save thee." He will forgive you, and God will provide for all your needs. This is His love He has for you. Be patient and put your trust in Him. **Hebrew 6:12** says, "That ye be not slothful, but followers of them who through faith and patience inherit the promises." We need to call on the Lord and ask Him to change our hearts, souls and minds, and to take away the world's system from our heart, and families. Let God be in charge of your household. Man and woman will become one in the eyes of God. His will is to become the head and the center of the families life..

Let's stop playing with God and fear Him. Go down on your knees and pray to God Almighty, "Lord, forgive my sins Oh Lord help me to turn my family around, and then guide us in the right direction. Lord, I want to go back where I first believed, back to where I was first born, into your kingdom and back into the House of God. Lord, I will trust you, I will love you, and I will praise your holy name every day of my life. Oh Lord, how can I ever thank

You. Help me grow stronger in Your faith". Jesus answered "father, provoke not your children to wrath: but bring them up in the nurture and admonition of the Lord." Children, obey your parents in the Lord: for this is right. Honour thy father and mother, which is the first commandment with promise. Love is the most important ingredient in holding a family together. Father and mother, I pray to the Almighty God, father love your wife, wife love your husband, and both must love your children with your whole heart, soul, and mind, and God will bless your heart.

Families Growing Up without the Love of God

GOD YOU gave us your word on how to bring our children up in the nurture and admonition of the Lord. Throughout life raising a family is not easy during these last days. There are so many things of the world, trials and temptations, which can come against a family not rooted and grounded in the love of Jesus Christ. Their lives are controlled by Satan and not by God. There are two types of families raising their children.

Family number one: This family is starting out raising children without God as their savior. The children are growing up with the mother and father both working. During the weekday the kids are dropped off to a babysitter and are raised by someone else. The mother or father picks up the children in the afternoon. In the evening the mother and farther have other activities that take them away from the development and growth for the love of the child, and this calls for another babysitter. During this time the children are growing up with very little tender love and care from the mother and father with no love of God in their hearts. As these children continue to grow up, the parent lets them control themselves involving all kinds of worldly things. The parents still don't have quality time to direct and guide their lives in the right direction. As they grow older, the children begin to want things to fill there empty void in the hearts, because there is no love from the parents, and the worldly things. Their lives are too busy to show love; the worldly love they have will not replace God's love. So they continue to look to the world system to provide love for their children, by buying them things of the world that will keep them happy. Once the children get tired of things.

They are looking for real love from their parents, but they have it not to give. The children will continue to look for things to fill their empty void. When they can't find it, they will try anything. They become children of disobedience, foolishness, and disrespect. They become discouraged with their parents and start staying away from home, hanging out with bad groups and gangs. They get involved in situations that will bring harm and hurt to their parents, and then the question will come: Why are our children doing this to us? We gave them everything in the world. "You can't replace the world with God's love". There is no substitute for God's love. Only the love of Christ can change our hearts to love our children and they love us. Away from God is the work of Satan; apart from God man can't do anything. This is how Satan works to destroy a family that doesn't know the love of Christ Jesus. Satan has total control over this family. These problem accrue when we fail God because in this home children imitate their parents. Whatever they do or say the children do: smoking, smoking drugs, abusive language, drinking alcohol, gaming, what you watch on television, what you say on the phone, how you dress, disrespect, and no discipline. Parents are crying out "Where is my child?" Today children growing up with an empty heart of Jesus Christ and full of hate and anger. And these young people think they have the right answer about everything; no one can tell them anything different. Their parents have no control over them. In school they are out of control. The church has failed them by not going out and rescuing them. These children are preparing to bring more darkness into this world. "My God," "My God," how long will you let Satan have his way controlling your children and family. It is the responsibility of the parents to raise these children under the guidance and directions of the love of Jesus, and the family's first requirement is to call on the Lord to change their hearts. **Proverbs 28:13** says, "He that covereth his sins shall not prosper: but whoso confesseth and forsaketh then shall have mercy." **Mark 12: 29-31** says, "And Jesus answered him the first of all the commandments is, Hear, O Israel; The Lord our God is one Lord. And thou shalt love the Lord thy God with all thy heart, and with all thy soul, and with all thy mind, and with all thy strength. And the second is like, namely this; Thou shalt love thy neighbour as thyself. There is none other commandment greater than these." There is no reason why families can't grow up with the love of God in their hearts, soul, and mind. Jesus Christ was crucified on the cross, and freed us from sin, and gave us the gift of salvation. God has set us free from sin; everyone has the right to salvation. Jesus Christ shed His blood for your and my sin. I pray to God Almighty, families will you seek the Lord for a new way of life, so you will receive the blessing of the Holy Spirit of Jesus Christ. Lord, fill their empty hearts with the goodness of your grace and mercy, then lead us into a loving relationship with Jesus Christ. Children, its time to seek the true living God to fill the empty void in your heart. He loves us so much He died on the cross that we all might be set free from sin.

Provers 22:15 says, "Foolishness is bound in the heart of a child; but the rod of correction shall drive it far from him. **23:13** Withhold not correction from the child: for if thou beatest him with the rod, he shall not die, but shall deliver his soul and the parent's heart shall rejoice. **29:15** The rod and repoof give wisdom: but a child lift to himself bringeth his mother to shame." **v17** Correct thy son, and he shall give the rest; yes he shall give delight unto thy soul."

Families Growing Up with the Love of God

THIS FAMILY is rooted and grounded in the love of Christ Jesus. This family is rising up with the love of God, and a true understanding of His knowledge and requirement in raising a family. This is a working family, both parents work; the farther works outside the home. The mother works at home taking time to raise the kids in the right way by showing them love, tender mercy and the care of Jesus Christ. They receive the right meals, the right amount of sleep, they receive parent's love, attention, affection, and instruction. They learn respect and responsibility in how to carry out their duties and requirements. They understand right from wrong. Parents buy what they need and regulate their television time and shows. Parents attend church with their kids to show love. They enter them into church programs and activities with God's control of righteousness. Parents participate with school activities; they enter them in programs that will help build strong character, strong carriage, and strong physical conduction and responsibility, with a solid foundation of Christ.

I pray to God that His love will never depart, that they will continue in the house of the Lord and their involvement in Sunday school teaching and their involvement with other church actives. Families, have Bible study in the home teaching children a godly way of life.

Ephesians 5:1-2 say, "Be ye therefore followers of God, as dear children walk in love as Christ also hath loved us, and hath given himself for us an offering and a sacrifice to God for a sweet-smelling savour." In **V8-9 "**You are the light in the Lord: walk as children of light. Be fruitful of the spirit in all goodness and righteousness and truth." Teach them to pray and how to pray and what to pray for. Let them receive Christ into their lives with salvation to experience a new heavenly Father. As children grow up, some will drift away from God. Parents, don't worry about your children. Christ will watch over them, guide and direct their footsteps. They are going to be all right. Have faith and strong confidence in the Lord. Pray and ask Him to watch over them and lead them back into the house of God. Sometimes families worry too much about their children. This can cause sickness, diseases of the body, and breaking their hearts. Sometimes worry will hamper our spiritual growth in our lives. Parents through Christ you have done wonderful works raising your children in the eyes of God. They have a solid foundation; when they stray away they have a foundation to come back to. Don't worry give your cares to the Lord and pray. **1 John 4:4** say, "Ye are of God, little children, and have overcome them: because greater is he that is in you, than he that is in the world. In **John 12:36** says, "While ye have light, believe in the light, that ye may be the children of light. These things spake Jesus and departed, and did. hide himself from them."

Children are precious in the eyes of Christ. They belong to Him, but they are our responsibility to direct and guide them in the right way of the Lord. Remember, God is the only one who knows their future. He will lead them back home into the house of God in His timing.

Parents, set a godly example for you children while they are young. Be a tree of life, planted by the river of everlasting living water, that it will produce fruit continually in your family and friends. This will bring glory unto the Lord, and your heart will be enriched by the grace and mercy of Jesus Christ. Teach young children to give of themselves by giving things to less unfortunate children. Let them know there are children dying because no one will help them. Teach them to grow up and be Christ-like.

Running the Race for Christ

March 29, 2002, God brought this to my heart and mind, and said write how I prepare you to run your world races, and how I am preparing you to run this race for the Lord. While I was running marathons (26 miles and 385 yards), I had no idea it would be a building block to a strong foundation for Christ to run His race. He is preparing me for this race of trial and tribulation to run to bring glory and honor unto the Lord. This race would be longer because God has to prepare my life according to His will to bring my blueprint into fullness with hard labor and intensive patience. While preparing, it gives me an awesome feeling. This is the predestined goal of my life. It is this amazing and incredible training of God that leads me through this cause for my soul to take on a whole new meaning of life, according to the riches of His glory. It a building block of my faith, confidence, strengthen, physical condition, mental strong, committed mind, endurance, patience, determination, discipline, courage, and a complete understanding involving God's presence and future master plan for my life, family, and church, which is my calling to serve the Lord.

At the start of this race, the clothes I wore to the race, had to be taken off before the start, except my race paint. This represents God setting me free from sin by cleaning out my heart. Now I was free to run with no baggage hanging on my shoulder. Before I retired from the army, there were many bags I was carrying lots of trash, and all these things and more were weigh me down. I was in captivity, in bondage to the work of the world. After retiring from the army, God's brought me out and away from all those things I had to confront day by day. This represents all the burden I was facing day in and day out during my operation duty. These things were to help me prepare my soul for the future calling upon my life. Saints, remember wherever you are working, you didn't receive it on your own; God led you there for your future purpose in life, so please your boss and Heavenly Father. God had to wash me through the blood of the lamb and clean me from all unrighteousness. At the time I retired, I had no knowledge I was about to take on such an awesome and difficult race. "My plan, I'm free to go fishing, travel, go to church like everyone else I had it made; this going to be all right."

Actually one year and three month later, "I felt I was hit with a Mack truck going one hundred miles per hours." "Hold its," "you are going the wrong way, stop, turn around and come unto me." Your first journey is over; the next journey you are going to run My race, "I fell on my face and cried out, Oh Lord, why me?" What have I done to take on this awesome task?" "Oh Lord, I am not worthy, my soul is not right; I am a sinful man with unclean lips." "After all these years, I thought I would have a good time like all my friends after retiring. He said; You have a race to run and there is no one except you. Because of what I have already put you through, you have the endurance and patience to go all the way to the finish line. I have singled you out and set you apart from your family, especially for this race you are about to run."

At the start I was met with stiff resistance, right off my wife wanted a divorce. I said "Oh Lord, why are you destroying our marriage and family after all these years? Oh Lord I don't understand." The beginning of this race was not easy. I tried every way to stay focused on the course. This was not what I wanted to happen. As I ran this race, she would try in every way to derail my soul and deny who I was. At one point it seemed as if the whole world had come down upon my shoulder. **Hebrews 12:1-2** says, "We are compassed about with so great a cloud of witnesses. {It was beginning to seem every marriage was getting a divorce.} Let us lay aside every weight, and the sin, which doth so easily beset us, and let us run with patience the race that is set before us." "I called on God" Why are you letting Satan destroy our marriage? Answer my prayer and tell me why Oh Lord? No answer. I called, and I called, and no answer from God. I was struggling trying to make it. The weight was showing upon my shoulder, weighing me down. My wife would continue to slow me down with her cold evil spirit of her mouth. I begin to not see the road. Things were getting cloud; I could not focus my sight on the Lord. I felt I was running the wrong way. I was all-lone, and there was no one I could call on; no one to help me. I started becoming discouraged. Satan was troubling my mind, trying to make me quit. So, I said, "Lord, if You will not answer me, I am going to give in to her I can't take this anymore. I am weak, Lord. She kept up the pressure, saying Are you going to sign these divorce paper? "Satan was saying, "yes.....then you can be free to go your way. You can't trust God." "Sign the divorce papers and I will show you plainly things that will make you happy." Satan was doing a masterful job controlling my mind; yet God knew my heart. He knew I was not going to sign. He was right there with me all the time, I fail to recognize Him. God said "Be patient my son and wait. I am with thee."

I fell on my face and cried out to Him. Oh Lord, I am sorry. I am weak, I am not strong, and Lord please forgive my sin, and help my lack of faith and disbelief. Oh Lord make me strong. Give me your strength that I may have strong faith and confidence in You, that I may stand upon that solid rock. That rock will stand. I had taken my eyes off God and started focusing on Satan. Then the Holy Spirit begin to speak. Be strong, my son. I will help you endure this course. I will give you strength, I am right here. I won't leave you; I won't forsake you. I will carry you through. **Psalm 27:14** says, "Wait on the Lord: be of good courage, and he shall strengthen thine heart: wait, I say, on the Lord." As I remember the past marathon, and what it taught me, it gave me strength and courage to go on. As months passed, she would try news tactics, trying to trip me up. I am strong, now and nothing is going to stop me. I have been washed in the blood of the lamb, I have sacrificed myself unto the Lord, my life no longer belongs to me. God is my Heavenly Father and I listen to His instruction each and every day. I pray night and day, and ask Him to cultivate me with good soil to grow, and produce fruit. Lord I have been running this race ever since **July 3, 2000. Today is March, 2002,**and the race still has many stumbling block along the way. My wife has not spoken a pleasant or kind word to me since July 2000. As I continue to run this race, I can feel the presence of her coldness all around my soul. So I will pick up speed to run faster to stay warmer. I would continue to show her love with kindness, regardless how of she treated me. Attending college, and spreading Your Good News; these things kept me busy. But I remember God is with me, and I know He will be with me all the way. I have learned to avoid most of her tricks and to stay focused on His course. Lord, each day I get little stronger. Winds may blow, storms may come, and nothing will be able to hamper or harm me from running this race. I can say this race is harder than other races, but the reward is much greater. I am pleased to run this race and I thank God for using my wife as an obstacle, because this has helped strength my faith in preparing my life for Christ Jesus. Running this race it the reward I will receive from my Heavenly Father, Oh, I feel the joy, and peace that passes all understanding. God is saying all saints have a race to run, so get ready and face your run. Only God knows the distance and what type. **Acts 20:24** say, "But none of these things move me, neither count I my life dear unto myself, so that I might finish my course with joy, and the ministry, which I have received of the Lord Jesus, to testify the gospel of the grace of God." Lord, I'm in this race until the finish. The distance and time don't matter anymore; I am totally committed to do whatever is required of my soul. **August 8, 2002,** Each day, Lord I feel my race getting a little easier. I can see much clearer. The road is clear; there nothing to slow me down. I continue to help your needed, witness His word, I continue to preach, and teach, and I spread Your love, everywhere I go. Lord, You spoke to me; mid July, saying my trial and tribulation was a three-year test; one more year and I will cross the River of Jordan. It a joyful feeling, knowing the Lord will end this race someday soon. Lord, when you spoke to me about this, I felt a hundred pound weight lighter, Lord, I can run all the way to heaven; that is how good I feel. I thank you, Lord, for my wife. She doesn't treat me that way any more. I know you are working in her heart. Her speaking and attitude is much more peaceful and that is a real blessing. Oh Lord, I will keep on running, hoping and praying your light will continue to shine through her a little brighter each and every day of her life.

August 26, 2003, the darkness crossed my path once again trying to slow me down, but nothing she could say made any difference. I am not running this race for her; I am running it for the Lord. I have seen the future, I have seen the glory of the Lord, I have seen heaven, and I have seen hell; neither am I worried any more; it is for the glory of the Lord, and I am on my way to heaven. By being heavenly minded of righteousness, a mind of excellence of knowledge of Christ Jesus, through the heart of my faith, that I may know Him, and the power of His resurrection, and the fellowship of His sufferings being made conformable unto all glorious of His heavenly Kingdom.

On April 28, 2004, God spoke words during the start of God's plan for my life that He put destine between my wife and me, leaving me to pay all the bills except she continues to buy the food. Also, she stopped attending church, but God allowed me to continue paying her tithe to Jesus, as God led me to send money to help the poor I will send money in her name also. The husband must maintain the will of God as long as the wife and husband are living under one roof. It is the husband's responsibility to take care of the household requirement and maintain strong spiritual growth and love and duty in supporting his wife regularly whatever the situation. At marriage we made an covenant with God Almighty for good or bad; the righteousness of God must stand and not be broken, so I will stand upon that solid rock as long as I live.

In December, 2003, another burden was lifted off my shoulder. God has led me to complete Bible College. I feel much lighter and I can see much clearer. My wife's evil voice is not there anymore. Her heart is being softened by the powerful hand of God Almighty. I felt it just a short time before He released her completely back unto Him and me. Hallelujah to the Lamb of God. Oh Lord God, I praise you for Your mighty word as You spoke three years ago. Oh Lord Jesus, Your word never fails; it always comes right on Your timing. Lord Jesus, I thank You; I glorify and praise Your Holy name in Heaven and on Earth.

June 15, 2004, is a day of celebration unto Jesus Christ in heaven because from the beginning I prayed, and asked God to release that evil spirit from out of my wife's heart At that time He answered my pray. But the glory, the hallelujah praise, the glorious peace of mind, the blessing from heaven didn't come until nearly four years later. This is a day of salvation, deliverance, mercy, and grace. She has been set free from the hand of Satan and restored back into the kingdom of God. He took me to **Leviticus 25:10** says write, "And ye shall hallow the fiftieth year, and proclaim liberty throughout all the land unto all the inhabitants thereof: it shall be a jubile unto you; and you shall return every man unto his possession, and ye shall return every man unto his family." A day of rejoicing unto the Lord who has made all thing possible so let us give Him the glory. Wait have faith and be patience unto Christ, He is the key to becoming successful with the Lord. My wife and I have stood the test and made the grade, Hallelujah to the Lamb of Jesus Christ.

For it is the power the glory and the honor, due unto my Father Son and Holy Spirit for putting my wife and I through this race; it was all made possible through Your compassion and love you had for our soul. For this my Lord, I thank you with all my heart, mind, and soul.

I Saw Jesus Knee in Prayer

On June 3, 2002, God led me to a church while the choir was singing praises and worshiping God Almighty. I stretched my arms up toward heaven with my eyes closed, saying Thank you, Lord, I praise you. "Then God opened up heaven and I saw an incredible scene all around; then I saw Jesus Christ knee praying, looking up to heaven with His hands close together. I saw His back, His face was dark; I could not see, His hair was black, His robe was purple. There were tears of joy flowing from my eyes and the Spirit of the Holy Ghost was upon my soul. In **John 16:33** say, "Jesus speak these things I have spoken unto you, that in me ye might have peace, in the world ye shall have tribulation: but be of good cheer; I have overcome the world. Then He kneed these words speak Jesus, and lifted up his eyes to heaven and said, Father, the hour is come glorify the Son, that thy Son also may glorify thee." Saints, God was showing me how important prayer is to Him, as His prayer was to His Father. Prayer is most important to communicate with God Almighty. Churches God is calling on us to pray and have faith to know our Heavenly Father.

The Black Race Is Losing Respect for God Almighty

ON AUGUST 19, 2002, I heard these spoken words from the true living God! While in service my heart and mind were mostly focus on the mission of our operation involving command and control. Since my retirement, I see the black family and church completely differently from before I went into the army. It seems the true word of God's foundation has lost it standard, and Satan has taken charge and is controlling many black man to bow down and worship him. With such destruction their no morality, no respect, and no discipline. In most large cities the black man has found a place to worship gods and goddess, and "forgot where God had brought us from."

The **second week of May, 2003,** God woke me up at 3:00 a.m. and said read **Act 19.** Paul came into Ephesians preaching the Good News of Jesus Christ. There was a certain name Demetrius, a silversmith, which made silver shrines for Diana which made him wealthy, but Paul preached against these idle of evil gods and people were turning away from them and accepting Jesus. Paul told them there is no god made by hands. Those who didn't want to see their wealth leave from their Great goddess Diana, felt threatened by Paul destroying her magnificence. When the world heard this saying, they were full of wrath, and cried out saying, "Great is Diana of the Ephesians." They cried out two hours "Great is Diana." This world today is cried out each time the true righteousness of word of God comes against their evil goddess Diana or materialism through the world. Most of our cities are full with goddesses and our black races and the world are crying out, save our Great goddess of materialism. In Detroit they worship the Great Diana, in New york they worship Baalism gods, in Chicago they worship the false god Baal, in Los Angeles they worship the goddess of Satan, in Washington, DC they worship Queen Jezebel, in Baltimore they worship the idol god of idolatry, in Philadelphia they worship pagan gods, in Charlotte North Carolina they worship the Babylonian goddess, in Atlanta they worship the golden calf, and in Miami they worship the goddess Asherah. In **I King 18:19** says**,** "God is showing how the church is partaking and worshiping many of these goddess. Gather to me all Israel unto mount Carmel, and the prophets of Baal four hundred and fifty, and the prophets {minister of God} of the groves four hundred, which eat at Jezebel table denying God." "For three years I asked God; Why have our young black men and ladies have put themselves in a position to destroy their own race by worshipping other gods?" I was shocked to know, this black race of people on earth are dying fastest than any other race. We are being destroyed at the hand of Satan for our evil ways. We encounter more sickness and plagues than any other race. God has shown me how the darkness of Satan is using the young Black artist to destroy their soul. Satan is destroying God's church and family along with destroying other race and countrymen, because many are following after evil. **Jeremiah 13:10** says "This evil people, which refuse to hear my words which walk in this imagination of their heart, and walk after other gods, to serve them, and to worship them, this girdle is good for nothing." Oh God, what have we become? The family and church has lost control of God's commandment and become Baala, Diana, and goddess worship. Satan is using television, radio, Internet, and other ways to filter these evil things into every home and lives. Breaking down the true foundation of God. Their are only two or three program on television a family can watch with their children without destroying their moral ethics of God. Commercial have takes over with sexual, immorality, and indecency exploded, showing no respect for God and His people. Most all black stations are under the control of Satan worship and have no respect for God, with curses and evil language. These are false gods and idol worshiping by people controlled by Satan all around us. The pagan civilizations of the Old Testament worshipped many gods; this race has not turned from these evil wicked things, so this generation is no different We are the same pagan civilization. We have become a race of emral people, dying and filling up jails, prisons, and graveyards. This said the Lord, "Behold, I will bring evil upon this people, and upon the inhabitants thereof, even all the curses that come out of your mouth before God. Because they have forsaken me, and have worshipped other gods, that they may provoke me to anger with all the evil work of their hands, therefore my wrath shall be poured out upon this people." Black families, I pray you will seek the face of the living God and take control of your children and let the Lord save them from the wrath of God.

The churches see these evil things all around and are not doing anything to stop it, nor are they speaking out against their evil doing. God said the church's eyes have become blinded to these evil things. The hands of Satan sitting right in the churches are destroying God's families. They are inside the church with closed doors and people are dying right around them. Lord God somebody has got to do something to stop this evil race from destroying itself. Church, it is your responsible to go out and tell them about the cross, the blood, the resurrection of the Holy Spirit, and the love Christ has for them. Compel them into the church and teach them the truth of God's word, and ask God to overcome the darkness of this black race of people. Clean them with the blood of the Lamb, wash us in the living water, and create in us a pure and new heart. Oh Lord something must be done to save this race. Oh Lord, it hurt my heart so bad to see my race falling away, and not putting their whole hearts, minds and souls, in the hands of the true living God. I pray, young and old Christians, you will assemble yourself around strong faithful saints of God to stand and grow strong in the Lord, and pray and ask God to give you strength to resist the devil and he will flee from your soul. Don't continue to allow Satan to use you this way. Beware, there are some who say they love the Lord, but we are deeply involved with the same Satan worship. We go to church, we put on a difference attitude, we put on a difference face, we jump, shout, and praise the Lord. We depart church and change our lifestyle. No man can service two gods; you will love one and hate the other. But this is the church of today. What you do at home, around your friends, or on your job is going to be a reflection of what your church life will be like.

Last of August, 2002, God led me to a church. The pastor spoke of a vision about a church of God. The church was at a high note; the preaching was whooping and hollering. The church was singing the word of the world, mixed with one or two of God word, a drum was beating, people were shouting, jumping, and running around. They were worshipping the creation of man. Suddenly the floor opened up and a dark spirit came up and hovered above the pastor's pulpit. "I felt a strong feeling from God come over me" and Satan; said Church, thank, you for praising me; keep up the good work; then Satan disappeared. Suddenly the roof opened up and a cloud rushed in. "It was God calling His saints three times to come up to heaven. Nobody heard God calling; they were doing their own things and didn't hear the Lord. There was one old lady sitting in the back She stood up and say Lord, here I am, and she was taken up with Jesus."

When the pastor spoke these words God show me the same vision; then I felt the presence of the Lord come over my soul and tears running from my eyes. God spoke. "This is what I hear, I been trying to show you this about my church." I felt so hurt; my hearted was crush with such great compassion for all those so-called saints of God who were left behind. This vision is burn in my heart and minded, and I cannot forget it. Sometimes I can see it in my mind. Churches, God is speaking and I pray you will take heed to these words in **Exodus 20** and God speake all these words, saying. I am the Lord thy God, which have brought thee out of bondage. Thou shalt have no other gods' befor me. Thou shalt not make unto thee any graven image, or any likeness of any thing that is in heaven above, that is in the earth beneath or that is in the water under the earth." Evil music, evil speaking words, evil minds sexual behavior.

Sin is anything that takes you away from God. "Thou shalt not bow down thyself to things not of God: for I the Lord thy God is a jealous God, visiting the iniquity of the fathers upon the children unto the third and fourth generation." What God is saying; the evil the father and mother bestow upon our children can affect the next four generations. We must keep God's commandments. "Thou shalt not take the name of the Lord thy God in vain." Most black people today are using God's name in vain, with cursing if there is nothing wrong. God said you would receive your punishment at the gate of Hell; Lord who will speak out against their wrongdoing? "Woe is me! For I am undone; because I am a man of unclean lips, I dwell in the midst of me people of unclean lips." "Oh Lord, I try my best to please you Lord, by spreading Your Good News, yet all I do is in vain. Lord, I am a sinful man No one want to hear me, for mine eyes have seen the Kingdom of the Lord of hosts. He took a live coal from off the altar and laid it upon my mouth, and touched my lips, and He taken away my iniquity and sin." "I heard the voice of the Lord, saying, "Whom shall I send, and who will Go for me?" I said "Here am I Lord; send me." And He said, "Go and tell this people; they will hear but understand not, I will open up their eyes and give them understanding with a heart converted to love of Jesus Christ." Oh Lord please let these words into their hearts your people because I love them with my whole hearts.

Three months later God led me to another church and shows me that same vision again. I could not believe my eyes. What God was showing me was happening right in His house and those saints didn't know what they were doing. We think we are pleasing God, yet we are pleasing Satan. I left with a heavy burdened down heart. When will we believe the truth that we may serve the one true living God Jesus Christ, Lord of Lord and King of King. Lord, I pray they will let You open their eyes and hearts to see the glory of Jesus Christ's righteousness, and remember the Sabbath day and keep it holy: this means we must keep God in our hearts every day. He will help us do the right things pleasing to the eyes of God. On His Sabbath, I pray we will be able to keep it holy, and live our lives with the highest praise unto the Lord "hallelujah", and become holy unto the Lord God Almighty.

I pray that your love may abound more and more in the true knowledge that all things we do are excellent and sincere unto Christ Jesus, and that we will be filled with the fruit of righteousness in the glory of the true living God Almighty Amen.

Making God's Crosses

On March 23, 2003, God's spoke and said "Make crosses," I didn't quite understand what He meant. "Lord I don't understand" He led me to threes different churches. Each Sunday the pastor preached on the cross of Jesus Christ that was my confirmation to make crosses. I brought the material I needed to start making crosses. First I made three. Placing on a base, I told someone I was making crosses. He said Will you make me one. I did and I went to take it to him. He had not arrived for work, so I sat in my vehicle waiting. I asked God how much should I charge? suddenly the Holy Spirit came on me, saying, "Give them free to all my Christian. I have paid the price by taking on all your sins upon the cross and defeat death to sin that you may be saved by the blood of the lamb." I felt something come over my soul, I was so happy and so at peace with joy by the Holy spirit of God Almighty. I gave one to another saint of God and the spirit spoke to her to tell me to make single crosses and give them out. They are made with three nails with blood running down, supported with Bible verses. God has anointed each one with the power of His Holy Spirit. He has led me to make over five hundred by the hand of God, giving them to family, friends, churches, nursery homes, colleges and others. To work for Jesus and give to His saints is a blessing I can't find words to describe. **Philippians 2:8** say, "And being found in fashion as a man, he humbled himself, and become obedient unto death, even the death of the cross." God is speaking to you and me. **Luke 9:23** says, "If any man will come after me, let him deny himself, and take up his cross daily, and follow me. **Luke 14:27** says, "And whosoever doth not bear his cross, and come after me, cannot be my disciple." **Acts 20:35b** says, "How He said it is more blessing to give than to receive."